# Ian Chillcott

# Fanning The Flames

For my wife, Lynn-Marie, without whose strength, courage
and love none of this would have been possible. X

ANGLING PUBLICATIONS LTD

First published in 2016

Copyright Ian Chillcott Angling Publications Ltd.

British Library Cataloguing in Publication Data

Fanning The Flames – Ian Chillcott
1. Carp Angling
1. Angling Publications Ltd.

ISBN: 978-1-871700-94-7

Designed and produced by Angling Publications Ltd.

Printed by Gutenberg Press

# Acknowledgements

You will never know where you are going unless you know where you came from. So to my Mum and Dad in Plymouth, thank you for the life you gave me, I can assure you I live every day like it is my last!

Tim Paisley needs a very special mention here, and not only for the great friendship I have enjoyed with him over the years. His influence on carp fishing has been nothing short of biblical, and we all owe him a debt of gratitude, for sure. For me he has been a mentor and friend, someone with whom I have been able to share my most private of issues. And because there has never been anyone quite like that in my life, I will always owe him so much more than he could ever realise.

To my great friends, Steve Morgan and Kev Knight, at Mainline Baits. You have had to put up with me for over 23 years now, but while you continue to produce the best bait on the planet, you will have to put up with me for a lot longer yet!

To Paul Reeve, Shaun McSpadden, Scott Day, Lewis Porter, Harry Charrington and everyone at Fox International. 15 years of my life has been spent with Fox, and loyalty is probably the thing I seek most in life. Thank you for yours, and you know you will always have mine.

DHP have carried my articles almost exclusively for the last eight years at the time of writing, and I cannot express my gratitude enough. After all, it is where my writing career began, when the inimitable Jim Foster asked me to write an article on fishing in weed back in 1997. Here's to you all!

*Fishing.TV* has been a major factor in my life since 2008. David Hatter and John Dunford lit the fuse, and we have been at it ever since. So Rae, Tim and Paul, here's to the future.

I simply must extend my thanks to all those many people whose carp waters I have fished during the making of the book, many of whom gave special permission for us to film at their waters.

There isn't enough room to mention all those who make my life such a wonderful place to be, but my book wouldn't be complete if I didn't mention my friend Dave Lane, for just being Dave Lane, really, and Adam Penning for his friendship and his very interesting take on life. Mark Walsingham all the way down there in Somerset, for making my wishes come true in the most amazing fishing environment I have ever come across. Mark Browne and Mark Denton remind me of where I came from, and very definitely keep my feet firmly on the ground. Airborne!! Paul Bennett, whom I first met back in the 80s beside a carp lake, who has taken Lynn on a fantastic voyage of unforgettable memories with *Midsomer Murders*. And finally, to Tracey Brown and her sons, David, Stuart, Billy and Cameron for re-establishing my faith in humanity. They will know exactly what I mean!

A special thanks must go to all the people I have met along this amazing journey. I often feel that fishing is so much more than catching fish, and without the company of some great people, fishing just wouldn't be the fun it is always meant to be.

# Contents

# Stirring the Embers

As you read the pages that follow you will gather that Chilly doesn't suffer fools gladly, or at all, really, which explains why it is unusually flattering to participate in the double whammy of being involved in the production of this book, and writing the Foreword for it.

Evidently Chilly has a thing about conflagrations, not just in book titles, but in day-to-day life. His first autobiographical carp book was *Light My Fire*, and this book is *Fanning The Flames*; in real-life terms one fiery incident stands out from among many. Although he tends to talk down overseas fishing in the book, Chilly has done some, and I think his first latter-day French session was on one of our trips. (I say latter-day because there are areas of his previous life that must remain a mystery.) We travelled in separate vehicles, and agreed to rendezvous at the Calais port exit to travel to Goncourt, in the Champagne region. After a twenty-minute wait outside the port we began to get anxious. Had he been impounded for some incident in his former life? We sent a text. Where was he? The reply came back. He was halfway down the A26 with his hair on fire. That was handy, because he didn't even know where we were going! We rendezvoused at an A26 services, sometime later than originally planned.

The book revolves around four main themes: Chilly's former life; his life with his beloved wife Lynn, and her debilitating ongoing illness; his carp-fishing life, which includes his extraordinary commitment to the successful filming career he now enjoys, and, of course, his carp fishing. (There is a fifth theme I touch on later.) I've separated the carp-fishing life from his carp fishing because at times they are very different things, as the book makes clear. Unusually, I have asked for a number of pictures to illustrate the Foreword, one to make a point, and the others because I'm proud to be a friend of this remarkable man. Some time before Chilly's first book came out I was talking to a high-profile member of the carping community and he made a disparaging comment about Chilly's 'rumoured' military background. I smiled when *Light My Fire* came out because the lead picture spoke more poetically about that part of Chilly's background than any words of mine could! Arising from aspects of that background there is an anger in Chilly which surfaces from time to time, and I suspect that is because it is a past that he still struggles to come to terms with. There are references in the book that hint at the fuller, darker picture, and while it is not my place to elaborate on any of that, they help to explain why he is one of my heroes.

I have fished with Chilly on occasion, and marvel at his obsessiveness, his ability, his attention to detail, and his need to catch carp. I suspect there may have been a time when I aspired to all those characteristics, and if, at times, I no longer do so, I excuse myself on the grounds that the fire no longer burns as brightly in my aspirations to catch carp as it clearly does in Chilly's. I smoulder from time to time, but being there, and enjoying being there, have now become as important for me as catching something while I am there. Reading the pages that follow has emphasised how far short I am falling in the basic armoury of a day-to-day successful carper, and I'm sure many of you will feel the same.

I figure briefly in the pages that follow, from time to time, and I feel I must embroider a couple of episodes slightly. One is concerning the Redmire session we shared with Mark Walsingham. It fell on the first week of October, and some time previously I had become increasingly enamoured of Bob Richards' first big Redmire carp, the fish that brought the attention of Redmire to the world. He caught that fish on 5th October 1951, so I was wildly jealous when Chilly caught a carp on the anniversary of that capture, during what

*Chilly the para: I smiled when I saw this picture at the beginning of Light My Fire...*

*Filming is not easy. Chilly and cameraman John Dunford coming in from the cold and wet at the end of their Mangrove filming session.*

was our difficult week on the pool, fishing-wise. Then I got to thinking of my previous trips, and checked the dates when I got home. I, too, had caught a Redmire carp on 5th October, recorded in *More From The Bivvy*, so my jealously abated. Following our week at the pool that anniversary became increasingly significant in my mind, and when Tony Mears asked me to contribute to a new Redmire book – which is still in the pipeline at the time of writing this – the chapter is simply headed October the Fifth. Blame Chilly!

The other episode relates to the Mangrove May filming session, which receives some coverage in chapter 14. What Chilly doesn't mention is that the session, and the filming, took place during five days of the most hideous spring weather imaginable, and Chilly's swim happened to be on the receiving end of the cold northerly winds and torrential rain. The level of the mere rose 2ft during the session, and there was snow on the high ground in Shropshire a couple of miles away. Chilly, and cameraman John, coped admirably, if uncomfortably, and managed to come up with a meaningful and entertaining programme in extremely adverse conditions.

Looking back, I'm surprised by the number of fishing and social sessions I've shared with Chilly. They are occasions I have always looked forward to, and will always look back on with great affection. The two trips to the USA for the World Cups of 2005 and 2012 hold a special place in my memories. They were real adventures, made all the more special by the group camaraderie, and the fact that the winners came from our group on both occasions – the winners on the second occasion being Chilly and his partner Lee Jackson, of course.

There is an area of Chilly's carp-fishing life that is barely mentioned in the book, and that is the now defunct English Carp Heritage Organisation, founded by Chilly, to highlight, and counter, the dangers from the import, illegal and otherwise, of unhealth-checked carp that can be a hazard to our home carp stocks. In fact the venture gets just one page of coverage in

*One of my favourite overseas trips; the group who made the trip to the USA for the 2011 World Carp Cup so memorable. From left: George Csonka, Paul Musson, Tom Duncan-Dunlop, Briggsy, John Lilley, yours truly, Chilly and Jacko making plans.*

the three books Chilly has now written, because, as Chilly puts it on page 432 of *Light My Fire*, 'I didn't want to cloud that picture with what many will perceive as a political agenda.' I'm not sure I understand that, because carp fishing needs a political agenda, and in support of Chilly's successful efforts two remarkable carp politicians emerged from the creation, and running, and success of, ECHO. The organisation ECHO was successful in increasing the awareness of the seriousness of the illegal import of carp in the corridors of power, with a resulting step-up in preventive measures. One of the politicians was Ruth Lockwood, whose comet flared hugely successfully, and all-too-briefly, across the angling political scene. Hopefully, in the fullness of time, she will return to the political arena, because she is fearless, and special. The second was Mike Heylin, now an OBE, whose effectiveness as a politician I am well aware of because I work with him on the board of the Predation Action Group, and have done so for the last seven years or so. I think it is fair to say that ECHO represents the biggest success story to date in carp politics, and the aftermath is one to learn from. The lesson is that people burn themselves out, either through achieving their short-term objectives, or finding that the responsibility of carrying the political burden is too onerous, and too thankless, and too unrewarding in material terms, to run with for ever. The problem is that politics represent a changing lifetime scenario that needs understanding, and tackling head on. But to expect the politics of carp fishing to be handled expertly, and over the long term, on a voluntary basis shows a failure to understand the time-consuming complexity of all the aspects of the carp and angling scene. This comment is simply by way of a tribute to Chilly, Ruth and Mike, so I won't extend at length the thought process involved there, but there is a simple one. Carp fishing needs effective full-time political representation beyond that provided by the Angling Trust. It is something a handful of us are trying to work towards.

What follows is a big book by a remarkable man, who happens to be

**Receiving an ECHO award from Chilly the politician at an ECHO AGM**

a remarkably successful carp angler. I hope you enjoy reading it as much I have enjoyed my friendship with the big man, and working with him on its production. May his fire continue to burn brightly for many years to come.

*Tim Paisley, August 2016.*

# Introduction

*If angling helped me escape the world, then carp angling is the greatest escape of all!*

As soon as I typed the last words of this, my third carp-angling book, I wrote the word 'Introduction' as a heading on a new file. I wanted the emotion of what follows to be included in this important piece of any publication. Emotion, now there's a word... a word that I never realised was something I was capable of, if I was being honest. For much of my life I operated without the hindrance of feelings, or emotion, and in many respects that changed me quite fundamentally, as I am sure anyone who knew me back in the day would testify to. But even back then, I would allow my fishing to act as an outlet for my feelings. From the Caribbean to the Indian Ocean, and from Colombia's River Magdalena to Lough Erne in Northern Ireland, all would, in one way or another, save my sanity, and probably my life. However, no matter where I was I would always dream of Richard Walker's 1952 carp record. It is probably hard to imagine, but at times that image dominated my thoughts. I can never claim that carp fishing hasn't ever taken over my life, because it certainly has, from time to time. However, all I have ever really wanted it to be was part of my time on this planet. In the early years it helped me come to terms with issues in my life caused by my service of this incredible country of ours, and, of course, helped me get away from things in my personal life, too. Like everything I have ever been involved with, I had set myself goals, and this tome starts when my carp-fishing dream became a reality. But what happens when you achieve all that you set out to do? For me, it was all about finding something else to chase, and conquer, but when all was said and done, there was only one constant throughout my existence, and that was fishing, or, to be more precise, my carp fishing, in all its various forms. It's a bit like my military career, actually; I just want to experience it all, and to that end I have often become tired of fishing in one environment. I want to move on, fish different places in different ways, and just as importantly, meet different people along the way. I could think of nothing more boring than sitting on the same lake year after year, fishing for the same fish. Conversely, although I love to catch big carp, I have no wish to sit it out for years trying to catch one individual carp. Life is far too short for that kind of thing in my world, and therefore what follows is not a look at one water, to catch a particular carp, then on to the next. It is about the life of someone who makes a living by going carp angling, which isn't quite as simple as some would have you believe. You will read about my wife, Lynn, the greatest catch I ever made for sure, and some of her incredible health struggles along the way. To a much lesser extent I have had my problems with carp fishing, but in the end that is what has made this part of my journey so incredibly interesting. To that end, may I suggest you hang on to the arms of your chair just a little tighter; it's been a kick-arse ride!

*Ian Chillcott, August 2016.*

# Chapter One

## Dreaming is Free

*Time to dream.*

Somewhere back in the mists of time, a very young lad gazed at the base of a Christmas tree. There were several presents there for him to open, but only one held his attention. He knew what it was, and was totally convinced it was the answer to all his boyhood fishing dilemmas, because in that parcel of glittering paper was, what would become, his angling bible. Once his mother had given him permission to attack the pile of presents, he launched himself upon the package and ripped the paper away. Within seconds Richard Walker's *Still-Water Angling* lay before him, and moments later he was leafing through its hallowed and life-changing pages. Indeed, so engrossed in its contents was the lad that the rest of the presents remained unopened, until once again his mother gently encouraged him to investigate the remaining gifts that waited for him under the tree. With what was for him a time-wasting chore taken care of, the young lad retired to the television room at the rear of the house, and, until his concentration was broken with the promise of a turkey dinner, he became lost in the great book's pages. Life was just about to take on a very

*Most of my childhood was lost in the pages of Walker's remarkable book.*

new meaning, one that would in many respects, change things forever. The boy had no idea, of course, where this journey would end, or indeed where its long and winding road would take him, but for now all he wanted to do was dream, and that dream always centred around the pictures of Walker and his remarkable capture of a 44lb common carp from Redmire Pool in 1952. It was an impossible dream, of course, but one day he promised himself he would catch a common carp of that stature, although he could never have realised that the dream would meander through his life for the next forty years.

There was another interesting thing about the book that always added more fuel to the already burning desire, and that lay in the titles of the two chapters referring to carp. The first was simply titled 'Carp', whilst the second was called 'Big Carp', and his mind boggled at the possibilities. He also wondered why there should be a separate chapter for those topics. It took a while, but he was eventually going to find out. There was one problem with all of this dreaming: the young lad had absolutely no idea where he would find a water where a carp lived! Coming from the West Country, as he did, no one in that part of the world even knew evolution had invented carp, let alone someone who had caught one. Not that it mattered, it didn't cost him anything to dream, and all he could think of doing was to spend his time chasing monsters of whichever species, and they would guide and help him when his name came up on the carp-catching wheel of fortune.

It is impossible to calculate just how many times that book was consulted over the ensuing years, but I am looking down on that very copy right now as I type. A torrent of memories rush through my mind every time I look at it, and every one of them makes me smile the smile of a lad who first opened that famous tome one Christmas back in the sixties. There

*The 1973 37lb Plymouth conger eel.*

is also the not insignificant number of miles that book did over the years; it literally went everywhere with me, man and boy. All that was left to do at that time, as far as a six-year-old boy was concerned, was to simply catch fish, and so that is exactly what I did. The first species that grabbed my attention was trout. They were incredibly easy to catch, especially if I poached them from the River Chew where fly fishing was the only legal method of angling. I could never understand why people wanted to make life so difficult for themselves by chucking a bit of fluff around, when a big fat lobworm, suspended under a home-made grayling float, worked so much better! There was also the fact that my neighbours, much to my parents' chagrin, bought my stolen trout from me. This became a thriving business by the time I reached my teens, and I ventured farther afield to ply my trade at Chew Valley Reservoir. Pike were next up on my list for monster training, although I didn't find it too challenging to be honest, often catching the same fish several times in a day. However, my pike-fishing expeditions were carried out with friends, which meant learning about so much more than just fishing. That was when women started to enter the game... thankfully!

Amid the courting, I eventually found the next stage of my big fishing dreams, and that revolved around the Bristol Sea Anglers, at which point my dreams went into overdrive. Everything centred around conger eels, and when a fellow Bristolian caught a British record from Plymouth of 108lb, on a baited pirk, whatever that was, my whole life revolved around catching one for myself. This all came to fruition when in 1973 I landed a 37lb conger from a Plymouth reef, qualifying me for the British Conger Club. Again my mother had given me the inspiration and, this time, the tools to complete the mission. I cannot for the life of me remember the name of the rod, but the reel was a Mitchell 624. There is an incredible story connected to that reel, one that took me another forty years to unearth, but maybe

*Evidently, mullet were impossible to catch, which only made them more of a challenge.*

that is for another time. My family spent the summer holidays in Beer in Devon, and being so close to the sea meant I could spend most of my time fishing in a variety of ways. The most important species was mullet. Everyone told me they were impossible to catch, and no one was more surprised than me when I landed three at the first time of asking. In my world I was now a specimen hunter, although I could never have guessed how far off that I really was. And as I still didn't know anywhere to catch a carp, I focused on barbel. Once again, I turned to Walker to guide me through the whole intriguing process.

Eventually that dream was crossed off the list at Sutton Benger, near Chippenham. It was only months before I was to join the Army, and I was trying to cross as many things off my bucket list as possible. I wasn't sure how much time the Army would allow for angling, but believe me, it was an incredible shock when I realised the limitations that would be placed on all aspects of my life. My best friend then, and still a friend to this day, was a guy called Dave Stratford, and he lived just around the corner. Not only was he a couple of years older than me, which gave him, and subsequently me, access to lots of women, but he also had a car. It was a yellow MK1 Ford Escort which became the fishing wagon, and the reason I was in Chippenham in the first place. I spent the day chasing chub around with cheese paste, when eventually a barbel broke the cover of his snaggy margin. I watched open-mouthed as the fish glided across the sparklingly clear, shallow and weedy stretch of river and engulfed the hookbait only a yard from my feet. At 7lb 2oz this veritable monster remained my personal best for over 35 years, but as soon as I got home I flicked to the Big Carp chapter in the bible. Maybe I just needed to dream a little harder?

*Still-Water Angling* was first published in 1953, and for many of today's carp angling community it would be difficult to understand just how hard it was to catch a carp back in those days, and for many years after. There was one paragraph in Walker's book that, in many respects, not only shaped my fishing, but many of the challenges I undertook, and faced, subsequently. But my, how things have changed, and I quote;

*"The carp, being the most difficult of all freshwater fish to catch, is not a favourite with the majority of anglers. In recent years, however, the number of carp-fishers has begun to grow, and with it, the increase of knowledge, while one hears of more and more waters being stocked with carp. Its difficulty of capture is a spur to greater efforts and study, and carp-fishers will feel well rewarded by the capture of one or two big ones in a season; while the passing of a whole season, or even several, without such reward will cause no dismay."*

I really needed to understand just how that difficulty of capture felt. Trout hadn't been much of a challenge, and pike had begun to be less exciting because the fishing was rather predictable, and easy. It needed to be a carp because it was hard to catch and it was, most pleasing of all, a challenge. Now all I needed to do was find one. Infinitely easier said than done! There were a couple of problems that started to get in the way of my angling desires, and one was the fact I wanted to join the Army, and jump out of aeroplanes. In the main this ambition was because that was a challenge too, but mostly because I needed to get away from people who seemed happy to just accept the hand that life had dealt them, ploughing on without ever experiencing the joys and pleasures that life presents. Anyway, that was their problem and at sixteen years of age I joined up, although it wasn't until I got to Aldershot that my fishing life could continue. The area was stuffed with various lakes, several rivers and a canal. All the hunting ground I would ever need really, especially in the incredibly limited time the Army would provide me with for fishing, a point of interest that still makes me smile to this day. You would be very surprised to know that I get told several times every week how lucky I am to spend the time that I do fishing. Whilst I am not always that bothered by what others think, I have to tell them about the time, or severe lack of it, the Army offered for a spot of fishing. Several times during the 1980s and '90s I would leave for a tour of Northern Ireland in June, not returning until December or January. A whole season's fishing gone, and when you throw in numerous operations and tours in many other areas of the globe, you begin to see that for many years fishing was a very rare activity for me.

One other interesting aspect of Army life was that I was just about the only person I knew who was into fishing, and became the brunt of everyone's jokes and mickey taking. Over the years I probably didn't make life too easy for myself, being late for work in the mornings because of the need to photograph a fish, only added to the delight of my colleagues as the extra duties mounted up. However, the dream continued, only this time I would be chasing crucians for a couple of years, interspersed now and again with a few smaller carp. Now, this was a time when it really didn't matter how big those carp were, it just mattered that you had caught one, but I didn't want to tell anybody. You see, the secrecy that shrouded carp fishing was fierce, and I thought it would be the coolest thing on the planet to keep things to myself, so that is exactly what I did.

All of those thoughts and memories were exactly what was going through my mind as I pushed my barrow away from the Double Boards Swim on Frimley Pit 3 in March of 2007. I had left some money with a couple of the lads there so they could raise a can, if they wished, to my capture of a lifetime's dreaming. Charlie's Mate had turned the scales around to 44lb 4oz , a whole 4oz bigger than Walker's 1952 record. An irrelevant fact really, but it was a common

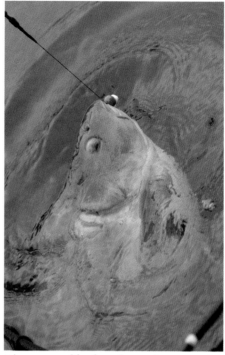

*Back then it didn't matter how big the carp were, as long as you caught one.*

*It's moments like these that make me wonder why I would ever want to give up carp fishing!*

carp comparable to the great man's, and for so long my very existence had revolved around this one moment. Their excited chatter faded the further I barrowed my gear from the swim, and in short order I was left to my own thoughts. It dawned on me that the first carp I ever landed as a soldier, shortly after arriving in Aldershot in 1978, had lived in a water not a mile from where I was right now. It made me smile, and as I turned the top corner of the lake to make the last leg of the journey to the fishery gate, I stopped in Swim 3. Every single time I had arrived at this lake I would stop in this swim. It gave a great view of the majority of the pond, and I very often made decisions based on what I spotted from there. This time, though, I put my barrow down wondering where, and probably more importantly what, I would do next. I was delighted, to say the very least, but something was chiselling away in the back of my mind.

In the space of a few short hours, after three winters' worth of effort, I had landed the one fish that was the pinnacle of my fishing dreams. Much like everything else I have done in my life, once I had got where I wanted to go, it was time to move on. At that very moment I had absolutely no idea what I would be doing in the future, but for the life of me I couldn't see the point in continuing to carp fish. This might sound a little strange to some of you, so let me explain. I had caught an awful lot of big carp, but it has always been the ones that are special to me that counted. Jack from Horton, Single and The Dustbin from the Car Park Lake at Yateley, Mallin's from Wraysbury, Shoulders from Horton, and of course, Charlie's Mate, to name a few. I have never wanted, or needed, to rack up a huge number of big fish to create a list to wave at others, and blow smoke out of my own backside. I have fished how I have to satisfy my own desires, and what others think of that has little relevance to me. To that end, with this one capture I had left myself nothing else to achieve in angling as far as I was concerned. But what, in God's name, would give me the satisfaction that carp fishing had over the years? The incredible people I had met and been influenced by over that time had made it so enjoyable, as had the spectacular places I had visited and fished. It had been, as the saying goes, "emotional". Be that as it may, as I lifted my barrow to complete the journey back to my car, I had decided that I was no longer a fisher of carp: I would wipe the slate clean and start again. At what, I had no idea, but I knew it would be exciting and challenging, just the way I want everything to be!

I loaded my gear into the back of my old Mondeo estate, for what I considered the last time, and arrived home some five minutes later. Yes, I lived that close to Frimley, and as I pulled up outside the bungalow, I smiled even more broadly as I gazed upon all the balloons and banners hanging outside the front of my home. Lynn and a couple of the local lads had strewn the place with congratulation banners, and it just made things even more complete, and, in many ways, made my decision to move on a little easier. Once I had accepted the applause from a couple over the road, I closed the front door behind me. It was at that time I couldn't help thinking about the impact on Lynn my fishing may have had over the years, certainly over the past few months, as every thought in my head had been about Frimley and catching Charlie's Mate. Now she had her husband back, and we could start to do things together once again. Make no mistake here, that one carp had taken over my life and it was this, I feel, that made me come to the decision to quit carp angling for good. Lynn is far more important than any carp, and over a cup of celebratory tea, I told a rather incredulous wife about my plans. Once I had stopped she simply sat there and shook her head. Yes, it was nice to have her husband back again, but I needed to take a little time to sort my head out. And there was only one way for me to do that. Within the hour Lynn and I were cruising down the road on my Harley-Davidson, collecting a few flies in my teeth and believe me, there is no better way of clearing my mind than that! We had lunch in a pub the other side of Guildford, during which Lynn reminded me what carp fishing had done for me over the years, and how much I loved the very idea of going carp fishing. To be honest she had a point, and on the long ride home I came to the unavoidable conclusion... I would probably die holding a carp-fishing rod, and that would do for me!

Once I had ensured that Lynn was happy with me continuing my chasing of dreams, I started to think about the future. At the time I was writing a carp-fishing diary for Carpworld, and monthly technical articles for Crafty Carper. My relationship with Angling Publications has nearly always been a good one, apart from one person who simply believed he was the best thing that ever happened to carp fishing; maybe I will tell you about that a little later on in this tale. I wanted the diary to continue, so that was one box ticked. Secondly, as so many unfortunately do in this game, I couldn't write about carp fishing if I didn't go, could I? Thirdly, I was still involved in the political scene through The English Carp Heritage Organisation (ECHO), but my involvement was getting less and less. In fact, it was the draining and very often unappreciated work we all did that would lead me to never want to be involved in the politics of angling again. What we so nearly achieved was breathtaking, and although we never quite got where we wanted, ECHO's influence is responsible for the way that angling is being represented today. Although I would never suggest that it was the be-all and end-all, we have never been thanked by any of these new money-grabbing idiots who are only in it for their own gains. The PAG is a completely different thing entirely, and will always have my support, for all that is worth, of course. Don't worry, that is the last you will hear of politics from me. Was it worth it? Yes. Would I ever get involved again, no... nuff said!

As my mind cleared, I started to think about the carp I would like to fish for, and having my head buried in the proverbial sand at Frimley for so long, I had no idea just how many big carp there were around to catch. Whatever I did, and wherever I ended up, all I wanted was for my fishing to be fun, and very soon I had the basis of a plan forming in my head. Although I suspect there are a few sorry little people in carp angling who would like to see the back of me, they weren't going to get rid of me that easily.

*The action at the North Lake was incredible.*

For a couple of years I had access to a lake, the name of which I was not allowed to divulge. I could show pictures and write about my fishing there, but that was as far as it went. Dave Lane and Keith Jenkins had had tickets for some time, which meant I could fish there as a guest, but I had eventually got hold of a winter ticket the year before. I would love to tell you that it was a hard water, but it wasn't, it was quite simply a great water to fish, and the social fun was second to none. All in all, it seemed the ideal place to kick-start the new phase of my carp-fishing life. The problem, if I can call it that, was I couldn't start fishing at Mercers Park in Surrey until later on in May. For the next six weeks or so I guessed the best option was to use my cover-all CEMEX ticket, and as my mate Mick Barnes was the head of that establishment, I reckoned it was time to give him a call and see what was new. Because I had basically turned my back on the world at Frimley, I had little idea what had been going on over at the Yateley complex, or more precisely, the North Lake. Mick asked if I would have a go on the newly revamped lake and see what the fishing was all about. There were a couple of other 'worthies' who could fish there, and in the end it turned out to be the perfect panacea for my Charlie's Mate hangover. The lake was being opened to the general angling public at the beginning of April, and in doing so CEMEX had to carry out extensive work. It had to be made more accessible, and that meant removing large amounts of the bankside foliage and snags around the numerous islands. As alarming as that first looked, I am pleased to say Mother Nature very quickly began retaking her territory, and it started to look in fine fettle quite rapidly. The problem was the knockers (aren't there always a few ill-informed idiots to rock the boat?). No one had any idea what CEMEX were supposed to do with the lake, but to leave it as it was after the death of Basil would have been a waste of time and money. There is little doubt that it is one of the most historic lakes in carp-angling history, but didn't others deserve a chance to fish in its unique atmosphere? Redmire was the leader of the pack, creating in the main the industry that surrounds carp angling, but when Ritchie McDonald landed Basil from Yateley North Lake in 1984, a new generation was born – a generation, incidentally, that led the knocking, of course. Thankfully, I believed CEMEX had done exactly the right thing, and although my time at Yateley is over, it remains to this day a wonderful syndicate that carries the torch for Basil, and all the other famous carp the complex was once home to. Long live the North Lake!!

Stocking-wise, they had introduced 25 stunning Sutton carp into the lake and, a while later, a further sixty fish were added from the same source. However, you are never going to be able to run a day-ticket water with such a low stocking level. To that end, CEMEX stocked forty fish from the Blue Pool at Reading, and did the same again the following year. Everything was settling in well, and although a lot of the stock fish were in the 8-10lb range, the future looked very bright indeed, and all that was left for me to do was go fishing. I put my feet up for the rest of the week after catching the big Frimley common; there didn't seem to be much of a rush to get the rods out. That was until I had a chance encounter with Barry Hearn and Ian Russell, who had been fishing the North Lake recently. They had landed a cartload of scaly carp, and were loving the fishing there. That was enough for me. I planned to do a couple of nights the following week, and once I had gleaned enough information from them, I prepared for action. I had never fished the North, but had seen it many times when I fished on the Car Park Lake. However, it was still a bit of a shock when I turned up to see how much work had been done. I was shocked a little more when Simon Scott and his crew from Sparsholt turned up to do some more. It needed doing, of course, before the first punters arrived, and it also allowed me to go out in a boat with Simon to have a good look around the lake. Now, the intention was not to take things too seriously. I just wanted to put my feet up and do a little angling, just for me. The first night I did was a blank, which, as

*This 24lb 12oz Sutton stockie simply took my breath away.*

always, was a red rag to a bull, and by mid-morning I was all set up in a swim a little farther up to my left, the Corral. Well, that was an inspired move because several hours later I had landed about fifteen carp, all stockies, but who cares? It made me smile and, as I have already mentioned, that was all I needed from my fishing. After a quiet night, I was doing battle at first light, and this fish felt like a different species. After several heart-stopping moments the fish decided to put me out of my misery, and slipped into my net. It was one of the first Sutton stock fish, and at 24lb 12oz he simply took my breath away. I am often billed as a big-fish angler, although I am actually nothing of the sort. I am a carp angler who occasionally catches a big fish. I get just as much satisfaction from catching good-looking fish, whatever their size, and this fellow couldn't have made me happier. That evening I sat and put my feet up on some of the stumps at the side of the lake. If ever I needed reminding just how much carp fishing meant to me, and just how much it was a fundamental part of my life, then this was it. In those couple of hours before darkness fell, I made some plans. I thought about some of the fish I would love to catch, fish that aren't necessarily the biggest around. I don't want to chase a fish just to put a certain weight in my diary, I want to catch them because they mean something to me, because that is what really matters. However, just to put a little extra spice in the next stage of the journey, I did nominate the next fish that would provide me with all the inspiration I would ever need. Second only to Walker, Chris Yates has provided many moments of inspiration, and to that end I could think of no better fish to try to emulate than his 1980 capture of the Bishop from Redmire Pool. I was living and operating in another world at that time in my life, but I still remember hearing and reading about him catching the then British Record. Now, if that fish couldn't spur me on to greater things, then nothing would! At that moment in time the wheels of fortune had already started to turn in my favour, although as regards to this particular fish, I simply could never have realised how soon it would happen! Plans were made and all was well with me in my carp-fishing world. I just hoped Lynn wouldn't regret her decision to let me loose, encouraging me to once

***Chris Yates has provided so many moments of inspiration.***

again chase my dreams. There was also the fact that her illnesses and subsequent restrictions could be compounded by a focused man. But as Lynn said, "There's only one way to find out, husband!" I couldn't have agreed more, and anyway, I assured her, at least dreaming is free.

*The incredible Mercers Park was the next leg of the journey.*

Chapter Two

*Re-Light My Fire*

*A stunning 22lb mirror that ensures the North Lake's future.*

With my head back on the right way round, I decided that fishing the North Lake was quite a good place to waste a little time before my Mercers Park ticket became usable, which was about three or four weeks away! That fishery was run, in part, by a good friend of our little group, Bob Bolton, and whilst running around trying to catch as many scaly Yateley carp as possible, I probably made his life a bit of a misery. I was constantly on the phone to him, mainly to talk about the fish and the fishing I would be doing on that lake. There was also the not-insignificant point that Long Tall Bob (LTB), as we referred to him, could fish the lake occasionally during its short springtime shut-down period, and of course I was keen to see what he was catching. As I said before, I had fished the lake as a guest, but having a ticket of my own in my pocket put a completely different slant on my fishing there. As much of a distraction as that was, I was determined to concentrate on my own fishing, and soon enough I was back on the North Lake. As the lake was still not open to the public, it gave a few of us a chance to do some magazine and promotional work. I am never keen on myself, or anyone else for that matter, doing magazine work on lakes that no one has access to. If we can't catch them on everyone else's terms, then we really shouldn't be doing what we are, should we? In this case, I reasoned it was okay because the whole point was to do some advertising on the lake for CEMEX. And things worked out very well indeed.

One other bonus of not being pushed for time at that moment, was that I could do a few charity events. I have responsibilities at home and another life to live outside of carp fishing. Many believe that all I do is go fishing, but nothing could be further from the truth, as I have two or three days a week to get all the material to write about. The first event was down in Chelmsford, and we were raising money for The Meningitis Trust. One nice thing about this event is that I could meet the very person who had inspired it in the first place. Ellie watched fascinated as I tucked into my bacon sandwiches which her mother had made, and that was all it took to realise how important events like these are. Yet still in today's carp-fishing environment, so many give so little of their time and effort to raise funds for those less

**At 33lb 6oz she represented so much more than just another carp.**

fortunate than ourselves... ho hum. Anyway, it was a great event and we raised some £5,000 for the charity. I even caught some carp, which is a hugely rare thing for me to do at fund-raisers!

Back at Yateley, the fishing just got better and better. However, I was a little concerned that I hadn't caught any of the bigger fish in the pond. They had been stocked from the Blue Pool to over 35lb, and I was keen to see how they were getting on in their new home. One in particular had captured my attention. When the fishery manager, Mike, had been introducing the fish he mentioned a mirror they had recorded at a weight of over 35lb, suggesting that no one knew the fish and maybe it was an escapee from Burghfield next door. He said it was a stunning, scaly carp and right there and then he became my target. Also, I couldn't help thinking I had seen this fish already in several stalking situations. I visited the lake a few more times, catching plenty of fish and thoroughly enjoying myself, but was still a little concerned about the lack of bigger fish. I turned up early one morning for my last serious session on the lake, and with visions of scaly 30-pounders swimming around in my mind I set off for a look around. The first person I bumped into was a bailiff called Mark, and he had just landed a beautiful black common of 31lb 8oz. As he was about to pack up, it made sense (to me anyway) to move into that area of the lake. I didn't fish that swim, but eventually settled in a swim further up to the right. Mark hadn't used any bait at all, so in time-honoured Chillcott tradition, I let 'em have it! Three kilos of my Pulse boilie mix found its way to three spots and I settled down to wait. Nothing happened for the rest of the day apart from the Bash Street Kids, an affectionate name I had given to the shoals of stockies that marauded around the lake, clattering through my lines every now and again. All three of my rods were fishing on the bait, but as I gazed around the area I noticed some serious fizzing and bubbling just round to my left, no more than two rod lengths out. The carp were tearing the bottom to bits, but the water was becoming so murky it was hard to see any individual fish. About ten minutes later the fish drifted away from the spot, and as quickly as possible I positioned a rig there, along with a scattering of boilies and Response Pellets around it. As darkness settled over the lake,

# TACKLING CARP
## with
*Chilly Chillcott*

*Ian Chillcott*

**To say it has been difficult would be a biblical understatement!**

the two rods that remained on the bait started to produce a few bites and by the early hours I was several fish to the good, the biggest of which was a 22lb mirror. I sat rather bleary-eyed just before dawn, looking accusingly at the short-range rod, wondering why the carp hadn't returned. I reached for the kettle, and as I did so the rod heaved round and the buzzer sang its tune. Not until I saw the fish did I think it was anything other than a catfish, so brutal was the fight. It was something of a surprise to see a rather large mirror making its way begrudgingly towards my outstretched net. I knew which fish it was, one that I had attempted to stalk a few times; she was the fish that Mike had mentioned when he stocked it into the lake. Later, I discovered it was an original Burghfield fish, but for now I marvelled at her dark flanks coated with the most amazing golden scales. At 33lb 6oz she represented so much more than just another capture, she meant the lake held some truly great prizes. I landed a couple more fish that morning before I packed my gear and headed for home, but I knew the following week would be my last visit for a while as Mercers would be fishable the week after that.

One other incredible moment in my life was just about to take place around that time, and that was the release of my first book, *Tackling Carp*. To say it had been a struggle would be an understatement of biblical proportions: I had no idea these things took so long and how much impact it would have on my life. Somehow I had kept my diaries going in Carpworld and, more importantly, Lynn had survived me being at home so often. Quiller Publishing had just sent it off to the printers, and it was as if a huge weight had been lifted from my shoulders. I had not been that proud of anything for a long time, and neither had I been so surprised that I managed the self-discipline to do it. You live and learn.

It's not that I'm Billy No Mates or anything like that, but I do tend to do most of my fishing on my own. To that end, I have a set way of doing things, and as much as I enjoy a good social, I am also very comfortable with my own company. For the most part I am happy with this situation; I can concentrate on fishing and not be swayed by other people's opinions and reasoning. I experiment and find out things for myself. There are times, however, when I am pleased to fish alongside someone else, and the following week was just such an occasion. My old mucker, Keith Jenkins, had told the company he worked for that they weren't the kind of people he wished to be employed by, which resulted in him being told he could leave with a whole month's money in his pocket. I, for one, could think of no better way than to invest a little of that money on some decent red wine, and then we could spend a night or two putting the worries of the world to rest. So, with the wine and menu sorted, we arranged to meet up at the North Lake the following Monday. We might have mentioned the fishing, but at least the important things were sorted first! Now, Keith has always been the ultimate Weekend Warrior and we had arranged to meet up at my place at 5.00 a.m. However, as the years have advanced

*Jenks hollered when the scales read 31lb 10oz.*

it has done nothing to expel the child that lives in him, and soon after my alarm clock had kicked me out of bed at 4.00 a.m. and I filled the kettle, I saw his motor pull up outside the bungalow. He was just like a kid, and as I opened the door I was greeted with a huge Jenkins smile. He hadn't been able to sleep because this was the first time he had fished in the week for years and he was truly excited. That is what I love about this fishing thing; it keeps you young.

As with many lakes at this time of year, the carp were full of the joys of spring, and I wanted Keith to see their early-morning antics. The weather was set to be fair and I had no reason to believe they would not follow their familiar routine. The carp, however, had other ideas, of course. The lake was now open to the public, but it was empty, which left us plenty of time for a look around. The only signs of fish we saw were in an area just up the way from the car park, which was kind of handy for two reasons: one, it was an area I was very familiar with, but secondly and most importantly, it wasn't far for us two old buggers to lug our gear... happy days! One problem, if you could call it such, was that Keith's daughter, Christine, was expecting her first baby, and that monumental event would make him a grandfather. The little mite had been in the departure lounge for a couple of days and I was more than a tad concerned about how I was going to get Jenks to the hospital, if that became necessary. Thankfully, that amazing event didn't take place during our time at Yateley, but it wasn't far away. Once we had set everything up and were angling, it was time to sort out the world. It had got in an awful state since our last session together and things needed to be discussed. We were debating the merits of Jeremy Clarkson becoming the next Prime Minister, when Jenkins got a bite. It wasn't the biggest fish in the world, but what it lacked in size it made up for in beauty. He was suitably impressed, as I knew he would be. At which point our youthful exuberance caught up with us, and on the verge of falling to pieces, we decided to retire to our brollies for a snooze. As soon as I was awake Keith was called back into action. While he huffed and puffed I readied the net, and the fish, as they normally do here, tried to pull his arms from their sockets. Eventually I scooped him up into the mesh, and it really did look like

**By 6.00 in the morning I had evened the scores.**

a good fish. We both let out a holler when the scales spun round to 31lb 10oz. I must admit I winced a little as I was sorting out the scales, when I spotted a bottle of the finest Chardonnay placed strategically in the corner of his bivvy. Oh well, if we must! He made the cover of Carpworld with that fish, but what never gets mentioned is the poor photographer. I slipped and sank rapidly into the silt trying to get the perfect shot, and eventually ended up soaked to the skin and stinking like a cesspit. That said, it was good to see the old boy enjoying life.

The problem I now had was that when Mick Barnes arrived for a chat, he was told by Keith we were having a friendly match, something I was totally unaware of until he had gone two fish ahead. And it got even worse when, as he was telling Mick how much he was enjoying kicking my arse, he landed another fish! The swim I was in only seemed to produce fish in the early to late mornings, so whilst we had a cracking evening, I knew my time was fast approaching. A good kip was followed by an incredibly hectic morning. By 6.00 o'clock I had managed to even the scores. The fishing was frantic, as it sometimes could be, and Jenks wasn't about to let me rest on my laurels. His next fish was a stunning 29lb common, but as we sorted that out I was called to action again. The low-20 mirror evened the scores, but again as we sorted that one out, he was soon battling a cracking 26lb mirror and restoring his lead. Things settled down after that, but unfortunately, as we drank tea, my phone chirped into life and all of a sudden I was being summoned to Essex by his Lordship, Kev Knight. Although I moaned and cussed about the whole thing, I had to leave for a few hours. In cricketing terms, bad Knight had stopped play! The rest of the trip only resulted in one more carp, and that was a 20lb mirror for me, and the scores were even. Keith was away by mid-morning, and I wished him all the best. It had been a brilliant social session, and no matter how big you think a carp needs to be to make you happy, moments like that are infinitely better than any carp I have ever caught. I stayed on a bit longer, and I doubt that Jenks had even locked the gate behind him when I had another 20lb mirror, followed shortly after by a beautiful 28lb 12oz scaly mirror. It had been the best session I had

*Jenkins had only just left as I held this 28lb 12oz cracker up for the camera.*

experienced in years, and I drove away a happy man. I was also thinking that this was the last time I would visit the lake, but unbeknown to me, I would be back for one last blast.

It was time to move on to Mercers, although the opening day fell on a weekend, and I wasn't keen on fishing a packed lake. To that end, at daft o'clock the following Monday, I loaded the car and set off along the M25 towards Reigate. Mercers Park nestles in the Surrey countryside, and exists because of sand and gravel extraction. At around 45 acres it's a fairly large pit, with depths down to around 36-40ft. There's one island, a shallow end, and a deep end, but apart from that the bottom of the lake can seem totally uninteresting to the uninitiated. That would change for me very quickly, as certain messages sent up the line by a dragged lead would lead to much improved catch rates. There was a publicity rule in place back then, but at least I could talk about the carp I caught. The problem, as it invariably is for people who want to keep their lake a secret, is that most people know where it is anyway. Everybody I spoke to knew exactly where I was fishing, but if that is what the management wanted, then that is what they would get. And of course, there were the fish themselves. No one I ever spoke to knew how many carp there were in the lake. Estimates ranged from about 100 to 250, but no one knew for sure. Many years before, the lake had been run as a match fishery, and several hundred carp had been purchased to satisfy the market. Nothing big, all the fish introduced were around the 5-7lb size. The club had tried to buy some bigger fish and actually purchased six fish from a source that dragged carp from the Continent. It may sound a little strange for me to say so, but I smiled when I learnt that those fish were dead on arrival, much like the thousands that died during the importation process. At least all the fish in the lake were born in this country. The only problem was that the lake was a snag-infested environment, and the carp weren't shy about getting caught. In the end the mouth damage was horrendous, in some cases, as they were dragged through countless barriers under the water. The problem was eventually addressed, but unfortunately the damage had been done. Once the lake was turned into a syndicate the carp were afforded a greater level of care, and their health had boomed from there on in. Best of all though, they still loved the bait and fought like lunatics. All in all, a perfect world for yours truly!

It was a Bank Holiday Monday, and, as I knew I would, I met several of the members either packing up, or just about to. I spent a large part of the morning just chatting and getting to know the other guys, all of whom seemed to be great company. One guy in particular was packing up from what was generally considered one of the best swims on the lake, and it would have been both rude and stupid for me not to set up in there. The fishing at Mercers is invariably at very long range, which can give you a few things to think about. Even more so on this water, as leaders of any description are banned, and you are not allowed to use leads heavier than 4oz. The problems, for me at least, were overcome with the use of a 17lb braid. I have no idea who made it, but it was recommended to me by someone I trust, and I cannot tell you how much of an impact it had on my fishing. I could launch my lead massive distances without a leader, and in fact I'm sure it was the curvature of the earth that stopped me seeing the lead land at times! There was another rather dodgy ruse that made a difference. One tackle company applies so much coating to their leads, and as long as you check first of course, you cannot read the weight of the lead. To that end I could get away with 4½oz leads which did make a difference. With a marker on my line, the farthest I ever landed a carp from this lake was 201 yards, so all the subtle changes had a great influence on my fishing. And before I move on, there was one other massive edge that was available to every angler on the lake, which was the use of the sailing club's safety boats for putting bait out. For a small fee, you could freight up the area you were fishing with as much bait as you wanted. And for me it doesn't come much better than that. The carp at Mercers loved boilies, the more the merrier in fact, but that in itself could cause some a few problems. There was a 48-hour rule, in that you could only fish a swim for that length of time, and then you had to move. You could stay on the fishery as long as you liked, but not in the same swim. What many did was to bait heavily at the very limit of their casting ability, but they were then unable to bait up again with a spod because of the casting distance involved. It soon became apparent that once the fish had cleaned out your bait, they never came back until there was more bait to entice them to feed. To that end, although I enjoyed catching carp at ridiculous ranges, I eventually ensured that I could rebait in the night, or if the boat was unavailable. Again, it was something that made a huge difference to my results. Anyway, that was all still to be discovered when I arrived that Monday, and I sat with a brew staring at the area of my hookbaits some 160 yards from shore. Let the games begin!

My first fish came an hour later, and at 28lb it was a great start to proceedings. A 24lb mirror and a small common completed the captures for the day, and with the rods reeled in I legged it round to the out of bounds headland (out of bounds for fishing, not baiting up) to bait the area. And although I knew the spot was very unlikely to do a night-time bite, I repositioned the rods on my return. As expected the night was remarkably quiet, but shortly after redoing the rods at first light I was called into action. The demented fish kept me busy for ages, but eventually a rather rotund mirror of 33lb 10oz lay in the folds of my net. I got a neighbour to do the honours with a camera, and I only mention that because at the time self-take photography was a thing of mystery to me. I was just getting into it, but wasn't sure of the technique just yet. I landed a few more fish before it was time to obey the 48-hour rule. I ended up at the far, much deeper end of the lake, but all the action I saw was only a few yards from the bank, and when you are expecting everything from extreme range, it is great to be fishing at the bottom of the marginal shelf. Seven more carp made the move worth the effort; no monsters, but a stunning 24lb linear completed the action early the next morning. The swim seemed to die after that, and I made the move back to the first swim I had fished. Again a great idea, as I ended up with mirrors of 31lb 2oz and 26lb. I was more than

**I liked it at Mercers... a lot!**

happy with my first visit and packed away, smiling like a Cheshire cat. I liked it there... a lot.

My voyage of rediscovery was, by now, starting to pick up steam. But as much as I wanted to be fishing for myself, there were still things that I had promised to do some time ago. One such event was the Fish with the Stars (cough, cough) down at Chilham Mill in Kent. It is something that I have always supported, but as usual, I get a little miffed when I see the same anglers supporting the event. Why do so many take so much from carp angling, and never give anything back? The event as always was a huge success; I even managed a carp, and we raised over £6,000 for charity. However, the event will be remembered by me for completely different reasons to fishing. We all arrived the day before the event for one reason: the social. However, I was completely knackered and for once I was all tucked up on my bedchair by 11.00 p.m. that evening and very quickly in the land of Nod. That was until 5.30 when I was woken by a very excited Jenkins. Daughter Christine had gone into labour. Oh Lordy, here we go! Two stiff cups of coffee and we were on the road, and at a rather alarming rate we soon found ourselves at Redhill Hospital. We quickly got our bearings and ran like a pair of nutters to the delivery ward. Once we were there I announced that Keith was the granddad and I was the assistant granddad. I have no idea what the nurses thought of these two scruffy old gits who marched into their world, but they took care of us. Within minutes of our arrival little Ayla made her first foray into the world. I was invited in, which I didn't expect, and WOW, this was the newest baby I had ever seen and she took my breath away. Ben, the father, asked if I would like to hold her, but my bottle went. I explained that I would probably break her, and started looking for an escape route. Thankfully, some matriarchal nurse came in and demanded to know why there were so many people in the room. I tried to explain, of course, because it seemed she was unaware that a baby had been born. For my sarcasm I was shown the door. Some things never change, eh? It was a spellbinding thing to be involved with, something that I had never had the chance to experience. And do you know what? Carp fishing had so much to do with that, and talking of which, Keith and I were back at Chilham about three hours later.

I was absolutely busting a gut to get back to Mercers. I had no individual fish in mind, and with a kind of carefree attitude to it all, I just wanted to enjoy my fishing. The decision to continue life as a carp angler was proving to be a good one, but there is always something that tends to get in the way, isn't there? I am not one to labour a point, and to be honest my wife wouldn't let me get away with it anyway, but on so many occasions my life, and to a lesser extent my fishing, has been affected by many years of looking after her whilst she is recovering from one of the countless operations she has had to endure. Throw in the fact that she had a left side weakness as a result of two strokes back in the nineties, and that she is registered blind, you will be somewhere near to understanding what my being away from home can mean to her. Now, believe you me, I am now in deep poodoo for even writing that, but this book is about life, just as much as it is about carp fishing, and at that moment in time Lynn had had to endure another operation. She doesn't like people knowing, and spends much of her life ensuring that no one knows she is even ill. It's remarkable really when I listen to some moaning and whinging about their lives, and she never mentions the traumas of her own. Let's face it, it can't be that good having me around, to be honest, and for a couple of weeks I was at home hoping her recovery was complete. That said, I never get to sit around for too long, and as soon as she was able to sort things out for herself, I was shown the door. "Oh, if I must, I'll go fishing then, dear."

The weather had been appalling of late with more and more rain. Evidently, the lake was very high, and the ground around it was completely waterlogged. Be that as it may, I was going angling and once the waterproofs and wellies were loaded into the car, I was racing towards Mercers early one Sunday morning. Not having been able to get to the lake for a while, it made sense to arrive on the Sunday to have a word with whoever was fishing. At the very least I could see how the water was fishing. It was early doors when I arrived, and the few members who were fishing were still knocking out the Zs. To that end I set off for a lap or two, but the only fish I saw seemed to be the small commons that inhabit the lake. It wasn't until I arrived at the large out of bounds bay that is the home of the sailing club's boats and equipment, that things got a whole lot more interesting. And being out of bounds is very often a refuge for the carp. Indeed, as I sat at the top of the ramp I could see plenty of very big carp going about their business. I was tempted to go and get some boilies but I can see little point in putting bait in where I cannot fish for them. It encourages them to stay in that area waiting for the next meal. No, if they wanted bait then they would have to come out into the main part of the lake and find me there.

Eventually I found someone who was out of his pit, and I drank his tea for a while. The popular swim was still just that, and had done a few bites over the weekend. Being new to the lake I had no wish to fish the same swim all the time, but hey, a few bites are always good for morale! The occupant was leaving in an hour, so I went and barrowed my gear down the slope, and waited. By mid-morning I was on my own and ready to rock and roll. Because it was such a popular swim I didn't want to put too much bait in to begin with. To that end I trotted round to the point and baited the area with a kilo of Pulse boilies. Once I was back in my plot, I launched my two hookbaits into position and sat back to wait for events to unfold.

It was around 2.00 in the afternoon when the first bite came. Now this fellow was angry and nothing I could do would stop its race for freedom. It was ages before I had him heading my way, and not for one second did it stop trying to dislocate my shoulders. I lifted the mesh around him eventually, and he turned the scales round to 32lb 8oz. A nice start! A couple of small commons and a 28lb mirror completed the action for the day, so I baited up once more and positioned the rods, hoping for some early-morning action. I was up and drinking tea

*The biggest of a fantastic brace. The Big Lin at 36lb 12oz.*

before first light, but it wasn't until a couple of hours had passed that I had to try to get control of another angry carp. The battle was tense and long, but after two pin falls and a submission I wrestled him into the net. It was a lovely old fish of 34lb 12oz and he deposited a huge amount of my bait on the mat. Confidence was high! However, the little commons moved in and by the following morning I was on the move. I had seen fish on the other side of the lake and, in short order, I was pushing my barrow into a swim that covered the area. The action was about 120 yards out and once I had a marker in position I rang the sailing club who kindly sent the boat over. I hadn't really let rip with the bait so far, and even though I would only be in the swim for one night, I decided to put everything over the side of the boat. Ten kilos of Response Pellets and around six kilos of boilies were deposited around the marker, but I had ensured that I kept a little bait in the bucket to top up the spot should I need to. The water levels were rising rapidly on the lake and real estate was becoming a problem, so to that end, I had a very close neighbour by 5.00 in the evening fishing the swim next door. However, that was to be a bit of a bonus, because as the light started to fade I had a blistering run. Deep and hard she fought for some time, and just as I was leading her into the net, one of the other rods decided to join the party. I rather crudely winched the fish into the landing net and lifted the other rod. My neighbour looked after the first fish and informed me that it was the pond's Big Linear, and it was indeed looking big. The fish I was playing felt like a good one too, and eventually another good mirror ended up in the bottom of my other net. It took a while, but we did sort things out in the end. The Big Linear weighed in at a very respectable 36lb 12oz, and the mirror in the other net registered 31lb 13oz. A fantastic brace, and with the smile of a contented man I repositioned the rods and re baited the area. The rest of the session brought two more mirrors of around 25lb, and several small commons, and I really couldn't wait to get back.

It was on the next trip that I decided to investigate the areas I had caught carp from a little more thoroughly, and they all had one thing in common. It's a very old Army saying, and so very true: 'Time spent in reconnaissance is seldom wasted'. Most of the lake was just plain sand, but every now and again the lead would skip over, what felt to me, like pieces of slate. It seemed to be the key to getting more than just the odd bite, and from then on it was that kind of feature I was looking for all the time. And it seemed to work, too. The session brought several fish, and it was then that I was sure I could go on to catch some of the really big fish in the lake. There were probably six 40s to go for at the time, but that wasn't why I wanted to fish it. I am a carp angler, of course, and very often it's the targets that drive us on, and all I wanted now was a 40 from Mercers. However, time for the next couple of months was just about to become very limited. *Tackling Carp* had come back from the printers and I had a few book signings to take care of. It's not something I ever thought I would do, and I cannot tell you how proud I was to do so.

So, amid book signings, and half the country reporting the deaths of thousands of carp through disease, I tried to carry on as before. The water levels at the lake were becoming worse, in the main because the gravel and sand company had stopped using the lake to wash off their product. This process had been controlling the level for years, and as much as it was affecting the angling, the sailing club was now in trouble. The other thing was that the rods had to be fished out in the water a little way, which meant when I got a bite, I had to wade. It's not a problem for me and invariably, come rain or shine, you will find me playing a fish in my bare feet and underpants, especially if the bite has dragged me from my slumber. I watched fascinated one day as a fellow angler got a bite. Calmly, as the line was literally ripped from his spool, he took time to pull on a pair of chest waders and casually waded out to the offending rod. I was amazed and it begged the question; why the hell do you bother carp fishing if a screaming buzzer doesn't get you excited?

Anyway, I digress. My next session would be my last for a while at Mercers; not that I was aware of that as I arrived, but to be honest, by the time I left three days later, it was obvious I needed a rest. Whilst the sailing club were very kind to let us use the boat for baiting up, the relationship with the anglers wasn't always good. I had set myself up in a less popular swim, basically because I had found another area of 'slate' and wanted to see if I could catch from it. The problem was the boats came in so close that my rods were constantly being wiped out, to such an extent that I eventually lost around £450 worth of braid... and of course, my temper. I let the management have it, and whilst it didn't do a blind bit of good, I felt a lot better for venting my spleen! The session itself produced no less than 47 fish, the vast majority of them being small commons, and as I sat wondering what I had to do to catch one of the monsters, my phone rang. It was a very good friend of mine, an ex-1 Para soldier called Mark Denton. I knew I was in need of a change, because for some reason I get a little bored fishing the same lake all the time. To that end he said I ought to ring the guy who ran the small estate lake near to his home. I had fished it as Mark's guest a couple of times, but never thought I could get a ticket. One, they were very limited with around 15 members; and two, I didn't think they would be happy with the publicity. Nothing ventured and all that, so I took a deep breath and gave Andy a call. I'm not one for dancing round the handbags and got straight to the point. I needed a change of scenery and could I have a ticket please? You could have knocked me down with a feather when he said he would be delighted to see me there, and that I could get straight on with the mission whenever I wanted. It was the change I really needed. The syndicate had been great; there were so many carp I wanted to catch and a few of the other members had been wonderful company, but I needed to move on. I would be back later in the year, but for now I was Northampton bound... and I couldn't wait!

**The boats at Mercers could be a real pain!**

# Chapter Three
# A Walk in the Park

*The peace and tranquility of Melchbourne.*

The seven-acre estate lake was situated in the wilds of Northamptonshire, and I had fished there before. Again, it was as a guest and whilst I had caught a few carp from there, no one really knew what the lake held in terms of the fish population. This is probably the biggest thing that led me to want to fish the lake on a more permanent basis. Interestingly, I had done a Crafty Carper feature there a couple of years before, with a very young and keen Mat Woods, and had landed a cracking mirror of 24lb with two massive C-shaped golden scales, side by side on one flank. It became known as Chilly Chillcott, and as much as I never want to catch the same carp more than once, we would meet again some way down the line. In the short term, Mark had sent me a couple of the very few catch shots from the lake, and one fish in particular caught my eye. There were two shots of it, one as a small double and another at just over 30. I believe the first picture was from a netting, and the other was the only time it had ever been caught on rod and line. Right there and then she became my target on this particular mission. Not that I needed one really, I was just looking forward to the peace and quiet I knew I would get at Melchbourne. All that was left to do was sort out my gear, and prepare for the start of a new adventure the following Monday morning.

I arrived shortly before first light after an uneventful one and a half hour journey, stopping on the winding road that leads down to the lake to take in the scenery. I was amazed that I had not slept the night before, so excited had I been. In fact the alarm didn't have to wake me as I was up and about well before it was due to do its work. The seven-acre lake is about 500 yards from the massive house on top of the hill, and is relatively open, for one good reason. The people in the house want to be able to see the water, and who could blame them? To the left was the shallow inlet arm that sees water run under an old stone bridge into the lake. It's about 20 yards wide, at most, and runs for about 150 yards before it widens out into the main lake. There are two islands, and behind them, far to the right, is the dam wall, which has an outlet facility that feeds a rather overgrown and shallow mere just below it. The water isn't deep at all, with around five feet the deepest I ever found, and it's silty and featureless, too. The only things I found were a sunken snag on the house side of the lake, and now and again the odd patch of Canadian pondweed. It was all I could do to start my motor and drive the short distance to the bridge, but soon enough I had my wellies on and was making my way around for a look-see. As the sun rose and the mist wafted from the water's surface, it quite simply took my breath away. Whatever the water held I was certain that I had found something of a spiritual home; it just felt right.

After an hour or so I had seen very little apart from a couple of possibles, and eventually settled on a swim that gave me access to both of the islands. There was no one else on the lake, and neither was there likely to be. I had it all to myself, and I couldn't have been happier if I tried. I fished two of my rods on the gravel at the base of the island margins and one in the open water. Pulse was still my bait of choice, and I scattered about 100 x 15mm boilies around each hookbait. The ridiculously tranquil environment was sucking me in. I had not felt this contented in a very long time, and as I slackened off my lines, I wondered what this adventure had in store for me. The only company I had were the sheep; the little lambs danced around my rods for ages, whilst the parents watched me with a suspicious eye. That was until Mark decided to join me for the evening. He only lives over the back of the estate, and as we hadn't fished together in ages, joining me seemed the right thing to do. He fished way down the other end of the lake, to my right, and that evening he brought me up to speed with events at the lake during the two years I had been away.

Eventually, tiredness took over and I was in the land of Nod as soon as my head hit the pillow. I was woken by the odd fish boshing out in the darkness, and the occasional liner had the pulse rate racing at times. However, the bite didn't come until around 4.00 in the morning.

*Mark Denton is a little like the lake's guardian.*

I was fishing locked up on that rod because of a snag a few yards to the left of the spot. It was nothing I couldn't cope with, or so I thought, but I needed to be careful. I was on the rod in the blink of an eye, but although the rod was arched over, all I could feel was a little frantic headshaking. I said a prayer, hoping that it wasn't one of the small commons, but no sooner had I muttered the words, than the rod took on an alarming curve as a powerful fish headed directly for the snag. And of course, it found it! For several minutes I tried to get the fish moving from as many angles as I could. I didn't want to be too heavy-handed, but every time I tightened the line I could just about feel some movement from the fish. Stalemate! There was a small boat on the lake for just such emergencies, and about five minutes later I was off after the carp, using the rod to gently reel myself to the snag. The problem was the wind. With the boat being so light I was in danger of ending up getting farther and farther from the area I needed to reach. With much effort, I eventually got the bow of the boat stuck on the island with my line running under it and into the snag. For a full fifteen minutes I tried to get the fish out, cussing and swearing all the time. A couple of times I did manage to free it only to see it immediately return to its sanctuary. Just as I was beginning to despair, Mark wandered up, all cool and unflustered, and asked what all the noise was about. And just as he was going to get a bit of abuse from me, the fish dashed from the snag and raced into open water. Finally, a minute or two later there was a lovely mirror on the surface wondering why I hadn't netted it. The problem was that as I moved away from the island, my landing net got caught on a branch and now I was 20 yards away from it. Oh bollocks! Mark switched on immediately and ran down to the wooded area and quickly retrieved an old inflatable boat. Thankfully it still had air in it, and in no time he was making his way out to me, and as he pulled alongside I stupidly asked if he had brought a net with him. He shook his head and gave me the most withering

**At 37lb 2oz this fish meant as much to me as any other.**

of looks. The scene looked remarkably like something out of a *Carry On* film, and whilst we tried not to laugh, it was impossible not to. I got the fish into the net eventually, and thought that maybe the mirror was an upper-twenty. Whatever it was I was happy, and back on dry land I started to sort things out while Mark held the fish in the net. As I was getting the scales and mat ready, all I could hear was him saying that the fish was a lot bigger than I thought. When we lifted it out of the water I could see what he meant, and as we lay her on the mat we admired her in total silence. There wasn't a lot to say: it was the fish that I had made my target, and she looked spellbinding. At 37lb 4oz that fish meant as much to me as any other fish I have ever caught, and as this was only her second capture, it was a truly special moment indeed.

Once I was happy she had swum off strongly, we sat and looked at the pictures and I turned to Mark and said, "If I ever write a book, that will be on the cover." Who says dreams don't come true, because only a couple of years later she decorated the cover of my second book, *Light My Fire*! I am not a pretentious person and would never have thought I would be writing a second autobiographical carp-fishing book, and whilst I never even spoke of her capture in that tome, she deserved that place of honour. She was my only fish of that two-day session, but I wasn't complaining. I had found somewhere that felt like home, and I was comfortable with that. A little later that day it dawned on me I was not going to have to share the water with anyone, although a couple of funny things happened on that estate whilst I was fishing there. It was just me, the sheep and a whole host of remarkable wildlife, and in my world carp fishing doesn't get much better than that. That said, one of those funny things involved a very famous female radio DJ, or rather her other half. She spent her weekdays down in London, whilst her other half stayed at home. What, if anything, he did for a living I have no idea, but every now and again he would arrive and fish as far

*My first appearance on TalkSport's Fisherman's Blues.*

away from me as he could. It was all very cordial as he would wave and I would wave right back. Up went his brolly with its back to me wherever the wind was coming from, and he would wait. Eventually, either a beautiful black Bentley or a red Ferrari would arrive and a stunning woman in her high heels would stumble across the sheep shit and grassy stumps to his 'fishing' position. At which point, although I never got the full screen version, she got the good news. After some 45 minutes, she would stumble all the way back and ride away into the sunset. Ten minutes later he packed away, too, and every time he turned and waved to me. How very civilised! A bit later that day it was back to the real world for me – more book signing, of course – but that just fuelled my fire for a bit more Melchbourne serenity.

Due to a whole host of other commitments it was two weeks before I could return to Northampton, and the last of those commitments was a trip to the TalkSport studios and a guest appearance on Keith Arthur's *Fisherman's Blues*. I had spoken to Keith a few times, and whilst there may be the odd thing we disagree about, I find myself in total agreement with him much of the time. And, my goodness, does he know a thing or two! It's not bravado at all, he simply knows everything, and the only other bloke I know like that is my old mate Keith Jenkins. Now what that means to a radio virgin, as I was, is that Keith picks up all the pieces if you get something wrong, which, if your name is Ian Chillcott, is very handy indeed! It was great to meet Porky Parry and Andy Townsend as Keith (Arthur) handed over his show to them. It was a great day out, but all I could think of on my way home was getting back to the estate lake. And when I arrived on the Monday morning I was determined to find out a little more about it. Once parked up I started out on the first lap, and for some reason I didn't take a rod and net, as I normally would. If I found a fish to fish for then it would probably have gone by the time I got a rod. As I neared the completion of the first lap, I spotted the flank of a fish only inches from the bank. I couldn't believe my stupidity, but I ran as fast as I could for a rod, net and a little bait. Five minutes later I was lowering a small PVA bag of boilies and pellets onto the spot, then slackened off the line and stepped back from the water's edge a few yards. I hadn't even made myself comfortable before the rod slid through the long grass and the reel was hissing at me. It was a lively but short battle, and soon enough a golden 17lb common lay in the net. Not bad; ten minutes of fishing and I was one fish to the good. I couldn't find anything else to fish for, so it was best-guess time. I hate setting up on a wing and a prayer, but sometimes it's all we can do, and I wasn't surprised to wake up with no action the following morning.

I reeled in and promised myself I would look until my eyes bled before I set up again. Two hours later I had found what I was looking for, and had set two traps in the shallow arm of the lake. It's a fairly open part of the lake, so there was no hiding place to stop me seeing what was going on. All I could do was move back a few rod lengths and hope I had it right. I was just thinking that the carp had done the off, when one of the rods ripped into life. The fight was spectacular, and as it neared the net I noticed a big mirror grazing unconcernedly on the baited area. He didn't seem to recognise the danger until my fish raced past him, at which point he tore off, leaving a wake similar to a Severn bore. Exciting stuff for sure, and my 22lb common was the icing on the cake. The activity fizzled out after that, and even before I loaded my gear in the car I was thinking of my next session.

After attending the Stoney & Friends event at Yateley at the weekend, at which we raised over £20,000 for cancer charities, I loaded the car and set off for the estate. The hot weather had been replaced by a strong south-westerly wind and rain. Bloody hell it looked good, but I must (rather selfishly, I might add) admit to being a little taken aback to see another bivvy on the lake. The only thing to do was share a brew with him. Whilst we chatted I noticed a good fish show in the edge on the far bank. It was very near to a snag I had found, remembering that it must surely be a good holding area. It looked as if it could be the case when another fish boomed out in the waves. Within minutes I was pushing my barrow around there, and very soon I had three hookbaits in the edge surrounded by a couple of handfuls of bait. I sat wringing my hands in anticipation, as you would. I was so confident of a bite, but still nearly jumped out of my skin when one of the rods heaved round. It was on for only a short time before the line parted on some underwater obstacle I was unaware of. It felt like a good fish too… oh shit! It wasn't until first light that I was once again called to arms, and this time I let the fish run into open water before I attempted to draw it towards me. It worked too, and after a spirited battle, a cracking 25lb 10oz common was being held up for the camera. A little later a fish transferred the hook into a tiny twig, which always leaves me wondering… how the hell do they do that? A small common during the night confirmed the fish were still there, and at first light I landed a truly magnificent linear of around 14lb, a fish that was born and bred in the lake, and one that ensures the water has an interesting future. Mark popped down to do some pictures for me, and as we waited for the rain to clear, he told me he had never seen the fish before, which obviously makes any capture that little bit more special. Just as the skies cleared, I got another bite which again found something to get stuck on. It took a long time, but with Mark's help I got it moving towards open water, and I could take a big gulp of air. A lump of wood was wrapped on the line for a minute or two, and with Mark constantly taking the piss, I slipped the mirror into the net. With much relief we sorted out the incredibly long fish, and at 32lb 2oz it represented something of a result. He looked glorious as I held him up for the camera, and as you can imagine, I was falling more and more in love with the place.

As an angling writer, you sometimes have to be very careful about the way you pen things. I would never agree that I am a lucky man, because I have had to graft for everything in my life, including my fishing. However, I agree that I am fortunate to be able to make a living from something I love doing. That said, there are always a few things that tend to get in the way of

***At 32lb 2oz she represented something of a result.***

the fishing that you really want to do, most of which I enjoy anyway, but when I am on a bit of roll on a particular water, the last thing I want to be doing is casting a line elsewhere. And that is exactly what occurred when I got home from the latest session. Carpworld wanted me and a couple of other guys to fish at the Blue Pool near Reading for a few days, to do some filming for them. I couldn't say no, really, and actually ended up having a bit of a carp-catching bonanza. It happened to be a good week, but incredibly knackering, and all I wanted to do when I got home was sleep. There was also the problem for Lynn that my mind was in another place for the days I was at home, and she therefore ejected me from the house the following Monday.

As I always do, I was on the motorway at daft o'clock heading for the little estate lake. I am not normally a fast driver, but by the time I arrived my hair was on fire, and to cool off I spent a fair bit of time looking around the pond. There was only one other person on, so I took my time, eventually finding two areas of disturbed silt, but no carp. They had been there for sure, and I set up accordingly. I had been getting my bites from certain spots, and all of them felt the same as I donked a lead down. Not too soft and not too hard seemed to be the order of the day, and once I was happy with where the three rods were placed, it turned into a pleasant waiting game once again. I was still waiting at 8.00 the following morning, and all I could think to do was risk a peek at the spots to see what was going on. It was so open that I had to bivvy up well back from the lake, and to that end I crawled on my hands and knees to the water's edge. To my surprise the water was a very pale brown colour, and I could make out the vortexes of several carp as they fed. As quietly as possible I retreated back to my bivvy; surely I was going to get a bite. And I did. The nearest rod ripped into life, but once I had it in my hand I could make little impression on the fish. In the shallow water she had no depth to play with and contented herself by stripping line from the reel for a while. As is the way of these things, steady pressure and patience soon

***Disturbed silt led to the downfall of this 27lb 10oz estate lake common.***

had her wallowing in the bottom of my net. It was obvious that the 27lb 12oz common was completely spawned out, but she looked fantastic as I held her up for a picture, or three.

Charity work was the next thing to keep me from the estate, but again, if I am going to take anything from this carp-fishing game, then I should be prepared to give something back. It was the Naomi House Charity Event near Southampton run by a Guy called Clint. It was a great success, but one thing made my blood boil. The 'star' who he had invited had charged him a couple of hundred quid plus expenses for being there. It was a bloody charity for Christ's sake, and not one person in carp fishing is worth any amount of money for such things! Perhaps the angler concerned needed a payment for the wife who had left him, or the spaniel needed a shampoo, who knows? I had desperately wanted to get back to Melchbourne, but there was one other promise I had made. Lynn used to have a hairdresser come to our home to do her hair, meaning that when she was poorly she could at least still get her locks washed and sorted out. The woman had a son, and I often heard stories of how his juvenile arthritis was hindering him, and how painful the condition was. It took an age, but eventually I found out he liked carp fishing, although he had done very little. I didn't know how to help at first, but after my visit to the Blue Pool I thought that it might just be the place to take him. After a lot of organising, I arranged to take him midweek for a night, which would have been longer but I had to record a *Tight Lines* show on the Thursday. As it happens I think we spent exactly the right amount of time there, and what an incredible, if not heartbreaking, trip it turned out to be.

Although Isaac had caught a few very small carp before, the object of this particular operation was to get him doing battle with something a little more substantial. After making sure he had everything he would need, a bivvy, a bedchair and rods, I sorted out all the bait we would require. I have to admit I was probably as excited as he was, and couldn't wait

**Through the pain, Isaac held on to his prize.**

to get going. To that end I picked him up from his house at 5.00 o'clock on Wednesday morning. He was buzzing, but right now the best thing was that his mother had packed the most enormous box of goodies for us. We definitely weren't going to get hungry! I wanted to sort out the night-time accommodation before we headed off stalking, but the area I wanted to fish was occupied at the time. We booked the plot, and quickly set off to find some fish to fish for. The Blue Pool has always been a great place for stalking, and as much as I was worried about landing him a carp, I really had no need to be concerned. Things simply couldn't have gone any better. We carried one rod, and a few essentials, and began our detailed search for carp, which didn't take that long, really. I had briefed Isaac on how this was going to go, and once we had found a likely-looking area that was being visited by several fish, we got a trap set in the deep margin. With the line slackened off, we moved back from the water's edge and waited. At this stage I don't know who was more excited, him or me! We were just giggling about something really stupid when the rod hooped round, and the spool fizzed at incredible speed. Once he had the rod in hand it soon became obvious that we had a small problem. The arthritis made it difficult for him to play the fish in a normal fashion. We overcame the problem, although I had to be a little more forceful than I would have liked, at times. The little fella was in pain, but not once did he complain. I didn't know whether to laugh or cry, but I did know that I thought I was going to burst with pride at any moment. As the battle raged on one of the bailiffs arrived on the scene, and what happened next reaffirmed my faith in human nature. The guy trotted back to his car and got his video camera, capturing the whole thing on film. Not only that, he made a 100-mile round trip to come back and present Isaac with a disc and a few stills of the momentous occasion. Vic, I salute you and will be eternally grateful for your generosity. I owe you one.

The smile on the young lad's face was a moment I shall never forget as he held his 18lb mirror up for the camera . We sat and chatted about playing fish for a while, and the next time he joined battle it went a lot better than the first time, for sure. And when the scale ran round to 21lb 10oz I thought his ears would disappear in the biggest grin I had ever seen. We landed eleven carp whilst ghosting around the lake, and eventually we set up for the night. And again the fish didn't disappoint. However, by around 10.00 in the evening it was obvious that Isaac was wracked with pain, so much so that I reeled the rods in once I knew he was asleep. He needed some rest, and to be honest, so did I! We left the lake at around 9.00 the next morning and I cannot tell you how happy I was with the way things had gone. God, I love carp fishing!

As much as I didn't want it to happen, I knew that my time on the little estate lake was coming to an end. We had been developing some exciting new rods and reels at Fox and they needed putting to the test, and the intimate nature of the Melchbourne water was not the ideal place to put the distance setup through its paces. However, I did have a ticket for a lake that would fit the bill very nicely indeed. With a heavy heart I set out the following week for one last blast, but with a horrible northerly wind blowing I could find nothing of interest, and had to rely on my best guess. Unbelievably, I was in action shortly after setting up, but the damn thing fell off after playing it for a few minutes, and as I settled down for the night I did so with a scowl on my face. However, in the morning I landed another fish that no one had seen before, and at 21lb it made a fantastic end to my time there, for that year at least.

The following Monday I was on the road to Mercers Park once again. If I was to test things to destruction then this was the place to do it. That first trip was a bit of a bittersweet pill due to some errant boats and a couple of lost fish, but I did land a few up to 29lb. Most pleasing of all, though, was that the gear had performed even better than I thought it would. Next time out I wanted to take things to the next level, and in essence that is a large part of my job as a consultant. The thing is, I cannot say something is good if I have not used and abused it, can I? It does neither me, personally, nor Fox, any good if I do so, but more crucially, it does the most important people no justice at all, and they are the anglers who purchase the gear.

Next time out I was surprised to find a nice warm south-westerly blowing, rather than the expected north-easterly. The new marker rod and spod rod had no trouble finding the area I wanted to fish at extreme range, and with that task taken care of, I positioned all three hookbaits in the area. The night was quiet to begin with, but around 3.00 in the morning the first fish made a mistake. It was a small common, of course, and as I slipped him back I couldn't help wishing he was the last I would see. And he was, for a while at least. Two hours later and I had landed four more fish, all mirrors up to 29lb. The new gear had handled everything, and even immersing the reels in the sandy margins for a few hours couldn't hamper their performance. I really didn't have to think about them any more, thankfully. As I rebaited the area, I was kind of hoping for one of the lake's larger residents, and as darkness fell I crossed my fingers and drank inordinate amounts of tea... as I do. A mid-20 mirror had me wading to the rods around midnight, and I sent him on his way with a message for his big sister. She took her time responding, but eventually she must have got his message. I was up and about

*Perfect in every way, the 40lb 15oz leather.*

before first light, just as the wind picked up speed to catch up with the dawn. I watched a couple of fish crash out in the baited area, and couldn't help thinking a bite must be on the cards. It was, but it still took me by surprise as the buzzer howled its early-morning call. I detected a little headshaking and was convinced it was another common, and whilst I prepared to winch it in from the distant spot, the fish decided the far bank was a much better place to be. On and on it raced, and the more it ran the more I knew it was a much bigger fish. Long and hard she made her bid for freedom and it was an age before I had her within netting range. She looked big, but it wasn't until I looked down on her that I realised just how big. She was an unmarked and very dark leather, perfect in every way, and the fact that she weighed 40lb 15oz was simply the icing on the cake. My voyage of rediscovery was nearly complete!

My intention for the rest of 2007 was to fish the deep sandpit at Mercers Park up until Christmas. For one, I wanted to have a good look at my options in the New Year, and secondly the deep lake had a history of fishing well up to the festive season, and then switching off completely until spring arrived. I was busting a gut to get back to the syndicate because I couldn't help feeling I was on a bit of roll. I had been having a debate with myself about which bait I should be using. Don't get me wrong, boilies would still be the mainstay of my attack, it was just that I wanted something to keep the fish rooting around a little longer in the baited area, and to that end I had included about three or four kilos of hemp into my mix. Believe it or not, I am not a great lover of the stuff, but apart from my Response Pellets, I couldn't think of anything better. I had also purchased a trendy set of rubber sandals, not because I am a follower of fashion, because I am certainly not, but to save my feet from feeling like I had walked the circumference of the globe over broken glass when playing a fish. They slipped on easily, and meant I could actually walk without a limp! In an effort to keep the fish coming

*The water levels were starting to make the fishing very interesting indeed!*

*A beautiful mirror of 35lb 2oz.*

I decided that I would launch half a dozen spods onto the spot every couple of hours, which seemed like a plan, but initially I was offered little chance to test out my theory. A 25lb mirror started the proceedings off, and although I didn't know it at the time, it would be my smallest of the night. By 3.00 in the morning I was shattered, having landed several more fish of 27lb 8oz, 28lb 1oz, 28lb 7oz, 28lb 8oz and 29lb 4oz. With the rigs in the butt rings, I decided to launch twenty spods-worth of bait onto the area, and once the hookbaits were back in position it didn't take long to start catching again. Within an hour I had landed mirrors of 29lb, 29lb 2oz and 32lb 1oz. Because of being constantly immersed in the cold water the feeling in my legs had long since left me, but it was interesting to note that the fish were steadily getting bigger. I wrote in my diary that I had not had so much fun with my clothes on (well half of them anyway) in a very long time! The action slowed for a while, so I busied myself clearing up the devastation in my swim. All the action had come to the two rods fished on the big baited area, with my third rod fishing through a gap in the trees to the right of the swim. And whilst I had no bites on that one, it was about to cause me a few problems.

The next bite came on that very rod, and as soon as I picked it up I knew I was playing a big fish. Slow and powerful, she chugged around at range, and as I started to make some headway, one of the two rods on the baited area roared into life. Now I was in trouble! The first fish had found some weed at around 40 yards, so I casually (?) put the rod down on the rest and loosened the clutch. I then ploughed through the water to get to the noisy rod next door. I couldn't help laughing, the situation was so comical, but this one felt big, too. It was a very protracted fight, but all the time I couldn't help thinking about the fish on the other rod. What happened next still causes me a lot of concern about my sanity, but as the fish neared the same bank of weed that I hoped the other fish was still stuck in, I pulled the carp I was playing into it too. Slackening off the clutch and putting that rod on the rests, I rushed round

***The big girl dragged the needle round to 42lb 10oz.***

and joined battle with the first fish again. Madness! Mercifully the carp hadn't gone far, and with some weed covering her eyes I managed to bundle her into the net. I remember thinking I would never have done such a thing if I had known how big she was. Once secured in the net, I raced back through the water and as soon as I picked up that rod I knew it would be some time before I saw the fish. It had stripped about a 100 yards of line from the reel, and was now back in open water. Patience won the day, and eventually I had that fish in the net as well. Believe me, it's so much better to be lucky than good! A chap by the name of Dave came round to give me a hand and the smaller of the two was a beautiful mirror of 35lb 2oz, whilst the big girl dragged the needle round to 42lb 10oz. I was speechless. After Dave did the deed with the camera, as much as I should have fished on, I was just too excited and went for a walk. What a night... what a lake! The evening was punctuated with several smaller fish, and much as I wanted to go home in the morning, for some reason I decided to stay, probably because I needed to investigate more of the lake. To that end I eventually set up in an area I had never fished before, where I landed a 31lb mirror fairly quickly before the little commons found me once again. It was time to head for home, and I could not have been happier.

The following session was a lot quieter. In fact it looked as if, with the arrival of the cold winter weather, the lake was starting to slow down. A 33lb 12oz mirror known as Heart Tail cheered up proceedings, but it was hard work, especially as I moved several times in an attempt to find some fish. After that I had a busy schedule to attend to, including a visit to Holland and a *Tight Lines* interview with footballer, and all-round good egg, Lee Bowyer. Now the last occasion was a great chance to see how he fared at this carp-angling malarkey, and with the capture of a couple of carp to 37lb 4oz I'd say he was pretty damn good at it!

As the weather got colder and colder, I was seeing fewer and fewer people on the lake. That was all fine and dandy, but because the carp seemed to thrive on the bait, I couldn't help wondering if it would slow things down a whole lot quicker. To that end I started to use a little more bait, and in the main it was Pulse boilies of varying sizes. One area that caught my eye, simply because of the number of fish I saw showing there, was no more than 80 yards from the bank down towards the deeper end of the lake. The distance made it so much easier to bait up, so I probably put far too much bait in, or so I thought. In truth I wanted to bait this area for when the conditions really deteriorated, and wasn't expecting too much action. Famous last words! I landed 16 little commons, and whilst slowly losing the will to live, I decided that I would, in future, fish over smaller beds of bait, and put the majority in when I left. A 27lb mirror cheered me up no end, as did a cracking 30lb 10oz mirror, and thankfully, no more commons.

I fished like this for a couple of weeks with only the odd fish for my troubles, until eventually I decided I needed to invest my time elsewhere. I looked across at the centre of the opposite bank, and as Long Tall Bob fancied a bit of a social whilst listening to England's humiliating exit from the European Championships, I decided that was what I would do. Once the painful football experience was done, it was only minutes later that my middle rod decided to chase away our blues. After a bruising battle I was staring into the lens of a camera holding a bulky 39lb 2oz mirror. As I was straightening the line after the recast, it was ripped from my fingers, and I quite correctly reasoned that it was a bite! All thoughts of football were now a distant memory and again, after one massive struggle, I was looking down on a decent fish. At 34lb 6oz she completed a great brace. Christmas was fast approaching and I wanted to squeeze in a few more sessions. I had kept the bait going into one particular area, and on my next trip it was in this area I decided to fish. The carp were very evident there, and it was no surprise that an hour after casting I had a 27lb mirror, and a small common. Then nothing...

To be honest, I was getting a little fed up of being on the same lake for so long. I think I must have been an explorer in a previous life, because I get so bored looking at the same scenery and catching the same fish week after week. We are all different and we all want something different from our lives, and this is how I am made. To that end, I decided two more trips and that would be it. I would try a swim I had hardly ever fished before next time out, and as soon as I set eyes on the lake I saw a fish show in front of that very plot. Just as pleasing, my marker was in a clip at about 90 yards, coming to the surface only a few yards from where that fish showed. Nice! The spod delivered the bait and all too soon I was sipping a brew, full of confidence. It was a clear and very cold night, but I was encouraged to see a few fish showing in the moonlight at the distance I was fishing. At 8.30 that evening the bobbin on one rod lifted and fell, then did it again. The third time this happened I guessed something was attached, and sploshed my way to the rod. By the time I got there the line was out of the clip and the buzzer was howling. After a torrid battle I lifted my net around the fish, with some relief. Nearly falling in the lake, as I couldn't see the edge of the swim because it was underwater, I managed to get her on the mat and record a weight of 34lb 6oz. Now that would do very nicely indeed! After a quick brew I was soon back in my pit knocking out the Zs. It was midnight when one of the bobbins started to dance again, and I was soon rushing towards the rod. This battle took place under the rod tip for what seemed like ages, but a bit of patience saw a good fish roll into my outstretched net. At 32lb 7oz I could not have been happier and smiled broadly for the camera. A brace of 30s at any time of the year is a result, but in the middle of December? Both bites had come from the baited area, whilst the other rod, fished some 15 yards to the left of the bait, had not let out a single bleep. I was just attaching the bobbin to the recast rod when the single hookbait rod was away. Now, as I have mentioned, these carp fight, but this one took things to a whole new level. Not once did I feel in control of things, and if not for the weed at about 30 yards, I fear I may have

**An indignant 34lb mirror as the winter set in.**

been there for hours. Once the weed had covered its head, as nearly always happens, the fight was over. I led a big ball of green stuff, plus a carp, into the net and let out a huge sigh of relief. The tussle wasn't over and weighing and photographing the handsome, if somewhat indignant, 34lb mirror was something else again. I love carp with attitude, and to this day I feel he was the best carp I landed from that lake. Size isn't everything, but memories are.

I landed a few more fish before it was time to start singing *Jingle Bells* and eat too much until it hurts. I was off to Plymouth with Lynn to spend some time with my family, and I couldn't wait. My decision to continue carp fishing had been a good one, and I was having so much fun all over again. It wasn't simply a case of relighting my fires, because by now those fires were blazing out of control... just the way I like it!

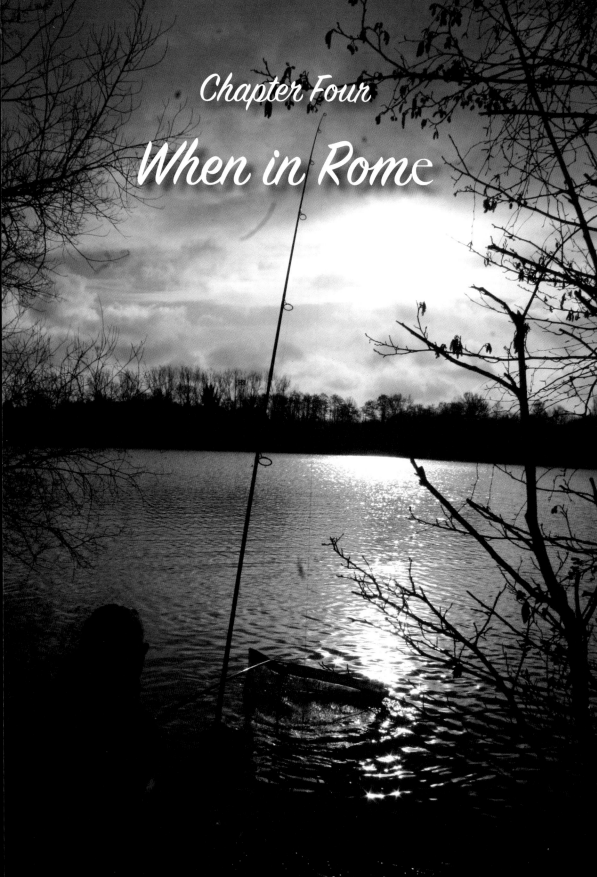

# Chapter Four
# When in Rome

*It was to be a very productive few weeks at Sandhurst.*

I have always found it difficult to get going at the start of a New Year, in the main I suspect, because of overindulgence. However, the weather and the conditions have a lot to do with it, too. I remember getting lost in my own thoughts on the drive back from Plymouth, and eventually ended up in a very moribund mood because the weather was cold, nasty and being dominated by high pressure. They were the worst winter conditions I can remember, and nothing happened over the next few days to raise my spirits. I had a whole host of waters running around in my head to have a go on, but I couldn't shake the notion that as Mercers Park had fished so well a couple of weeks ago, then why wouldn't I catch a carp from there now? We all make crappy decisions now and again, and I was just about to make a classic. In reality, I really didn't have a clue what to do, so the following Monday morning I packed my car and headed off to Mercers. Surely it couldn't be that bad?

The first key sign that I conveniently overlooked, was that no one was actually fishing the lake, and to be honest, none of the swims looked like anyone had been there for a while. Two hours later, and covered in mud, I hadn't seen a single fish; not even the small silver fish were dimpling the surface. If you will excuse the pun, it looked bleak, but undeterred I made my best guess and began setting up. Halfway through the process I decided that I didn't like it there, and moved a couple of hundred yards to my right. I sat in that plot for an age, but eventually decided I didn't like it there, either. To cut a very long story short, I moved four times over the next couple of hours. Why? I have no idea, because I saw nothing to make me do so. I think it was probably just a reflection of the mood I was in... confused! I settled a little later, and at the very least, I was angling.

The rods were cast into the lake, but I was far from confident. Unsurprisingly, I was knackered and in the land of Nod shortly after dark. That said, I have never been one to sleep too long when I am fishing, therefore I wasn't shocked to be sipping a brew around 2.00 in the morning. For an age, I sat and stared across the most lifeless of vistas. I could see not a single thing on the surface of the flat calm water, and after another brew I made the decision to get on my toes at first light and find another swim in which, I was sure, I could waste even more of my time. If anything, the day started colder than the previous one, but at least the move warmed me up a little. Once again I relied heavily on guesswork, and by midday I had set myself up. All I could think I was doing was drowning three hookbaits for a while, and didn't feel for one minute that I was actually fishing at all. Once that was done there was plenty of time for me to stew in my own juices, which was dragging me further and further into a mental mire. I had no idea what I wanted to do, but a chance phone call was just about to change all of that. I was chatting to a guy called Andy Thomas, who lives up the road from me in Aldershot, and during the conversation I asked him how Sandhurst at Yateley was fishing. His reply made me sit up a little straighter; I was instantly a lot more interested in carp fishing than I had been for the past two days, that was for sure. Basically, the lake had been fishing very well with plenty of good fish coming out, and at that very moment I decided I would be heading Yateley way just as soon as I could in the morning. I felt as if I had a reason to go fishing, and at that particular time, that would do for me!

Now, although Sandhurst is only a stone's throw from my house, I had done very little fishing there. About seven years ago, for reasons I won't get into too deeply here, I wanted to give up carp fishing for good. Lynn had been so ill for so long; many times I thought I may lose her, and I had just about had enough of everything. I hadn't been fishing for a couple of months, but I just happened to bump into Viv Shears one day, and he spent a little time explaining what the-then RMC were going to do with Sandhurst Lake. The last thing he said was, would I like to give it a try? Mmmm... now, let me think about that... a lake stuffed with very naïve carp that had never been fished... Oh well, I said, if I must!

Over the next few weeks I stuffed the lake with as much bait as I could carry, and in twelve nights I landed 128 fish. Sounds impressive, but in reality, it wasn't. As I said, the fish hadn't been fished for before, but there was one very positive aspect at the time, I found out how much I enjoyed carp fishing; it had been fun. It also made Lynn's husband a much happier man, which in turn cheered her up, too. And when Lynn is happy her recovery periods can be that much shorter. All in all it was a win-win situation, and I shall be eternally grateful to Viv for pointing me in the right direction. The lake has a special place in my heart, but apart from the odd social, it was several years before I ventured back. The winter before I had visited for a couple weeks, but on that occasion I had only caught a succession of bream. It wasn't long before I had made my excuses and returned to Frimley in search of a dream. That said, I vowed one day to return, and now seemed the perfect time to do so.

I arrived at some ungodly hour and was greeted by the sight of local angler, Dave Benton, fishing in the Car Park Swim. Now that was handy, tea and information readily available. Nice! Just the kind of start I like to my fishing days, and it got a whole lot better when he said he was leaving mid-morning. Normally I avoid car park swims like the plague, but according to those in the know, this particular one could be very productive at times. So with everything sorted we drank tea, and discussed tactics, until his phone chirped into life. A guy called Gary Lewis, who I had angled alongside at Horton a few years before, was fishing a little farther down the lake, and had bagged himself a 40-pounder: would we like to come down and do some pictures? Did we ever! The fish was called Cracker, and immediately rushed me back in time seven years. You see, it was the biggest fish I caught from the lake back then at 28lb, and it was wonderful to see just how well she had done. I left Dave to pack up and started to make a dent in Gary's tea supplies, too, and of course, to have a chat about the lake. Eventually, though, it was time for me to go and get set up. I knew nothing about the lake, really, so I fished it much as I do anywhere else. A spread of 15mm Pulse boilies covered all three hookbaits on the back of a shallow area at around 80 yards. I had left the Response Pellets out of the equation because of the bloody bream; I had no wish to go back down that route again. I have often stated that if there is a bit of a bandwagon on a lake that you can hitch a lift on, then more often than not, it's worth sticking out your thumb and going along for the ride. However, bloody-minded as ever, I chose to ignore everyone's advice about maggots, as just about every capture was being made through using them. First of all, I hate the damn things because it makes everything so fiddly and smelly. Secondly, in my experience, over the course of time they make the fishing harder, and the fish lose more and more weight. This was one bandwagon I wouldn't be climbing aboard, oh no. Famous last words and all that!

The next few hours did nothing to change my mind on the maggot front, because as a wonderful south-westerly raced across the lake, one of my alarms burst into life. I was playing my first Sandhurst carp for seven years! As nice as that was, there was one aspect of the fishing I had given no thought to, my main line. In the deep, dark depths of my syndicate water, although most battles on braid were fraught, they weren't that alarming. In 4ft of water, however, it meant there were plenty of sphincter-challenging moments; in fact I would go so far as to say, scary. Thankfully the fish found his way into the bottom of my landing net, and another guy I had fished with at Horton, Martin Pick, was on hand to lend some assistance. As we sorted out the 26lb mirror on the mat, I couldn't help thinking how similar he looked to some of the old warriors that lived in the Match Lake over the road. I never gave it another thought, well not for a while, and soon enough he was swimming off back to his home. One up for the boilie brigade! I would show those maggot-drowners a thing or two, I thought. That evening the head bailiff came around for a chat, and at some point I mentioned the carp I had landed, and he asked me to describe

**One up for the boilie brigade.**

it in detail. He immediately ran back to his car for his camera, and after trolling through his massive collection of pictures for a few minutes, he held the screen up for me to see. It was the same fish, and it had a story too. The fish had never been seen by him or anyone else for that matter until he had landed it the previous year at 24lb 12oz. Better than that, it was one of the lake's original 12 carp. I mentioned this to a few of the anglers on the lake, but sadly they couldn't understand why I was so excited. To them it was just another 26lb carp. Maybe it's just me, I don't know, but personally, he was a very special fish indeed.

Unfortunately, my boilie attack fizzled out after that, which had me thinking about what to do. Everything was getting caught on the little wrigglers, but eventually I came up with a cunning plan. Call me revolutionary... call me a visionary... call me an innovator, but the next time I came to the lake... I was going to fish maggots! To that end, the following Monday morning I arrived armed to the teeth with a gallon of 'germs'. Having spent the previous year fishing on my own, I have to say that Sandhurst was something of a culture shock. Bloody hell, it was busy. It wasn't surprising, really, because at the time the lake held an absolute cartload of 30s, and probably six or seven 40s, and all on a day ticket. The only thing that amazed me was the attitude of some of the other anglers on the lake. Call me old-fashioned if you will, but I always thought there was at least some etiquette and politeness in fishing. By trying to fish where someone else is angling is not only downright rude, it also ruins the fishing for both parties. It was a pressured lake, obviously, and loading more and more lines into an area was only going to add to the problem we were all trying to overcome in the first place. And bait boats, well, don't even get me started on those bloody things. To 'angle', is to cast a baited hook with rod and line, but it seems that 'angle' is another word that appears to be forgotten. There is also the problem that words such as respect and courtesy are instantly deleted from a bait boat user's brain when a purchase is made. Maybe I'm just getting old, eh?

My early-morning arrival was greeted with the sight of a packed car park. There was,

*It didn't take long before I was spodding out pints of maggots.*

however, a silver lining to the cloud, in that the area I wanted to have a look at was free. And as soon as I squeezed my car into the last remaining space, I raced round with my barrow to bag the swim. The forecast was for low pressure, strong south-westerly winds and rain. To be honest, I don't think I could have designed better winter conditions if I tried. With the lake being dominated by gravel, the object of the exercise was to find the siltiest area I could, and fish that. Like most day ticket waters, the obvious spots are as repugnant to me as they are to the carp. I discovered a nice silty gully at 55 yards into which I cast all three hookbaits, two about 5 yards apart and the third fished 10 yards farther to the left. The two rods fished together were baited with maggots, but the left spot was going to be fished with boilies; old habits die hard! Now, although this area was on the back of the strong wind and most of the action had been happening at the far end of the lake, I sat back extremely confident with my efforts. I was arming my maggot hookbaits with a large bag of the same, and the intention was to recast every so often. Interestingly, every time I did this I watched the line as it entered the water. For ten minutes or so it would twitch and flick, which convinced me that the huge population of silver fish were moving in and demolishing the bag as soon as it landed. After those ten minutes the line would remain stationary until I reeled in, or I got a bite. How often, I wondered, are the carp being caught on a single bunch of maggots? It was food for thought, for sure.

By morning, the maggot versus boilies battle was one-all. Mirrors of 21lb and 21lb 10oz had livened things up considerably, and at least I was getting it just a little right. A tench at 9.00 that evening had me smiling; if the old red-eyed critters were feeding, the carp couldn't be far behind. Sure enough, an hour later another 21lb mirror slipped into my net, followed at 2.00 in the morning by a 19lb common. A double-figure common completed the action for the night. The only problem, if I could call it that, was that the maggots were dominating proceedings, but I decided if the fish liked them they could have as many as they liked. To that end, every two hours through the night, I put out several spods of germs onto the spots, and in the end it started to pay dividends.

The problem with using maggots is that I seem to lack any kind of maggot management when it comes to looking after the little blighters. Several times in the night I had woken to find I had not secured the lid of the bucket and hundreds of the annoying little gits had made good their escape. And don't they get into everything? Just about every available crevice was infested with them, and it took me a couple of hours to clear my gear. Give me a bag of boilies any day! As I was removing yet another maggot from my teacup at around 11.30, I managed to get two bites at exactly the same time. It took a bit of knit one, purl one, but eventually I was returning two double-figure mirrors to their home. I kept up the two-hourly introductions of maggots, and the following night produced two more doubles. Forgive me here, because although the fishing was brilliant, I couldn't help wondering where the big girls were, but as dawn broke I got the answer I was waiting for. As soon as I picked up the rod, it was obvious this was a completely different kettle of fish. With no dramas to report, and after a monstrous tussle, a fine-looking common was staring up at me from the bottom of my net. At 34lb 9oz he was just what the doctor ordered, and as I waited for a photographer to arrive I played and landed a plump mirror of 26lb 12oz. Despite the incredibly busy nature of the lake, I was thoroughly enjoying myself, and as I packed up I simply couldn't wait to come back.

That would have to be delayed as a result of a telephone conversation I had had a couple of weeks before. A researcher from the BBC's *Countryfile* had rung because they were going to film a segment for the programme about a fellow in Devon who was organically breeding carp for the table. The alarm bells immediately started to ring in my head. However, the panic was over when he told me they wanted a carp fisherman to balance the programme, and tell

*At 34lb 9oz she was just what the doctor ordered.*

the audience what the fish meant to us, as anglers. My concerns were that they would not adequately convey just how valuable these fish were, and it would encourage others, not aware of their value, to eat them. The following Monday I drove down to Cullompton in Devon to meet up with the team, and presenter Adam Henson. The place was actually a holiday park, with loads of caravans and mobile homes for the punters. The most important thing was that there was a lake, and once we were by the side of it, the goalposts changed just a little. I had not been aware that they actually wanted me to catch a carp, but speaking to the production bloke, that is exactly what they wanted... Oh dear! The weather was cold and wet, but most important of all I knew nothing about the lake, not even if it actually contained carp! I was so convinced we wouldn't catch anything that I didn't even try to change the hookbaits, some old, dried out and smelly maggots were simply lobbed out into the lake. Adam, who is an incredibly nice bloke, asked if I could show him how to cast, which I was only too pleased to do, to break up the boredom. However, he didn't really get it, and eventually 'his' rod was left in the last place you would ever think of trying to catch a carp. I suppose the writing was already on the wall. I waxed lyrical for a couple of hours about how much carp meant to us anglers, and how we would never consider eating one, so in the end I was happy with what I had done – apart, of course, from catching a carp. The more the production guys wanted me to catch, the louder they got, shouting up and down the bank. I think Adam knew I was

*Countryfile's Adam Henson holding the carp he helped to catch.*

getting a little cheesed off with it, and eventually they decided to go a bit farther down the bank and he did a piece to camera reading from Isaac Walton's book, *The Compleat Angler*. I reckon old Isaac must have been smiling down on us, because as Adam did his thing the very rod he had cast ripped into life! No one was more shocked than me, and I was just sorry he wasn't on hand to play the fish. He did have a go but the fish was ready for the net at that time, and once in there I breathed a huge sigh of relief. Amongst many reminders that the fish had been landed on the rod he had positioned (and who could blame him), we finished off my part whilst he held up the 12lb-ish mirror. Then it was off to the farm where Jimmy and wife Penny were breeding the carp. I actually ate a little bit of carp that Penny had cooked, and it was bloody awful. If she hadn't overloaded the thing with spices I am sure it would have tasted like the silt it lived in. Be that as it may, they were great people and we had a brilliant time. It was just nice for me to stand up for carp in a programme with such a massive audience.

I had other magazine features to sort out over the next couple of days, and as I did so the weather turned to high pressure and frosty mornings. That was what confronted me the following week as I swung open the gate at Sandhurst. It didn't surprise me that no fish had been out for a few days, and nothing I, nor anyone else, did over the next 48 hours changed that. There was one highlight though: whilst I was trying to control and return to the bucket a squadron of mental maggots, my swim was invaded by a couple of horses. I have no idea where they came from, and all they wanted to do was eat grass around my rods. I had the very devil of a job to get them to move away, but they did so eventually, after knocking my rods off their rests and pooing everywhere... even on my bloody landing net! I wasn't going to do a third night, but Andy Little's son, David, and his mate Pedro came to visit to do some promotional stuff for Fox. And it was a good job too, because that night I had another 20lb mirror, one of four fish caught around the lake that night. As I packed up I couldn't help feeling that I was leaving just as things were starting to get interesting once again. All I had wanted from Sandhurst was to catch a 30-pounder from there, but once I had done that I got a little greedy. There were so many big fish in there at the time that I simply wanted to catch a few more. The culture shock of fishing such a busy lake had become a distant memory, and I was getting into the rhythm of the lake. However, things were going to get a whole lot more complicated in my little world, and the next few weeks would change the way I was going about things for a very long time.

With the release of *Tackling Carp*, I had been surprised by the number of people who asked when I was going to do a book about my own life and fishing. I hadn't ever really given it any thought, but the amount of inquiries simply took my breath away. I had been talking to Keith Jenkins about the possibilities of doing a book through his contacts. The short story is that Freebird Publishing was born, and the arduous second-book task was just about to begin, although I could never have imagined just how hard it would be in the end. *Light My Fire* was going to be a labour of love, and for those who have never done such a thing, the realities are a lot different from the popular perception of such an undertaking. First of all, my life had been a frantic adventure, and I had no idea how to portray everything that was involved with that. Then, when you throw in the fact that meaningful pictures from the early years were limited, and the difficulty of dragging long-forgotten stories from the dusty corners of my brain, it may just throw a little light on the task at hand. Be that as it may I was doing it, and I set out to do the best I could.

There was one other exciting prospect to get my head around, and that involved the TV cameras. A few weeks before, I had been contacted by *Onlinefishing.TV* (now known as *Fishing.TV*), who asked if I was interested in doing a series of programmes for their online fishing channel. Of course I was interested, and I became even more so when they said the aim was to produce content for mainstream TV. The fellow I was speaking to was David Hatter, and, unbeknown to me, he had an unbelievably good reputation, and massive amounts of experience, in the television world. We thought it was best for him to come and have a chat whilst I was on the bank, and set a date in the diary. With all that running around in my head, I turned to the one person who can make any sense of me, and the life I lead, and that was Lynn. I threw the lot into the melting pot; write a book, make a series of TV progammes, continue to write a diary on a monthly basis, and churn out a technical piece every four weeks. If that wasn't enough, I had to consider my loyalty to Fox and Mainline, and do whatever they needed me to do. Let's not forget, I was asking my wife, knowing that she had so many physical problems ongoing, many that would require surgery, as to how we were going to handle this, the most important thing of all, in my life. As Lynn said, we would handle it; we always did.

With all that swimming around in my head, there was still fishing to be done, and as it was still very much winter I rolled up to the Sandhurst gates once again on the first Monday of February 2008. The lake was busy, that much I could see, so the first thing to do was have a good walk around and see what was what. I was surprised to see the Bailiffs' Swim was free, and that it hadn't been fished since the previous Friday. I really wanted to be fishing other areas of the lake, but this seemed a bit too good to be true, so I dropped my barrow there and continued on my travels. With nothing having been caught for 48 hours, I set up as I usually did in that swim. The only difference now was that all my rods were being fished with maggots. Sometimes you just gotta go with the flow! I spodded out 20 or so spods then sat down with a brew, and in accordance with my plan I regularly recast the rods and topped up the spots with a spod or two of maggots every couple of hours. The liners started shortly after dark, and at 11.00 o'clock I had my first visitor, a feisty 19lb mirror. I recast all the rods and topped the spot up again, and soon after, I was landing a lovely mirror of 23lb 2oz. Forty five minutes later I was once again doing battle, and another 23lb mirror lay on the mat. It was interesting just how many maggots the fish were depositing on my unhooking mat. They were feeding hard, for

*I was in Rome, doing what the Romans do.*

*This 31lb common made a great inclusion in the Fox filming.*

sure, and by keeping the maggots going in I kept them interested. Saying that, it wasn't until first light that I was once again called into action, only this time the demented 24lb 4oz mirror wiped out all my rods. It was great fishing, and seemed to force all the other issues in my life to the back of my mind. Nice! Was I feeling guilty about using maggots? Well, maybe just a little.

David Little arrived again that day for some more promotional filming, for which I managed to land a 24lb common for the cameras, but as soon as he had disappeared I got sorted for the night. The action became very regular at this point, and several more good fish came over the net cord. Sleep eventually came but I was dragged from my slumber at dawn by a blistering take, and as soon as I had the rod in my hand it was obvious a bigger fish was making a bid for freedom. There could be only one winner though, and eventually a nice common lay in the net. David had just arrived to finish off the filming and the 31lb fish made a wonderful inclusion in the piece. With that part of the day over, I noticed a rather tall gentlemen waiting at the back of the swim, and rightly thought it was David Hatter.

I talked with David for a while, and gave him some interesting things to think about with regards to filming, prior to us having our own little meeting. To cut a long story short, they wanted to get going as quickly as possible, and I decided that we would start the week after next. My life was just about to change, and I really couldn't wait to get started. I kind of knew that this might be my last night at Sandhurst for some time, and I like to think the lake knew that, too. With my head still reeling from the earlier conversation, I just couldn't sleep, so was wide awake, drinking tea, when one of the rods melted off. The battle raged for ages, but with no sphincter-challenging moments I was able to get the fish bundled into my net. Once I had retrieved my headtorch I took a look, and what a sight it was! The Drop Scale Linear lay patiently in the mesh, and as one of the lake's original fish it just seemed the perfect way to end this particular part of my journey. She spun the scales round to 31lb 10oz. What a special fish! A couple more tripped up in the night and the session was rounded off with a cracking 27lb 12oz common. I packed away a very happy man indeed.

There was one other thing that was starting to arouse my interest, and it had all started because of my involvement with ECHO. There was a fellow down in Somerset who went by the name of Mark Walsingham, and he was heavily involved with various organisations that dealt with the betterment and well-being of the British countryside, and its inhabitants. He was a fount of knowledge who helped us to better understand the dilemmas that we faced as a politically-motivated unit. I had spoken to him a few times on the phone, and met him once, when he did a talk at the ECHO AGM one winter. He was such an interesting bloke to speak to, and although we weren't yet friends, I looked forward to speaking to him whenever it was necessary. You will understand, therefore, why I was so pleased to see his name on my phone one day. This time though, the conversation was around the lake that he had purchased near his Somerset home, Ashmead. Of course it was of interest to me. I had only just read of his capture of the lake's first 50lb mirror, but it just didn't seem to be the thing to do to ask for a ticket. He knew I was interested, and I left it to him to decide when, or if, I could have one. He had rung to get a recommendation from me for a fellow who I used to fish with about fifteen years before on a very exclusive syndicate near Aldershot. He was a great fisherman back then, a very nice guy, and I could find no reason to change that opinion. Yes, I said, I reckon he would love it there, and get on very well. The long and the short of it was that he was given a ticket that would start when the carp had stopped spawning later on in the year. I never gave it another thought, but unbeknown to me the wheel of fortune had just turned a little further in my favour. If, however, I had any idea about what was going to happen later that year, I would have been very afraid I had ruined any chance of ever getting to cast a line into Ashmead. More of that later...

*She spun the scales round to 31lb 10oz. A very special fish.*

*My biggest fish of the maggot attack. 35lb 3oz.*

*There will always be a special place in my heart for Sandhurst.*

I was nervous about the TV thing, of course. First and foremost it was important to show that I could do the do when needed, and land a few fish. I wasn't worried about the cameras; I had spent my life in front of sometimes thousands of soldiers briefing them, or instructing them in various ways, so that held no fear. The next thing was where to go for the filming, and that was sorted when I bumped into Mick Barnes, at that time still the CEMEX boss, at the Carpin' On show at Five Lakes in Essex . Why not give the North Lake a go at Yateley, he suggested. Why not indeed? And once I was home from the show I decided I would do a recce session there that week, and see what was what. That evening I managed to sort all of my gear out for the trip, and after setting the alarm clock, I was excited for sure, but somehow I drifted off to sleep. The next few weeks would change my fishing life forever, and I couldn't wait!

# Chapter Five

## TV Dinners

*North Lake reconnaissance.*

I understood that the filming of the series was going to dominate much of my life for a while, so I needed to sort a few things out. First of all was my monthly diary, which in all honesty, didn't need that much thought. The filming would simply put a new slant on things, and in many respects jazz it all up a little. Believe me, there is nothing more boring than writing that I went fishing one week and caught some carp, then writing that you caught some carp the following week too, and so on. I hate reading that kind of thing, as well, so a bit of derring-do and life in front of a camera would add some variety to my carping. There were also the venues for the five programmes to consider. I wanted to fish as many varied environments as I could, as it would liven things up to a great extent. Probably most important of all was that I have never wanted to, or ever will, have a swim shut down and baited for me. It's only done because those who do it are frightened that they don't have the ability to catch carp on everyone else's terms. To that end, all I wanted was permission to actually fish and film on the water, and I would sort it out from there. There was to be one anomaly to that train of thought, which I will tell you about when we get to it, but it didn't involve anyone baiting up for me, or swims being shut down. I even open the programme explaining honestly why I was where I was.

The last thing on my mind was the way that I was going to fish. I have spent a lifetime shaking my head at the utter bullshit that I read about people's ideas of rigs, their uses, and how it is the only thing that catches carp. Complete rubbish, in my opinion, and again, only done to try to convince the reader, or the watcher, that the perpetrator of this crap is a carp-fishing god. They aren't, of course, they are simply good salesmen, and that is always something to bear in mind. All of which meant that I would choose five different venues, as different from each other as possible, and fish in exactly the same way on every one of them. Same bait, same rigs, same colours of the components, same lead attachment, same size lead, and the same short leader. It was the setup that I used for 90% of my fishing, and I couldn't think of a better way to prove what I had been writing for years. Confidence in what you are using is vital, and changing things on a monthly basis, and emptying your wallet in the process, is no way of gaining confidence in anything. So, probably for the only time in this book, and before I lose the will to live,

A Size 8 SSC hook No-knotted to six inches of brown Cortex coated braid, a long Hair which would be armed with a 15mm Pulse boilie tipped with a piece of yellow plastic corn. A lead clip would carry a 3oz Flat Pear lead, and a 3ft length of leadcore finishing it all off. Not once did I change things, although I did have to use different gear when fishing on the top, of course. Now, that was the plan, and all I had to do was put it into action. Let the games begin!

Although the weather was cold, it was a lovely morning when I turned up for my recce at CEMEX's North Lake at Yateley. As nice as it may have been, I could find absolutely nothing to fish for as I looked around. Eventually I set up in a swim that afforded a good view of the rest of the lake, and if anything moved I could get myself on it. I had fished the lake on a few occasions at the same time the previous year, and the place had been remarkably good to me. I was hoping for a bit more of the same. The best thing about this session, and many more to come, was that I didn't need to use maggots. The wriggly little critters had driven me mad at Sandhurst, and I was looking forward to fishing with some good old boilies. I was still using the Pulse, so confidence was high. One thing that made me smile was that the lake had received very little in the way of pressure for months. All the other lakes in the area had been busy during the winter, but for some inexplicable reason no one wanted to fish the North. I have no idea why that should have been so: the stock and the stocking levels were fantastic, and its shallow nature made it a good bet in the colder months. Bear in mind, I was there as a recce for the following week's filming, and it was my intention to only bait one area. They hadn't seen anything in the way of food for ages, and I hoped that

*The recce went well. 24lb 12oz.*

by keeping the bait localised they would keep coming back for more. To that end, I baited a silty area behind a long shallow bar rather heavily with 6 and 10mm Pulse boilies, along with some Response Pellets. All three rods were being fished on the bait, and I sat back hoping I had got my part of the equation right. As day turned into night I still hadn't seen a thing, but around midnight the liners started in earnest. They had obviously found the bait.

It wasn't until 2.00 a.m. that I got my first bite. A lively battle ensued before I was able to slip the net under one of the stunning Sutton stockies. I was buzzing, and it may surprise some of you why I was so excited. I suspected that it was one of the second stocking with these fish, and as they averaged 12lb the previous year, they were obviously piling on the pounds, and looking magnificent. Things went quiet for a while and it wasn't until first light that my indicators assured me the carp had come back. A little later I was once again leaning into a fish and a lively scrap resulted in a lovely dark, ex-Blue Pool fish, of 24lb 12oz. I got some pictures taken, and as I sat with the photographer the most remarkable thing happened. Only feet in front of us a Sparrowhawk clattered into a thrush, and grappled it into submission. I have always expressed my love for carp fishing, but it is hard to make some understand, sometimes, that it is so much more than simply catching carp. It is not very often, in any walk of life, that you are privileged to have a ringside seat to such an event. I reckoned it was a good omen of things to come, and shortly after I was packing up and heading for the gate. I baited the spot again, and only hoped the lake would smile on me the following week. With the recce over, I was pleased with the result; those two fish alone would have made a great programme. All I needed to do now was keep the bait going in, which is easier said than done when you haven't got a swim, or half the lake, roped off for you. I also had a lot of writing to do, and when all I wanted was to go fishing, I had to really bite the bullet for a few days. I baited up twice, the last time on the Sunday before the filming started. Again I saw nothing and my prayers, to whoever listens to them, were getting just a little more urgent, to say the least. The problem was that all that effort and bait went to waste; the elements and the carp were just about to change everything.

With it all arranged, I headed off to the lake amidst the worst storms this country had seen in over 40 years. Things, as they say, did not look good at all. I rang David Hatter to tell him about the situation, and he thought I was mad. That may well have been the case, but I want my fishing to reflect what everyone else has to do. If this was a busy man's time to fish, then he was going to fish. Anyway, once I had convinced David that I was in control of all my faculties, he said that if I was prepared to do it, then so were they. Top man! With gusts of up to and over 80 miles per hour I tried to sort things out, but it was proving frustratingly impossible to fish the spot where the bait had been going, not with any degree of accuracy anyway, but as I sat on my bucket with my head in my hands, a very obliging mirror carp came to my rescue. No more than 15 yards to my left he launched half his body out of the water and sploshed back down, followed shortly after by another smaller fish. With no cameras there yet, I could take my time with this, and a little later I had two rods fishing the spot with a light scattering of boilies around the hookbait.

All the while my Evolution Bivvy was trying desperately to relocate itself in the gale-force winds, and it wasn't long before I had the first of many disasters. I was determined to get a long-range rod on the baited spot, and when there was a slight lull in the wind I rebaited it, and was just about to cast. The rod was leaning up against the bivvy and, as I grabbed the rig in my left hand, a sudden gust tore the bivvy pegs out of the ground. The hook was pulled viciously into my hand as the bivvy soared into the air. As I grabbed the rod I brought the full weight of everything to bear on the hook and the rod, and something had to give. Unfortunately it was the rod. With a resounding crack the pressure was off and I watched in amazement as my living accommodation disappeared towards the car park, some hundred yards away. Bloody hell that hurt, but it was nothing compared to me ripping the hook out with a rusty old set of pliers! I have no idea how I did it really, but by mid-afternoon I had everything sorted and nailed to the ground.

It was then that I met up with the cameraman, John Dunford. I could have no idea then, but we would be spending an incredible amount of time together, both home and abroad over the next few years, and he would become a great friend. For the moment though, I just needed to bring him up to date with the friggin' mayhem that had begun that morning. I also told him that, in the very unlikely event of me landing a carp, I would eat my fishing rods. Little did I know that come the morning I would be reaching for the ketchup! Most of the night was spent trying desperately to hang on to everything; it was very bad indeed with trees coming down and massive branches falling on our bivvies. To be honest it was a little scary, and you may be wondering why we stayed and did what we did, considering that the wrath of the gods was raining down upon us. Well, I for one have just about had enough of contrived TV programmes. It would surprise a lot of you to know what goes into some fishing-related (cough, cough) filming. It just doesn't, not by a million light years, represent what the viewer can do. We wanted to be honest with this thing, and this was about as honest as it could get. Faced with having limited time to fish, the normal guy must suffer whatever the weather is doing if he wants to go, and I hoped what we were doing reflected that.

Anyway, after a long night the dawn finally arrived, and John headed down to the gate to let David into the complex. I was knackered and simply pulled the bag back over my head; I wanted more sleep, but there was little chance of that. A single bleep had me gazing at the rods. You see, during the night I had removed the bobbins from my line, the incessant bleeping

**Chilly On Carp got off to a great start.**

nearly drove me mad. I looked a little longer, hoping the single bleep would result in a nose-bleeding run, but it never did. As the guys arrived in my swim armed with all the gear they would need, I decided to swing my legs out of bed, at which point I could see that something was not how it should be. The line on one of the rods was pointing in the wrong direction completely. I hollered at David to get a camera on his shoulder, and John to start preparing the rods for my breakfast... we had a fish on! A rather bizarre fight, due to weed and branches all over the line, eventually resulted in the first carp I landed for the series, *Chilly on Carp*. It was a fantastic moment for all of us, and we whooped and hollered. All I could think was that this was probably the greatest carp I had ever caught, all 21lb of him. The rest of the day was spent filming, and I did no more fishing until the evening. David isn't the kind of guy who was ever going to slum it and stay on the bank, oh no, which just left me and John to see if we could catch another, about which I still wasn't sure. However, as we sat and chatted about John's limited time spent carp fishing, one of the short-range rods ripped into life at 10.30 in the evening. The battle was a rather dour affair, and I was soon looking down on a substantial mirror, bigger than the last, and at 28lb 12oz he certainly was. It was dark, but we got all the footage we needed, and I slipped that fish back with a huge sigh of relief. We had done it; against all the odds we had put a programme together. I packed away first thing in the morning, a very happy angler indeed, and said to John that I just couldn't wait to do it all over again!

The following few weeks were all about promotional work, and filming for Fox. There was also the task of getting some pictures done for a few technical articles I had written for various magazines. And when you throw in the fact that my book-writing was now full steam ahead, there was very little time for doing any fishing just for me. It can be a little frustrating at times, I admit, but the people I work with are all great guys to spend some time with, and even if I really didn't want to do it, I always enjoyed myself in the end. I did land some cracking fish for the camera, though, and that is always guaranteed to make me smile. So my writing was punctuated with a few trips to the North Lake, but most of the time I was thinking about the next venue to do our second programme on. I have no idea, or interest for that matter, in most things of a technical nature. My brain just doesn't want to handle it; all I was ever good at really was shooting straight, running very long distances, jumping out of aeroplanes, and lifting heavy weights. To that end, I had just about lost the will to live as the guys informed me how the broadband television was going to take over the world. All I wanted was to talk about fishing, and where we were going next. As it happens, a gift horse with probably the biggest mouth in existence stepped into my life, and as I stared down his throat I couldn't help feeling that if I passed up this opportunity I would be a fool... so I didn't! We were going to be allowed to fish at Mercers Park.

To this day I am still not sure what happened to make it possible, but when I was told I could film there, I wasn't about to say no. There were problems, though, and for a while I didn't think it would happen at all. The lake, as I have mentioned before in these pages, was starting to flood, and this made fishing from the recognised swims not only impossible, but incredibly dangerous, too. Bankside erosion also put an unpredictable slant on things, but in the end we sorted something out. I have said before that I didn't want anything to be contrived, and if it was then I would be honest about what was going on. To that end, just in case you are thinking I am better than I actually am, I was given permission to fish an area of the lake that used to have a swim in it, but had been shut down for some time. As much as the carp were under a lot of pressure, being able to fish a bank that hadn't been fished in ages meant that I was probably fishing for carp that weren't quite as spooky as they normally would be. And I told the viewers all of that at the start of the programme. I still had to catch a fish or two though, and the pressure was well and truly on. The plan was to cover short-session angling, and I would fish from 5.00 to midday, Monday to Wednesday. What happened over those days left me breathless, and no doubt will live with me forever; it simply could never get any better... could it?

John Dunford and I arrived at the lake at 4.30 on the first morning. We really were like a pair of schoolkids setting off on some adventure. He quickly set up the HD camera kit, and once I was wired for sound we headed off to the swim. Five minutes later I was pushing in the banksticks, and swinging the first rig into position. I was fishing about 20 yards out, slightly to the left, and in around 16ft of water, and the plan was to use the same tackle and tactics as the North Lake session. Once I had placed the rod on the buzzer I turned and went to grab the second rod. I would only be using two. I had seen nothing, and hoped they would turn up and whilst I wondered, John locked his camera on the rods. It was our intention to film every bite and not end up as so many do, having someone in the lake pulling the line to look like action! What we could never have imagined is how quickly the first bite would happen. I had just picked up the second rod, when the bobbin on the first pulled up tight. Not being too slow on the uptake, I was on the rod in a flash, and within 25 seconds of starting I was into a fish. We battled away for ages, and the sound of my gibbering was accompanied by the knocking of my knees. It is as much pressure as you will ever be under in a fishing environment, with a camera shoved up your left nostril. All went well, and soon enough I was staring down on a big mirror, a 32lb 2oz mirror to be exact, and all of a sudden the pressure was off. Once again, John and I giggled away, because it really was a special moment. Once the dust had settled, I managed to get both rods back in the ball game, but it wasn't long before one of them made a bid for stardom. The cracking 24lb linear looked superb as we posed for the camera. We took a short tea break and spent a little time trying to get our breath back, and I remember saying to John that surely it couldn't get any better than that? I was wrong, it did... and then some!

***41lb 10oz for the cameras... Oh Lordy!!***

We sat around for another hour, and I could feel the nervous tension leaving me. We were able to leave the camera running because the digital HD setup allows you to delete stuff every now and again if nothing has occurred. John had just carried out this task once again when one of the rods heaved round and the buzzer sang. I remarked that this was quite simply a different kettle of fish entirely, and settled down to play the beast. On and on the fight raged, 27 minutes to be exact, before I was able to rather shakily lift the net around my prize. Bloody hell, it was huge! It took a few moments to catch my breath and sort out the scales and mat for the fish. There was a pregnant pause as I saw the reading... 41lb 10oz. Oh Lordy! I could never have dreamed of such a fish, and she behaved impeccably on the mat. Once she was back in the lake, I quickly got things sorted out again, and then it was time for handshakes and backslapping all round. I even punched myself in the face a few times (I didn't think a pinch would do the trick) just to make sure I wasn't still asleep and dreaming. A few minutes later I was releasing a feisty little 21lb common, and in accordance with the plan, thinking it was about time to pack up, I managed to get one more bite for the day. The fish showed me no mercy whatsoever, and all I could do was hang on for grim death. What a scrap! Yet another big mirror, which spun the scales round to 39lb, rendered me speechless. All I could hope for was that we could get just a fraction of this action the following day.

We were ready to go once again at 5.00, and although I thought the conditions were favourable, the carp didn't show up for some time. By about 9.00 we were beginning to think that I had used up all my luck the day before, when out of the blue one of the rods was away. After a short tussle I was soon showing off a rather strange-looking 27lb mirror, but however odd she may have looked, she was a real character. The final fish of the second day came shortly before packing-up time at midday, and this one again led me a merry old dance. The sun shone brightly as I held up the 38lb 12oz mirror for the camera, and

*A 40lb 5oz TV mirror on St George's Day.*

it was a great end to proceedings for the day. And as much as I would have loved to have got my head down, there were several opportunities that we simply couldn't miss out on.

We found some fish in a very snaggy and flooded corner of the lake, and managed to get really close to them. The footage shows a number of very big fish, including the 41 from the day before, going about their business. Both of us were blown away by all that had happened and so, as you do, we had a beer or three. We sat and chatted well into the night and viewed some of the footage, which looked absolutely awesome, especially as we had every bite and battle on film. Those two mornings were all about getting the action stuff, and the following morning David would arrive to do the important footage to link it all together. And so, at 4.30 John and I, with slightly thick heads, set off for the last time. I got the rods out in short order, and we settled down to the business at hand. David ensured we were all singing from the same sheet of music, and just as I thought I may be starting to understand some of it, one of the rods was nearly torn from the rest. With a few cameras now recording events I knew the footage would be spectacular. The 36lb 12oz mirror made us all smile. David had never seen a fish that big and his reaction was priceless. The day wore on with no more action and just as I was trying desperately to get the last bit right, I noticed a few carp just over the cameraman's shoulder. As you would, I asked to be excused and got a spare rod sorted. I positioned the small PVA bag as quietly as possible no more than 2ft from the bank, and no sooner had I relaxed than the rod skidded across the sandy ground. We got it all on film, and the immaculate 29lb 3oz mirror made everything complete... or so we thought.

Eventually I got the last section of the programme right, the boss man was happy, and as we discussed the future I got one last bite. Now, I have hooked fish that have shocked me with their power, but never – and I mean never – anything like this. At 40lb 5oz the mirror meant that I had caught two over the magic mark for a single programme, but the fight... well, I really don't think words will ever be able to describe it. I really do hope that you get to see it one day, and then you will know exactly what I am trying to say. It was April 23rd, St George's Day, and we could think of no better way to end the programme. As I said, it really doesn't get any better than that! It's interesting, because the following week I had to go off and do a feature for *Crafty Carper* with my good friend, Lewis Porter. Some may think that the fish I caught up to 24lb would have been something of an anticlimax, especially considering the size of those I had landed the week before. Nothing, however, could be further from the truth; I found it just as enjoyable, and satisfying, as I always do. I can only hope and pray that that feeling never leaves me.

Actually, I couldn't have been happier with life right then. Most importantly, Lynn was doing well, despite all the problems that still continue to interfere with her health. The book-writing was carrying on at breakneck speed, and I was even starting to enjoy shining my backside on the computer seat for hours on end... honest! And of course there were my commitments to the companies who support me. Steve Cole, the-then media manager at Fox, had blagged the use of the North Lake at Yateley for a couple of weeks to do a whole host of work for DVDs and website-related stuff. Once that was organised, I simply wanted to disappear for a little, and I had the perfect place to chill, Melchbourne. It may surprise some people that I don't spend all my life chasing individual targets. Yes, every now and again a fish comes up on my radar that I want to catch, but mostly I just want to enjoy my time on the bank, and if a carp or two come to the party that's just the icing on the cake. To that end I sorted out my gear and filled the air-dry bags with plenty of boilies. Once the alarm clock ripped me from my slumber one cold and dismal Monday in early May, I headed north. I was in a hurry, and with the pounding of Guns N' Roses at the correct decibels, and the sound of tortured air rushing through the car's radiator, I made it to Northampton in record time. Once again I sat on the inlet bridge for a while until I noticed a couple of bivvies, which kind of broke the spell. I knew both the anglers, which meant I could drink tea and catch up on what had been happening on the little Estate Lake. One of them had a double-figure common in his net, and as we did the pictures, I realised I had seen this fish a couple of times, and it dawned on me just how few of the maybe 50-60 carp in the lake actually got caught. It was interesting, and certainly lit my fires a little more as I tried to address that problem, although I just didn't know how, at the time. I saw one fish and set up in the area, but the problems initially had nothing to do with catching carp. The sheep had had their lambs, and these fluffy little gits were just about to make my life hell. Amongst a whole host of other issues, an hour after casting out I received a belting take. Trouble was, the rod was fast disappearing up the field in the mouth of one of the lambs. Huffing and puffing, I eventually rescued the thing, which seemed to excite the little buggers even more, and they started to use my other rods as hurdles to leap over.

They got bored in the end, but they were lucky not to end up in my freezer! And it wasn't just the lambs that caused problems. A little later that day I was chilling out, when an alarming bleat got my attention, and I gazed open-mouthed as I watched two sheep drifting down the lake in the lake's little fibreglass boat. I couldn't stop laughing, even when the farmer arrived. He was fuming and it took an age to get them back on dry land. Crazy! Once I had repositioned the rod, I didn't have to wait long for a bite, the problem though, was that it was a little mirror I had caught several times before. I hate catching the same fish over and over again, but to get to the other fish I guessed that was what would happen from time to time. A small common in the night meant I was getting things right, of course, but I wanted a fish I hadn't seen before, and later that day I landed a splendid-looking mirror of 21lb 10oz that fitted the bill quite nicely. My friend Mark was with me at the time, and

*This Estate Lake 21lb 10oz fitted the bill quite nicely.*

he didn't recognise it either, which at last meant I was getting somewhere. That said, I had a book to write, and suitably rested I spent a few days tickling the computer keys.

Whilst at home a little problem arose, and I had to make a doctor's appointment. Not that surprising, you may think, but when I tell you it was the first one I had ever made in my life, you may just see what I mean. I have simply never been to a doctor, not unless they carried me there on a stretcher. The problem was that I was going for a pee a lot more than I normally did, so my wife and just about all my friends, started hounding me to see a doctor, so I did. Oh, I so wish I hadn't! There were a couple of other things I needed to talk about, too, one being that every joint in my body hurt like hell. It's the end product of a life spent jumping out of aeroplanes, of course. 22 years of living in the slipstream is bound to take its toll. The aches turned out to be arthritis, and I can live with that. What I can't live with is what happens when you tell someone you pee a lot. I ask you, why in the name of all things holy, do they have to stick a digit up your backside? And why does someone, two chicks in this case, have to watch you take a leak? I couldn't help thinking that these medical types have extremely warped minds. Then there was the fact that they needed to take a whole armful of blood, and then test just about every other bodily fluid they could lay their hands on. At the end of the day I looked remarkably like a sucked maggot. I can guarantee I will never go again... ever!

With a couple more chapters completed, and my embarrassing visit to the doctors fading nicely, I was once again patrolling around the Estate Lake. A nice mirror head-and-shouldered about 100 yards to my right, and that was where I set three small margin traps an hour later. It all looked spot on, and around midnight I was slipping a 17lb linear back to his home. Yet again it was a familiar fish, and a little later I had landed a common of similar size that I was practically on first name terms with. Again, I spent a

***Although I rarely saw other anglers at Melchbourne, I was never really alone.***

long time wondering about the fish I was seeing, and wondering why I wasn't catching them. One in particular sprang to mind, and that was a mid-30 fully-scaled that I had seen several times patrolling around the edges. It was just one of those carp that you would walk a million miles over hot coals to catch, but how was I going to catch it?

Dawn came and went (bless her!) and by 10 o'clock I was getting itchy feet. The plan was to spend the day looking, and then looking some more. I was just about to set off when some movement caught my eye. Several yards down to my left I could see a vortex on the water, and as the area was fairly open, I crept closer on my belly. And there, just under my chin, was the fully-scaled ghosting in and out of the margin. After a few minutes I could see a pattern emerging, and as quickly and quietly as possible, I flicked a few Response Pellets onto the spot. My jaw nearly hit the deck when she returned and hoovered up the lot. Again, I acted quickly and got a rig positioned; surely now I was going to bag this stunning carp? I had to wait 40 minutes before the rod hooped round and a huge bow wave surged towards the middle of the lake. The battle was a rather drawn-out affair. I took my time, as I didn't want this one falling off. I positioned the net in the water and the carp broke the surface for the first time. It was a big fish for sure, but I couldn't help wondering where all the scales had gone. I heaved it into the waiting net and could see immediately it was the big mirror I had landed the year before at 37lb. I was a little sad to begin with, one because I don't like catching the same fish, and two, because I had missed out on the fully-scaled once again. That said, the fish I landed looked glorious, and at 35lb 6oz after spawning I really shouldn't complain too much, should I? A plethora of commitments were to keep me from my own fishing for some time, and it would be a while before my return.

I talked of a young lad with juvenile arthritis earlier, and it was around that time

***I had a PB barbel after 35 years.***

I had begun to get very angry with the-then editor of *Carpworld*. When I opened the magazine that I expected, quite rightly, would show several pictures of Isaac playing and holding fish despite his crippling disability, I was nauseous. I was shocked to see the opening full-page picture was of the editor weighing and dealing with a carp he had never caught! There was also the fact that about fifty per cent of the article was about that brave lad, and that session, yet he had seen fit to only include one postage stamp-size picture of him. I said nothing at the time, but I was seething and eventually I had had enough. Basically, I told him where to go, which was one of the saddest things I have ever done in carp fishing. You see, Tim Paisley is a true friend, as are his staff and family, but it was just impossible for me to work with such a self-promotional individual. Loyalty is everything to me, but if I couldn't be true to myself then it really wasn't worth carrying on. It was time for me to move on, and in the end I agreed a deal with David Hall Publishing to do my diary in *Advanced Carp Fishing*, and run a technical series in *Total Carp*.

With all of that upsetting my rhythm I decided that we really needed to do another TV programme and eventually, in an effort to change things as much as possible, I contacted David Burgess who ran the Royalty Fishery on the River Avon at Christchurch, in Dorset. It had a great track record with carp and he was more than willing to help. Having never caught a carp from a river, I needed as much help as I could get! I was also excited because many of my boyhood heroes had fished there, but I could never have realised the biggest problem when fishing for carp on this river. You see, carp can survive in the sea, not just brackish water, and very often the fish would swim from the Avon to the Stour via Christchurch Harbour. And that is exactly what seemed to have happened prior to our filming. I only saw two carp during the two days we were there, and amazingly I got a bite from one of

*I told Lynn I would catch it, and on the recce I did. Scaly at 26lb 2oz.*

them, which just happened to fall off! Now, this was the one time that I started to learn a little more about those who live and work in the business of 'show'. David Hatter went into meltdown when I lost the fish, and I seriously thought he was having some kind of spaz attack. In fact he was delighted, and reckoned it was going to make great viewing! I wanted to punch him, several times in fact, but as he was so orgasmically pleased with events I decided to spare him a beating... for a while, anyway. It was a wonderful outing on that river, and reminded me of my youth on the Bristol Avon chasing barbel. Indeed, even though a carp proved a step too far, I did land a personal best barbel of 10lb 7oz after about 35 years. I was also amazed to see the number of mullet in the river, another fish I angled hard for in my youth, and vowed one day to return and land a mullet and a carp in the same session.

Whilst I was sitting on the bank on our last day in Christchurch, I happened to have a chance conversation with Rob Hughes, who runs a small syndicate on his land in Shropshire. I asked if I could do some filming there, and he agreed immediately, so we arranged for me to go there by way of a reconnaissance the following week. We wanted to do a small-water piece, covering the inherent problems such waters can throw up from time to time. At two acres, and just about as silty as it gets, this seemed to fit the bill nicely. The trip would also give me a chance to do the pictures for my first technical piece in *Total Carp*, so I arranged for Jon Bones to meet me up there. I arrived the day before, after first making one fish my target for this particular mission. I had seen Mat Woods holding a cracking mirror called Scaly at over 30lb in a magazine a month or so before, and he would be the fish I most wanted to catch. It was interesting fishing, to say the least, and most of the night was spent dealing with about ten of Rob's new stock fish. However, early in the morning I found myself playing something a whole lot different. It chugged around for an age before I scooped up a lovely-looking carp, and on the mat I discovered that it was the carp I went there to catch,

*I informed Lynn I would ring when I landed the Black Mirror... so I did. 29lb 10oz.*

Scaly! At 26lb 2oz she had lost a lot of weight due to spawning, but I wasn't complaining, and she made the front cover of Total, too, which made a great start to my time at DHP.

I couldn't wait for the following week to come, and after looking at the scrapbook of fish in the lodge before I left, I designated another fish as the next target. It was highly unlikely that I would catch it, of course, especially with a camera following me around, but it's good to dream. So, the following Sunday I was on my way, having kissed Lynn goodbye and telling her that I would ring when I had caught the Black Mirror. The lake wasn't closed, of course, and I had to share the tiny, intimate pool with one of the members, which was exactly what I wanted. At around 7.00 John Dunford arrived and we set off to do a little stalking. I was amazed that after about an hour I had seen nothing, and started to become a bit concerned. At long last a good fish boomed out behind the island I was fishing to, and in the blink of an eye we raced round to get a rod or two on the spot. Fifteen minutes later I had cast PVA bags on my normal setup into the thick silt that showed signs of being fed on, and within ten minutes one of the rods was away. The fight wasn't too dramatic to begin with, but when I tried to lead the fish into my net, the tip of the rod got caught in a branch above my head. In the final edit it's not obvious, but the fish surged away and pulled the line out of the tree, and I didn't see it again for another 20 minutes. The next time it neared the net I was just a little more careful, and when I saw which fish it was, I probably became even more so. With a huge sigh of relief I drew the Black Mirror over the net cord and punched the air, yelling my battle cry. At 29lb 10oz he made a great start to proceedings and I couldn't help thinking once again, it's so much better to be lucky than good! I even made another prediction, in that I was going to catch the Kinky Back Common and, amongst a few other fish, I did just that. The filming was going so well, and with me proving the point about my rigs, especially in a situation when everything needs to be perfect, I could not have been happier. One other interesting point was that the

**It was great to get it all on camera.**

area was renowned for producing four leaf clovers, and would you believe it, I found one whilst we were filming. Maybe the fact that I was so fortunate was way out of my hands anyway, eh?

Book-writing, the Junior Event and the legendary Stoney & Friends bash at Yateley in aid of Macmillan Cancer Support, were all coming up next. Ironically, the morning of the event I had to take Lynn to the hospital for a check-up, and she really is a constant reminder of how important these cancer charity events are. I fished the Pads Lake as I couldn't see anyone fishing the far end of the pond. Now, the fishing can be tough when the lakes are so packed, and when you throw in a small gang of mad men and a few bottles of wine, things can get a little messy... which they did. However, along with having a wonderful time in great company and raising over £20,000 for the cause, I did land a couple of carp. A mirror of 25lb, and another of 30lb 5oz, livened up events considerably, especially a fellow that went by the name of Jack Daniels, and I left the event hoping he would never be invited again! I found out later that Allan Stone and his cohorts had, at the time, raised over half a million pounds for Macmillan, which just goes to prove what a remarkable man Allan is. A few days at Horseshoe Lake in Lechlade took up a lot of time at the Fox Carp Experience day, and one other strange task needed to be taken care of. I needed to do the voice-overs for the programmes that we had already done, which took place in my living room. But I must admit to being a little shocked when David Hatter asked me to 'camp' things up a little. I had to remind him, very calmly, that I was probably the last person on this planet he should ask to do that!

And then a little of the pressure I had put myself under at that time was off. *Light My Fire* was released and I was overwhelmed by the response from all of you. As much as I was excited, I was also very humbled by the way it was received. I am not the kind of man who is afraid to bare his soul, and neither am I someone who is frightened to say things exactly as I see them. The book was a little different to the normal, 'Look at me, ain't I

***A Stoney 30-pounder. A great event and a great man.***

the bollocks?' kind of thing, so to that end I wondered what people's reaction would be... I needn't have worried. Having it published was a very proud moment indeed.

I was now looking around for a lake, or a fish, on which I could concentrate my time, but I didn't really have a clue what to do with my fishing. I was having an absolute ball with the TV work, and all the other bits and pieces that were going on, but ultimately I wanted a target. I was looking for a carp that meant something to me, and not just another figure to add to an already burgeoning list. Lynn had been in hospital for three weeks, and whilst I worried hugely about that, I tried to sort out my future. I had a whole host of slide shows to do that winter, and it was whilst I was travelling north for one of those that the problem completely disappeared, as far as my fishing was concerned. It was early October, and I had stopped at a service station for a brew. As I got back in my motor my phone chirped into life, and I was pleased to see it was the Lord of the Manor down at Ashmead in Somerset. However, as pleased as I was to see his name, it didn't take long for a feeling of fear and trepidation to take over. He didn't sound too happy at all, and it revolved around the guy he had asked me about, and whom I had recommended for the Ashmead syndicate. No names, no pack drill of course, but angler 'A', as he will be known, had arrived for the start of the season, and set himself up on one of the islands. No problems so far. That evening the syndicate was holding a barbecue down by the lodge, at which angler 'A' and his buddy got completely plastered. It looked even worse when he retrieved a slab of lager from his motor, and with his buddy in tow, staggered off to his swim. Thinking he was probably a responsible kind of guy, although he had been a little rude to several of the partygoers, they let him go. At some ungodly hour of the night a buzzer was heard, and it kept on going for ages, until someone switched on and ran to the source. 'A' was completely unconscious and unable to do anything, and of course the fish was eventually lost. Come the morning a posse of angry anglers picked up 'A's kit and practically threw him out of the gates. Along with his friend, they would never be allowed there again, and quite rightly too. I listened horrified and, sure that I was going to suffer the same fate, I really didn't know what to say. But Mark, fully aware I suspect, of the discomfort I was feeling, saved the day. The problem was that 'A' had only paid half his syndicate money, which, if I am honest, only made me feel ten times worse. However, like a knight in shining armour, Mark slew the dragon and saved my blushes. If I paid him the required amount I could have a winter ticket for Ashmead, and therefore the ticket of my dreams. I was silent for a few seconds and he asked if I was okay. I just didn't know what to say, and my simple 'yes' seemed a little feeble at the time, but it was all I could muster. My ticket would start on 1st November, and whilst I was in danger of spontaneously combusting on the rest of my journey, my head was reeling at the thought. I had a fair few things to take care of before I could lose myself at Ashmead, but I could never have imagined what my time at this great lake would mean to me, and will surely mean for the rest of my days. I was just about to find everything I had been looking for from carp fishing and, I dare say, a fair bit more, too!

Lynn had been in and out of hospital for some time, and I was functioning because I had enlisted the help of the odd person, and a nurse who could visit Lynn at home. I couldn't rely on that situation forever, but at her insistence I was still making plans and trying to carry on as normally as possible. And believe you me, that was no easy task! If I say I am going to do something, then I will do everything in my power to make that commitment. If Lynn feels she is getting in the way, and stopping me doing things, then her condition can spiral out of control. What that means is that I try to keep her as happy as I can, at the very least; if her morale is high then it keeps everything on an even keel. I had been a very bad juggler for around eight months by now, but I still carried on, and had arranged to do a trip to Spain with *Fishing TV*. The finer details were yet to be sorted out, but I was really looking forward to finding out what the River Ebro had to offer, and not just on the carp-fishing front either.

Added to all that was the prospect that in the middle of October all the Fox team headed to Holland for the second Fox Carp Experience. I had a slide show to do, which was the first one I had done with an interpreter, and what a bizarre experience that turned out to be – because I don't think any of the funny stuff translated well into Dutch! We also got a chance to display all the tackle on a lake, and that occasion was so well attended that at times it was hard to deal with the number of people. That said, it was fun to get everyone together, and on both nights we had some tremendous brainstorming sessions. High on the list of things to discuss was the launch of the Stratos 12000e reels. I had taken the testing of these reels as far as it was possible, at Mercers Park, but we all agreed that we wanted to do something absolutely outrageous by way of another test, and as a publicity stunt. Some of the suggestions bordered on the ridiculous, and whilst we all laughed about them, it wasn't until we were on the ferry coming home that the final decision was made.

The weather was mild for the time of year, so we all spent our time on the poop deck of the ship. For the life of me, I cannot remember who suggested it, but by the time the ship was docking under the white cliffs of Dover, Steve Cole had decided that I should attempt to catch a conger eel from an English Channel wreck! As completely bonkers as that sounds, it really was the ultimate reel-test, and plans started to be made. We would be fishing from the Fox-sponsored boat, Brighton Diver, based, of course, in Brighton Marina. I think that skipper Paul thought we were all a little unwell, but readily agreed to take part in the madness. To ramp up the tension still further, the Sky Sports *Tight Lines'* cameras would also be on-board, and my old mate, Keith Arthur, would introduce the scenario to the audience. I spoke privately to Keith about it all, and he, along with everyone else I spoke to, thought it was totally impossible. Indeed, as Keith introduced the segment on the boat, he remarked that he really wasn't sure that it could be done. As we motored out into the Channel I remember being in a conversation with Shaun McSpadden, Steve Cole, Fox sea angler Alan Yates, skipper Paul, and the Sky production team. The skipper felt that it would look pretty bad on Fox because he was sure the tackle couldn't do the job, and when the production fellow said it was going on the programme whatever happened, I turned and looked at Shaun and Steve. To his eternal credit Shaun simply said, "What will be will be... let's crack on!" That was exactly the way it should be, and I continued to get my gear ready. We stopped halfway out and feathered for some fresh mackerel for bait – something that brought back wonderful memories from my youth – and with that done it wasn't long before I was lowering a mackerel flapper over the side. I was armed with a Stratos 12000e reel loaded with some 30lb braid, and a 4.5TC FX1 spod rod, and silently wished the setup all the very best. Evidently, the wind and the tide were slightly against us begin with, and I had the opportunity to warm myself up catching a few cod, whiting and a small tope. Poor old Alan Yates was clucking around me like an old mother hen, bless him, suggesting that I should saw the butt of the rod down to make things easier. I wasn't having any of that; if I was going to do this the tackle would be as it should be. Around midday I was joined by the skipper, and told that the boat was being moved to the other side of the wreck. With the tide and wind being perfect, this would be the moment. In technical terms, because of the conditions, I would be directly over the wreck, which would make the whole thing a lot more difficult. It was time to 'stiffen the sinews and summon up the blood'!

I had caught a large pouting a little earlier, and as I swung it to hand I decided that he would be the bait I would use when the time came. Once the anchor was secured, I lowered my 'flapperised' pouting into the depths, and it took an age to make the 250ft journey. With that done I waited and watched while a few conger came over the rail, the biggest of which was 62lb caught by Keith. As they were dealing with that, I received the faintest of knocks

*I had no idea I could have so much fun with my clothes on!*

on the rod tip. I let out a yard of line, and very carefully raised the rod to see if it was still there, at which point the rod heaved over and I was connected to a proverbial monster. It is impossible to explain just how brutal and painful the next 15 minutes were. For all the world, the rod and reel looked like they would shatter into a million pieces, a situation that didn't go unnoticed by those on board, so much so, that none of them wanted to stand anywhere near me! The only real way to keep the fish moving was to not use the rod at all to begin with, but simply lean over the side and use the reel to lift the fish. So many times I got it off the bottom, only for it to tear line from a clutch that I could not tighten any more. Every muscle ached and I was truly amazed that everything held together, but not as amazed as I was when a huge conger hit the surface! Paul slipped in a chin gaff, and it was brought into the boat to the most incredible round of applause and cheering. Even people on the boat who knew nothing about fishing found it fascinating! I was gobsmacked and had to check I still had my kit on; I had no idea you could have that much fun and still be fully clothed. What a way to test some reels, and what a wonderful day. Keith still feels that it was one of the greatest segments they ever showed on *Tight Lines*, and as it is no longer aired, I would like to take this opportunity to thank Mick Brais, the producer, and Keith for having me on the show so many times.

Unfortunately, Lynn had been admitted to hospital once again a couple of days before, and I had done the conger thing whilst they talked over what to do about the situation. The following day the decision was made for them, and they had to carry out emergency surgery. This, quite obviously, stopped me from doing any fishing; I just can't concentrate when there are infinitely more important things to take care of. As always though, as soon as she was able to speak, she was adamant that I should make the commitment that had been arranged a couple of weeks before. I was off to Spain to do some filming for *Fishing. TV*. Lynn came out of hospital only three days before I was due to leave, so with a couple of friends and a nurse on standby, I headed off to Stansted Airport. I met up with David Hatter and John Dunford, but it turned out we would be one person light to begin with. Mark Barrett, predator angler, had got stuck in heavy traffic due to an accident on the M11. I couldn't believe how expensive Ryanair was, for the service offered, but soon enough we were on our way. The plan was for us to do a couple of days' cat fishing, which is something I had never done before, and of course a little carp fishing. Once all that was sorted out we wanted to check out anything else the Spanish countryside had to offer. As guests of Catfish Capers, they met us at the airport and got us to our apartments in good order. It left us plenty of time to get the gear sorted, so whilst I organised the fishing gear, David and John got the cameras ready to rock and roll. We were also introduced to our guides for the week, Gaz and Paul, and I will never be able to thank them enough for their help; I had never met such a crazy and enthusiastic duo, and I christened them the Ebro Maniacs. In the end, that is the title we gave to the four programmes that ended up as a DVD.

Early the next morning we were up, and with some breakfast forced down our throats, we made our way to the river. In double-quick time, we were loaded up into two aluminium boats, and roaring up the river to one of the guys' favourite spots. Now, as much as the guides were there to help, I wanted to do as much as possible towards any captures myself, so it was a while before we were set up and angling. Four catfish rods were spread over the section of river, and each Size 4/0 hook was baited with a string of pellets, and the most hideous-smelling squid I have ever had the misfortune to allow near my nose. Once placed from the boat, half a sack of 25mm pellets followed them to the bottom. I waited, somewhat nervously, for the first bite. I have no idea why I was so nervous as I have caught marlin, sailfish and many other extremely angry fish, but, 'Hey ho, let's get going', was all I could think. The first bite was a small carp that I wondered about, firstly, how it was still alive in a

*At 133lb I was suitably blown away!*

**It was the Ebro boat battles that I shall remember the most.**

river filled with huge catfish, and secondly, how the hell it got that bait in its mouth in the first place. The next bite, a few minutes later, left me in no doubt as to what was on the other end. I had seen a few battles with these monsters on the telly, and I couldn't help thinking that the anglers had made a meal of the fight, over-egging it for the camera. I would like to apologise right now, because I now know that you weren't. Apart maybe from the conger eel a few weeks before, I don't think I had ever felt anything like it. It dragged me down the sandy banks, leaving me breathless at its power. It was around 15 minutes before Gaz was able to get a grip on its lower jaw with his gloved hand, and drag it onto the waiting mat. At 133lb I was suitably blown away. The footage was fantastic, and I think my reaction to the bite, and playing the fish, summed up exactly what those fish are all about. I landed a few more that day, and couldn't help having a healthy respect for them, but soon enough it was time to get back to civilisation. I really couldn't wait for tomorrow to come.

We met up with Mark, and spent the evening in the local tavern, where we found a fishing rod behind the bar. It was armed with a gnarly old multiplier. We christened it the Widow Maker because of the painful-looking butt you would have to place in your groin region to play a fish, and sure enough, the following day, we all stared at the tip of that rod with the bell attached waiting for it to ring... which it duly did. I landed a fish of 137lb, but it was the boat battles that I shall remember the most. The crowning glory for me, and the Widow Maker, was being towed around for ages by my biggest fish of the trip, weighing 144lb. Getting every savage bite and battle on film made sure the programming was complete. The only problem was, and it just went to show that we were right about that rod, were the bruises around my nether regions. With no butt pad it made the whole thing a very painful experience! As good as all that was, I am a carp angler at heart, and I

*My first ever Zander and the only one caught for the cameras.*

*The Ebro is stuffed full of carp and they are getting bigger.*

now wanted to move on and see what the river was all about on the carp-fishing front.

Mark had never caught a 30lb common, so the next plan was to bag him one. The river is stuffed full of carp, and they are getting bigger all the time, which isn't surprising really, as they have to run the gauntlet of catfish to over 200lb on a daily basis. Most of the small ones end up as catfish poo, I suspect. As everyone uses pellets on the river, it made sense to use the same, and with the rods constantly ripping off, we soon sorted out Mark's 30, and with that another programme was complete. One of the biggest highlights was the wildlife, and top of that list would be the golden eagles that soared above our heads on the thermals every day. The wild boars were impressive, if not a little scary, but thankfully they caused us no bother.

After that we wanted to go predator fishing, but things were certainly a little tougher on that score. Eventually, I caught the only zander for the cameras, my first of that species. Dragging it up through 80ft of water had me thinking it would die, but I was relieved to see it swim off strongly, after he made his debut on film. One spot our guides were keen for us to fish, and therefore give us access to Iberian barbel, was unfortunately occupied by a couple of German anglers who, after spreading their beach towels on the ground, started fishing for bleak. We left them to it, returning in the evening once they had left. The river had the barbel, of course, but I spotted the odd wild carp finning around in the current, and I spent an age trying to catch one, which I did in the end. I think everyone was bored with my self-indulgences by then, and somehow I convinced them to return in the morning. I lost a big barbel, but addressed the failure by landing another black wild carp. It was great fishing, and proves once again (for me anyway) that they don't have to be big fish to make you smile. The final day we just chilled out, catching countless carp until it was time to drive to the airport and hope that Ryanair could get us home safely. With that trip out of the way, I had absolutely no commitments to take care of, and at long last I could get back to fishing for myself.

# Chapter Six

## Serendipity

*It was probably the most perfect environment I had ever seen.*

The Ashmead ticket would start in a couple of weeks, but a call shortly after getting back to Blighty had me drooling at the mouth, and stopped me getting any sleep for a couple of days. Mark Walsingham wondered if I would like to go to Somerset as his guest, and get my first taste of angling on the chalky Avalon flats. The following Monday I raced down the A303 with thoughts of Guinevere and Lancelot racing through my mind. Legend has it that whilst avoiding King Arthur, they courted on the Avalon flats, and I was hoping that I would be making a date myself with a certain lady called Single Scale, at some stage. I was on fire but I had no idea that my carp-fishing life was about to become positively pyrotechnical.

I pulled off the A303, and after negotiating the roads through Ash, I found myself at the top of the track that led down to the lake. It was dark so I couldn't take in the magnificent

*The strange bridge made getting to the island very interesting indeed.*

vista across Somerset, but as I neared the gates I switched off the headlights. I didn't want an errant beam to spoil things, and annoy anyone who may be fishing near the entrance. There was only one car in the car parking area, and as I got out of mine the utter silence struck me. The first thing I wanted to do was have a good walk around, and as I did so, I couldn't help feeling that this was probably the most perfect environment I had ever been in. It felt as if I had slipped on some comfortable slippers, and, as weird as it sounds, I was home. I cannot (because I probably don't have them in my armoury) find the words to describe what I felt at that time. The feeling has only got stronger as the years have passed, and one day I will return to the lake. For now, though, I just wanted to take it all in; I was mesmerised.

A couple of years before my arrival, Mark had bought the venue and, after doing so, he and his right-hand man, Alan, started making plans to join the two little lakes together and extend the fishery to the extent of the boundaries. Goat Willow, the main lake, was about 2.5 acres, and just to its right was a smaller pool called Tom's, the history of which is Mark's story to tell, not mine. It seemed truly amazing that Goat Willow had produced such huge fish, but it had, and through an extremely demanding 18 months, Mark and Alan had joined the two lakes together, along with bringing the moat that ran along the fence that surrounded the property, into play. In all, the property of around 20 acres now had about 12 acres of water to go at, and it looked amazing as the light of the day started to chase away the darkness; and the more I looked the more excited I became. Eventually I came across a bivvy, and as I couldn't see any movement, I thought I would leave him to sleep whilst I continued my voyage of discovery. I carried on walking for an hour before I heard my first Ashmead carp break the silence of the misty dawn. It sounded like it had come from the area where I had seen the bivvy, and decided I needed to introduce myself in an effort to see the area of activity. Graham was awake when I got to him, and over the next hour we drank tea and chatted. Several more fish showed in the same area, and as Graham couldn't get to them, I decided it was time to push my barrow round to that side of the lake and start some fishing. The lake is very broken up, and although the fish were only 50 yards from me in Graham's swim, it still took me twenty minutes to get to where I could cover the spots. Due to the low-lying nature of the ground there, the mud was very thick and seemed to suck at the wheel of my barrow as I made my way round. The shock didn't end there either. When I arrived I found that the area I wanted to fish was on the other side of an island. The only way I could get there was to use a bridge that consisted of two telegraph poles. With all my gear this was going to be fun, but first of all I made my way across to see what I could see... I saw carp, and lots of 'em, that's what!

By talking to Mark I knew the lake contained around 150 carp; 60 from the original stocking and 40 that had been born and bred in the lake. These had been supplemented with 50 hand-picked stock fish, and whilst I couldn't see anywhere near that number of fish, I could still see a fair few. Most noticeable amongst them was a small white koi. No one knows how it got in there, but I can tell you he is the best fish-locating device I have ever come across. He went by the name of Shagger, and I couldn't help thinking that the rest of the fish must have hated him; he really did give the game away far too easily. Evidently, the name came from viewing the fish at spawning time; all you could ever see was this little white missile rushing around trying desperately to get laid. Top man! I sat and watched the fish milling around for a while before the urge to get a rod in amongst them became too much. It took a few very wobbly minutes to get my gear across the poles, but soon enough I was ready to go. Not wanting to go mad with the bait, I decided to fish just small PVA bags of 10mm Pulse boilies and matching Response Pellets. Due to the very shallow nature of the lake, it was easy to see the areas that the carp have been feeding on, and three small clay clouds had already been noted. As the carp turned their backs on each spot, I lowered each little bag into position, and as quietly as possible I dropped four similar bags around each of them. With the lines slackened off I sat back watching and wondering why the carp refused to visit my neatly laid traps, a situation that was to become all too familiar over the next couple of weeks. Mark joined me later in the evening and we chatted about the lake for the next two hours, and the more he talked, the more in love with the place I became.

I woke in the morning an hour before first light, and must admit to being a little disappointed at not getting any action. I had heard the odd fish in the night, so they were obviously still around, and to console myself I gave Lynn a ring so I could have a little moan... as you do. As we spoke, one of the buzzers let out a single bleep, and in the blink of an eye the rod ripped off. Lynn was thrown unceremoniously into the long grass, and once the rod was in my hands I concentrated on playing my first Ashmead carp. To that end, I probably took things far too easy, but I really didn't want to take any chances. It was some time before I was able to lead the stunning-looking mirror over the net cord and into the folds of my net. She spun the scales round to 20lb 11oz and it turned out that she was one of the fish that had been born in the lake, which only added to the excitement of the capture. Graham came around to take some pictures, and as soon as I could, I watched the special linear swim off in its home. Now that is what I call a great start!

A problem was that as much as the shallow lake allowed me to see where the fish had been feeding, it also enabled the swans to see exactly where I had placed my baits. For the next 48 hours they tried their best to make my life a living hell. The carp would not put up with the dumb white creatures feeding on their spots, and as soon as they arrived the carp would run for cover. It was imperative that I got away from them, so went for another good look around. Yet again it was Shagger who gave the game away,

*At 20lb 11oz that is what I call a great start.*

and I was able to set a number of traps in a small channel where he and about 20 of his mates were mooching around. As quietly as I had laid those traps, they were so aware of me that they eventually drifted away, leaving me fishless come the morning.

I had spotted Single Scale, the ultimate Ashmead target, on several occasions and all I could think about was getting back to the lake as soon as humanly possible. I spoke to Mark briefly on the way home and told him how the rest of the session had gone, along with telling him that I would bring the money down on my next visit for my winter ticket, although I don't think he had any idea that it would be the following day. I had never been so engrossed in a lake, and after being in my house for only a few short hours, Lynn said that it was obvious my mind was somewhere else, and why didn't I go back there tomorrow? The words had hardly left her mouth before I was in the freezer and packing the air-dry bag with a few kilos of 10mm'ers. I left at death o'clock the following morning and within a couple of hours I was making my way down the long, winding (and extremely bumpy) road. It was just about getting light, and for the first of many occasions I stopped at the highest point to take in the scenery. The West Country never looked so good, and with a spring in my step I opened the gate and had a good look around. Graham was the only angler on the lake and we shared a brew, but I had to get on my toes. There were carp to catch, and I wasn't going to do that sitting on a bait bucket, now, was I? I really wanted to fish a different area from last time, but as soon as I had crossed the poles onto the island I was confronted by the sight of several large carp chugging around in the margins. As quickly as I could I got a couple of traps set and sat back, convinced it was just a matter of time. The carp were very active, but nothing happened and eventually they drifted away. I wanted to have a more detailed look at this area, and ended up wading across a very shallow channel to the left of the island and climbing up the steep bank onto the next island in the chain. With my chest waders on, I sat in the long marsh grass for an age, and

**The long, winding and very bumpy road to my dreams.**

I cannot tell you how happy I was that I did. I watched in total awe as Single Scale hovered around a small weedbed, investigating the small open spot that was in about 4ft of water. I was only a few yards away from her and I could see every detail on the body of a carp well over 50lb. It was probably the best half an hour I had spent fishing in a very long time. Right there and then, and I have no idea why, I decided that if I was ever going to catch that carp, this was where the bite would come from. For the first time in a long while the thrill of the chase began.

Mark joined me a little later, and again I excitedly asked him questions about the fish. He even told me about a fully-scaled that resided there that he had never caught, and just as he stood to leave, I told him I would give him a ring in the morning and tell him how much it weighed. Well, we can all dream, can't we? I also made a decision a little later when I bumped into another member. He was someone well-known in the carp-fishing world, and during our conversation he mentioned that he would never use orange as a colour for his hookbaits, which I found a little strange. I also made the decision that every hookbait I used there would be tipped with orange plastic, just to test out his rather dubious theory. I got myself set up properly a bit later, and had a most peculiar bite at around 10.00 that evening. It had, in all likelihood, never seen a hook before, and after a crazy battle I had one of the stockies in the net at around 14lb. I had the rod quickly back in the game and got my head down, but my sleep was interrupted frequently by fish crashing out nearby. By 7.00 I was starting to wonder what I had done wrong. Surely I should have had another bite by now? I had just fired up the kettle when the closest rod hooped round and the alarm howled. This fish was taking no prisoners, and it was some time before I had any kind of control. Pressure and patience saved the day once again, and the fish slid into my outstretched net with no problem. It was a lot bigger than the last one, that much I could see, but when I peered a little more closely I nearly swallowed my tongue. There lay the fully-scaled that Mark had told me about the day

*The night before, I told Mark I would let him know how much she weighed.*

before! At 29lb 2oz she wasn't as big as some had thought, but when they look like that size is completely irrelevant. After suffering a certain amount of abuse from Mark, especially about the colour of certain parts of my anatomy, he said he would be there in ten minutes, and as I held her up for the camera she looked quite spectacular in the early-morning sunshine.

A little later, once I was on my own again, I decided to take a couple of rods, and try to find some fish to fish for. I had baited a small channel the previous day and wanted to see if anything had come to dinner. I was waylaid en route because I found a few stockies grubbing around in a tiny hole in some weed, and once I had a rig in position it took about ten minutes to get a bite. The problem was, through my own stupidity, it took only ten seconds for it to fall off! Disgusted with myself, I carried on and was amazed when I peered over some marginal bushes to look at the spot I had baited. There before me were all the large carp in the lake, and once again I marvelled at how huge they looked in such an intimate environment. Unbelievably, it took me eight hours to get two traps set, probably because I sat staring at them for an age, which was almost as good as a capture to me. I was so on top of the fish that I didn't even dare put up a bivvy, so, in mid-November I was spending a night under the stars. It was all to no avail, but as I drove out of the gates the next morning, I knew I was hooked just as certainly as any carp I had ever caught.

I returned the following week and managed to land two more of the stock fish. At the very least I was getting bites, but as much as I wanted to be there every breathing moment of every day, I had one very important thing to take care of. *Light My Fire* had been on sale for a couple of weeks, but the first time I had a chance to stand and sign copies was at the Carp & Coarse Spectacular show in Donington. I couldn't believe the number of books we sold that weekend. It was the last time I would have any nerves about *Light My Fire*, and I became the happiest man around. I was excited, and it was probably that excitement which got me

**Winter was in full swing and it was freezing on the Somerset flats.**

to agree to visit a water the following week. I had been invited as a guest to a water in Essex by a good mate of mine. It was something I should never have done, but he had had some great results from there, and he felt he may be able to sort me out a ticket. Unfortunately, buffoonery has always come relatively easily to me, and although I am not happy about it, I just have to put up with my inadequacies from time to time. Straight after the Sandown show, which was another cracking book-signing weekend, I decided, in my infinite wisdom, to do a recce trip to the lake in Essex. I should have been travelling down to Somerset, but on the Monday morning I was crossing the toll bridge and going to a lake I had never even seen before. The weather was getting increasingly cold and this, coupled with an imminent bout of man flu, ensured that the one night I did there was a very uncomfortable affair. Along with every other carp angler, I could never have imagined how long the freeze would last. That said, and although I should have been elsewhere, I hooked but eventually lost what felt like a good fish from under the ice. I couldn't wait to get away, but I had to do the pictures for a technical magazine feature before I could run for home and cuddle up to a hot-water bottle.

Every lake seemed to be freezing, including Ashmead, and as Christmas approached I just wanted this spectacular year to end on a high note. I even went over to Sandhurst again, but a night with those horrible wriggly, smelly, red germs had me doubting my sanity. It was time to go and spend some time in Plymouth with my parents, and to begin with I was more than happy about that. Until, of course, the weather warmed up and I received a call from Mark at Ashmead to tell me the lake had produced a few fish up to 34lb. There was little I could have done about it, but I must say it was all I could think about. And then, just as I thought I could suffer no more, the guy who runs the syndicate in Essex texted to inform me that he had landed a 43-pounder from the area that I was fishing the week before. Well, happy bloody Christmas!

By the time I got home everything was starting to freeze, and it would be two weeks before I could cast a line again. Being housebound is not my favourite pastime, and neither is it Lynn's. I was never meant to live indoors for long and as much as she loves me, she was starting to wonder when the weather would change just as much as I was! The next carp-fishing thing to do was the show at Brentwood on 8th and 9th of January, and as I drove to the event the weatherman on the radio said it was due to warm up late on that Sunday evening. I had sorted my gear out before I left, so if he was as good as his word, I was going back to Somerset. On the Sunday I left the arena for a break, and when I walked outside I could feel the difference, and noticed the increasing cloud was coming from the southwest. I was going fishing! The following Monday I was racing down the A303 for the first time that year, and I resolved that if the lake was frozen, the wind and rain I was driving into would soon clear the ice. It was dark when I arrived and the first thing I did as I got out of my car was lob a small stone towards the water. It landed with a horrible clank, and I just prayed that the far end would be unfrozen, as that was where the warm wind was now pumping. I put my gear on the barrow and made a quick cup of tea in the lodge, then, as the light started to fill the sky, I could make out the silvery shimmer of ripples on the water towards the far end. The problem, if I can call it such, was that this area was the one I had fished most but, as I reminded myself, that was where I had seen the big girl most, and hadn't I already sorted out the spot from which to catch her?

I got two rods fishing fairly quickly, normal setup, and baited up with three PVA bags of 10mm'ers once again. It wasn't until morning that I had any action when one of the bobbins pulled up tight. No line was taken, and in short order I had a tiny common of around 8lb in the net. With 3ins of ice on the rest of the lake, I stayed where I was and caught another small common the following morning. As small as they were, I was delighted to be getting some action considering the conditions. There was one other bonus of being in this area, and that was that I could bait the spot across the shallow channel. I had seen nothing to make me do so, it was just that I was sure it was where, ultimately, I would get action from the bigger fish. I watched a guy turn up over the top of a couple of islands in front of me, so the ice must have been clearing. The following morning I was packing up when I landed the biggest of the trip, another common of 14lb. As I made my way to reel in the last rod it simply tore off at a hundred miles an hour. It was very obviously a bigger fish, but as I slipped and slithered over the thawing mud the bloody thing fell off. I was gutted, and threw my rod into the bushes, before eventually retrieving it and making my way to the car. I stopped for a brew with the chap who had arrived the day before, and as we spoke he got himself a bite. In no more than thirty seconds he had a huge common waiting to be netted, which I duly did. It weighed 37lb and we were both suitably blown away. He told me that he knew I loved my boilies, but he was so much more confident with particles. Whatever, I was happy for him, but I couldn't help thinking about what he said. I was never going to put a particle in the lake; I don't like them, and rarely use them, but it was the confidence thing that made me think a little harder. I had been using 10mm baits there, and as much as they very often make a difference to results, I really needed to go back to what I did best, and the thing that gives me all the confidence I will ever need. From now on I would be using a spread of 15mm boilies around my hookbaits of similar size. It had worked everywhere I had fished, and I could see no reason to do anything different now. Time would tell, and again I had slowed the hands of destiny just a little more.

I have always found driving a very boring thing to do (unless it's on a Harley-Davidson or a big yellow Dodge truck, of course), and being honest, I find it just a means to an end. However, in carp-fishing terms it gives me time to think. Living as I do, surrounded by lakes that contain veritable monsters, it has not always been the case. Very often I don't get the necessary time to take stock of what has just happened, before the real world demands my attention. However, as I closed the gate at Ashmead and set the volume control to the necessary ear-bleeding volume for Guns N' Roses, I began to think long and hard about what I was doing. Maybe the little pellets, and a smidgeon of hemp that I had used so far were getting the attention of the stockies and the smaller fish, which destroyed the spot before the bigger fish arrived? There was also the fact that when I had found the bigger fish, they were usually on their own with no small fish for company. Once I had mulled that little lot over in my mind, I was sure the change to fishing just 15mm boilies would do the trick. Although the weather had been nothing short of abysmal, I had been on the big girl's case for a couple of weeks now. I had found her on every visit; indeed, one of the spots that I was concentrating on was the area she visited most. All I needed now was to give her what she wanted, and as soon as I was home I filled the air-dry bags with 15mm Pulse. It was the only bait that would be with me the following Monday, and I could only hope this was the answer I was looking for.

Early on at the start of the following week I was once again racing down the A303, trying desperately to stay on the road due to the incredibly heavy rain. It was so bad, in fact, that I couldn't really go above 50mph; not something I am any good at when I am on the way to a lake! The rain eased, thankfully, as I approached the lake and once I had parked up and started my walk around, I couldn't believe how mild it was. The place was deserted, so, taking my time, I ensured I looked everywhere. I really should have known that I would find fish in and around the area I had been concentrating on, but I wanted to make sure they weren't anywhere else first. And the one fish that gave the game away once again, was Shagger. Only this time it wasn't too hard to see that the little guy had company. I spent an hour or so in the trees watching the fish, including the big one, ambling around the area. All I needed to do then was set my normal traps, only this time I would put a couple of kilos of 15mm'ers over the spots. It took an age to get my gear round there because the mud had become too deep to use a barrow. Once sorted, though, around midday I fired up the kettle for the first brew of the session. I could only hope they appreciated the extra food. All the bites I had had from this area were early in the morning, so you will understand my surprise when one of the rods roared off at around 4.00 in the afternoon. In the shallow water the fight was rather protracted and there was little that I could do to prevent it disturbing the other two spots. As the fish raced over each of them, I spotted several big bow waves leaving the area. Eventually, I had the mirror in the net and, at 21lb 2oz, I couldn't have been happier with the stunning fish. I named him Ziggy Stardust, not because of the rig he was landed on, obviously, but because of the amount of tiny scales all over his body. As happy as I may have been, I couldn't help wondering which fish he had sent scurrying for cover. Apart from a small common, which had, of course, forgotten to read the script, that was all the action I got for that trip. I did leave them with plenty of bait to keep them occupied until my return, though. The water level was now as high as it had ever been, and consequently the spots were way out of the reach of the dreaded swans. On the drive home I made a decision once again. For the foreseeable future I would fish from my little island; it was where I had seen so many of the big fish. It wasn't a plan that I was entirely happy with, simply because I like to be mobile, but then again, what the hell do I know?

As usual, when there is a big fish on my mind, I must have been unbearable at home for the next three days. I could think of nothing else, and if I am honest, I really didn't want to. At long last the purgatory of domesticity was over by the following Monday morning, and after chucking the rods into the car I was soon dashing towards Ashmead. It was the only place I wanted to be, and unusually for me, there was only one swim I wanted to be in. On my arrival I had took a token look around, but I knew where I was going. I even found some fish elsewhere, but that group didn't contain what I was looking for. I crossed

*Ziggy Stardust at 21lb 2oz.*

the bridge onto the little island and quickly climbed the now familiar tree. There, 20 yards to my right, was a group of fish that would take any man's breath away. I stared at them for far too long, until I decided that I really ought to get my gear and fish for them. Knowing the area as I did, I managed to get everything sorted with the minimum of disturbance. The problem with being so close to the fish was that every twig that snapped under my feet sounded like a nuclear explosion. I was a nervous wreck by the time it came to introducing the rods, two of which were positioned at the base of the marginal shelf to my left, and baited with a kilo of boilies. The third was once again waded out to the island to my right . The spot was a hard patch in an area of soft silt almost surrounded by weed, and in around 4½ft of water. I donked the lead down a couple of times, just to make sure, and then added the hooklink with a large PVA bag of 15mm boilies attached. The trap was completed with the addition of a kilo of boilies and I walked the rod back the 20 yards to the swim. The line was slackened off completely and as soon as I was happy everything was okay, I returned to the tree. Remarkably for those cagey fish, they were behaving as if nothing had happened, and I even spotted the big girl circling the left-hand spot a few times before it got too dark to see.

The evening was incredibly cold, and as the skies cleared the temperature dropped still further. They weren't the most ideal of conditions, but I was truly excited, and gazed across the water, mesmerised by it all. I rang Lynn at around 7.00 in the evening, and the last thing I said to her was that if I did get a bite that night, I knew which fish it would be. Dream on, Chillcott. I found it very difficult to sleep and after making a brew at some unearthly hour, I received a single bleep from the rod to the left. Because of the way it was set up, it could only mean one thing, and with my trainers partially on, I raced to the rod. As I got to it, the spool on the reel was a blur and the buzzer was finding it difficult to keep up. As I picked up the rod all became solid for a moment; it had found a small patch

**I waded the rod out to my right.**

of weed. I should have left it there with hindsight, and waded across the channel with the net, because what happened next frightened the very life out of me. Applying a bit more pressure than I would have liked, the fish tore out of the back of the weed and at breakneck speed headed off down a narrow channel. It was a long time before I could slow its progress, and when I did the fish simply changed direction and disappeared behind a distant island.

It was at this point that I realised this was a big fish, but certainly I couldn't let it go any further. I clamped down and refused to give any more line, and for a moment or two the rod continued to arch over. Mercifully, the pressure took its toll and it moved back out into the channel. For the first time I could take a deep breath. The problem now was that I would have to play the fish across a gap between two other islands, so I braced myself for the inevitable. When it did make its bid for the gap it took my breath away, and again I had to lock everything up and hang on, hoping the pressure would bring it back my way. It worked, but by now I could feel myself shaking slightly, because the waves it had created were huge in the shallow water. Once that crisis was over, and the fish was in the relatively open water in front of me, the fight settled down into a more normal affair. Due to the high banks and the fact that I now knew for sure that I was playing a very big fish, I did something I had never done before. I shuffled along the bank to my Evo Bivvy and reached in for my headtorch. I had never used one to land a fish, because they always leave me feeling that I will frighten them just at the moment I want them to be as still as possible. I flicked on the red filter and concentrated on moving the fish towards the net, which kept on slipping down the bank into the water. I was just rescuing it for the tenth time when the fish surfaced and rolled in the red beam. From that moment on there was no doubt as to what I was playing.

She refused to come close for a while, but eventually she swam quickly in front of the net, but too quick to try to lift it around her, so I slowed her and turned her again. The net

*With Mark's help I got her onto the mat.*

**What a lake, what a carp, and I had caught her!**

was back in position and remarkably she swam straight into it, and all I had to do was gently lift the mesh around her. There, in the eerie red glow, was the biggest carp I'd ever seen in my landing net. We dream of moments like this, but for some reason we convince ourselves they will never come true. I never thought it was possible to become so emotional about the capture of a carp, but I had to swallow hard as I sank to my knees for a couple of minutes to take in what I had just achieved. As I mentioned at the start of this book, Yates's record was my next target after Charlie's Mate, and I wondered if he felt as I did right then. At 53lb 12oz she was a new personal best, and one of the most shockingly handsome carp I had ever seen. I reweighed her just to be sure, before zipping her up in a sack and wondering what the hell to do next. The mist and fog were descending rapidly, but first of all I had to let two very important people know what had just happened. My wife Lynn was first of course, and she was overjoyed, but the second I couldn't speak to immediately. I left him a message, and he was back on the line within minutes... he would be there in ten. Top man! Mark Walsingham arrived bang on cue, and with him came his right-hand man, Alan. It didn't dawn on me at first, but they were the two guys who were responsible for this remarkable venue. Mark had bought the place, as I have said, and Alan worked on it more than any man could. And there at their feet, stirring quietly in the margins, was total and utter justification for all their hard work. They were a very special few minutes, a passage of time that would never be repeated, and I couldn't think of two better guys to share it with. The three of us decided that I would do the pictures at first light, which meant I wasn't about to get any sleep; I had a rather large carp to babysit!

I smoked back then, and for the next few hours I sat on my bucket staring at the sack cord as it entered the water, demolishing a full pack of Royals. At first light Mark returned, and we prepared everything. With his help I got her onto the mat. She was truly enormous and didn't have a single blemish on her... perfect in fact. We gazed for a while, not saying a word; there isn't much you can say at times like that. She behaved impeccably for the pictures, and in no time at all I was lowering her back into her home. I stayed another night, but nothing else happened and I couldn't have cared less. Ashmead and her occupants represent everything that is so good about English carp fishing, the result of patience and a huge amount of hard work. She was born about 10 miles from my Aldershot home, and her whole history is well documented, which only made the experience much more special. What a moment, what a lake, but most importantly, what a fish.... and I had caught her!

# Chapter Seven
# Voodoo Child

*A beautiful sunset at the beginning of a new adventure.*

**W**ell, that wasn't supposed to happen, was it? For a few days I had absolutely no idea what to do with myself. For a start, I'd not been intending to fish at Ashmead until the following June. Whilst I wasn't entirely sure I would get a ticket even then, a little grapevine murmuring had me pretty much convinced. It was by pure chance that I got a winter ticket and, unsure of its winter record, I could have had no idea that I would land the carp of my dreams so quickly. It sounds so glib when I put it that way, but it is incredibly difficult to put into words just how hard I had fished that winter. Time spent watching the fish, and baiting the spots, had seriously taken their toll on me, and as hard as I tried to think of one, I didn't have a water to turn my attention to. Now, don't get me wrong here, I wasn't about to turn my back on Ashmead simply because I had caught the biggest one in there. I am not a bounty hunter, and I wanted to return to have a go at the other marvellous fish that swam in her depths. The problem was, I needed a change of scenery.

I write a diary as part of my living, and staying on the same water for months on end makes not only the fishing a little boring for me, it also makes the writing I can do about it a little dull, too. I have always tried to make my diary interesting, and, as far as possible, relevant to the guys and girls who will be reading it. A diary is something that is an intense thing to write, and is something of a unique carp-fishing article. It can dominate your life to such an extent that very often everything in life becomes secondary to getting something to write about. It also means that my fishing becomes a bit haphazard, especially in winter, as you are about to find out. I want you to see exactly what it's like to write such a series of articles for years and years, and what a complete disaster it can be from time to time. That said, I love doing it, although the pitiful wages the magazines pay sometimes has me wondering about my sanity. You see, I could sit at my computer and write a 2,500 word technical article, attach it along with about ten pictures with captions, in about two hours, yet the twelve to fourteen nights I do a month, and write about, receives the same remuneration. Mad really! Also, I have never been part of anyone's advertising stream. My work doesn't appear in magazines because the companies that support me demand that as part of their advertising agreement that my articles have to appear in the pages of their publication. Ninety per cent of what you read, regardless of the angler's ability, is there because of money, and many writers (if indeed they do even write their own articles) are billboards, and are very often discarded quickly once the public realise they know nothing. Take that how you will, but be very careful if you believe you can make a living out of simply writing about carp fishing; I would hate for any young budding carp angler to think that it is a possibility. It isn't, and anyway, how can anyone take a person seriously when all they write about is what they have read in another magazine? Best I move on before I give away too many secrets...

The Essex lake that I had 'guested' on had been a no-go for me. The local anglers didn't want someone like me fishing their water, and writing about it. As a consequence a publicity ban was placed on the anglers, and that was as much good to me as tits on a fish! I could have joined, of course, but I don't have the time to sit on a ticket that I can rarely use. I could only hope that something would come up on my radar, and as always a couple of phoenixes rose from the fire a few weeks later. Before that, with nowhere else to go, I returned to Ashmead, which was something I wasn't entirely happy with, because I am just so in love with the place. I reasoned that I would set traps as far away from the big one as I could (if I could find her of course) and thus lessen the likelihood of catching her again. Oh, the best-laid plans and all that! Not having to rush around the lake to get to the areas I had been baiting was a blessing, and meant that I could look around the lake without blinkers covering my eyes.

There were several areas of the lake that acted as junctions, if you like, and very often carp could be seen transiting through them. One such spot was at the top end of the original Goat Willow Lake. The lake there splits into a couple of other channels that lead to entirely different parts of the pond. And when it had been dug, the spoil had been piled up and had created a small hillock, on which I was standing one dark and dismal Monday in February. As the night turned into day I was a little disappointed not to see a single fish, but as soon as the sun hit the surface the carp materialised from all directions. I could easily have set a trap or two, but I wanted to ensure I found a certain 50-pounder before I did so. An hour later I smiled as I found her in a big ball of weed down near the gate end of the lake. Actually she couldn't have been farther away if she tried. Once back on the hill, it soon became obvious where I should put the traps, and in short order I was fishing. Sitting on the high ground I watched the fish going about their business, but none of them seemed to be interested in a snack. I was just thinking of a move, when a little movement caught my attention just down to my left. The slight ripple on the water obscured my view, and it wasn't until the fish was inches from the nearest rod that I realised which fish it was. I raced down the hill and quickly lifted the hookbait out of the water. Of all the fish to show an interest it had to be the one I was trying to avoid! It's not often, if at all, I have ever knowingly removed a rig from such a big carp, but I really didn't want to catch her again. She raced away whence she came, and, sure that she wouldn't return, I set a couple of traps, and settled down for the night. Two small commons later the next morning saved a blank trip, and if I was perfectly honest, my enthusiasm was starting to wane. Be that as it may, I had no other waters to fish, and as soon as I was home I sorted the gear for the following week.

The Carpin' On show in Essex, and then mine and Lynn's wedding anniversary, all conspired to ensure I was dog-tired as I stood once again on the high ground created by the digging out of the extended areas of the lake. For the first time in ages, the weatherman was forecasting low pressure and westerly winds. I could only hope that this would get the other big fish interested in a little munch. It seemed to be doing the trick, as over the next hour or so, several big fish glided around in front of me. And the best of it was that the one I didn't want to be there was nowhere to be seen. In fact I found her once again in the same weedbed as before, and although I knew she must have done so, it looked as if she had not moved a muscle since I was last there. I quickly got my barrow round to what had become known as the Second Point, and as quietly and quickly as possible got three traps set. I positioned my Evo as far away from the rods as I could, and settled down with a brew. Several large fish boomed out over the next couple of hours, and I was a little puzzled as to why I hadn't received any action. I didn't want to cause any disturbance by looking at the spots or redoing the rods, so sat on my hands. That was until one of the rods was ripped off the rest as a carp charged for safety. Having seen the second-biggest fish in the lake, Moonscale, earlier in the day, I was convinced that this was what I was playing and my heart raced. That was until a huge flank broke the surface which I recognised immediately. Now, I have no idea how some of you will feel about this, but all I wanted it to do was fall off! I had no wish to catch her again, but unfortunately the hookhold held and she eventually rolled into my net. I hate recaptures, because they not only take away the impact of the first capture, but, more importantly, they deprive other syndicate members the chance to fulfil their dreams. To that end, I wasn't going to make a song and dance about it all. Mark was interested in her weight so I quickly sorted that out and got a couple of shots of her on the mat for posterity. As soon as I could, I slipped her back home. My friends, people whose opinion I most cherish, agreed I had done the right thing. I have always thought that it was horribly crass for anglers to crow about catching the same fish over and over again. That's just simply rubbing the noses of other members in the dirt. I felt so bad about it all, and it was then that the real soul-searching began.

I sat and brooded at home for a couple of days. I think I knew it was all over for now but I still had no idea where else to go. I needed to get away from Ashmead for a while, but I didn't want to turn my back on the place with a bad taste in my mouth. To that end, I returned the next week, and just as if she was telling me what I already knew, I blanked. My heart wasn't in it, and I had paid the price. I spoke to Mark on my way out, and explained that I was not going to be back for some time. However, I was keen to tell him that I hadn't finished with the lake, because there were still some stunning fish to catch. Carp fishing is so much more than simply catching the biggest fish, but I knew as I closed the gate that things would never be quite the same.

*Single on the mat, and I had deprived another member of the chance to catch her.*

It just so happened that I had to go and visit a very good friend a few days later, and it was during this visit that, at long last, I started to get some direction to my fishing. I was having a moan, as you do, about not having anywhere to fish, and he came up with a couple of suggestions. The first one ignited a spark in my brain. It was a water I had fished in a charity event a few years before, and had several fish over 40lb, and also one that could do 50. My overriding memory, though, was of a fish I had seen a picture of at the event which went by the name of Hendrix. He was a big dark mirror of around 34lb in the photo, and I promised myself I would go back one day and catch him. My friend made several phone calls whilst I waited, and in no time at all, I had two waters to fish. The second was a lightly-stocked venue with one 50 in it, and several other good fish to go at. Unfortunately, the latter didn't last that long, and after only one visit, it was never worth fishing again. Now, in saying all of that, I have done nothing to enhance the theory that I am not a bounty hunter, but I can never deny that there is nothing better than a few good fish to fish for to get the old juices flowing. Hendrix it would be then, and along with a whole host of filming to do for *Fishing.TV,* my life, all of a sudden, had a new carp-fishing purpose. Spring was in the air, after probably the worst winter we had endured in a long time, and I just couldn't wait for the games to begin.

Before I could start my campaign at Cleverley Fisheries, however, I had a programme to do for *Fishing.TV*. I love doing this kind of thing, but I could never have imagined just how much this one single programme would impact on my time. We wanted to focus on catching a few out of your typical day-ticket water, so I made a few calls and decided that Yateley South Lake might just fit the bill. Now, never having fished the place, I surmised that I should do a quick recce, just to get a feel for the old girl, with the added bonus that I could get the pictures done for my next *Total Carp* piece. Two birds with one stone, if you like, although I could never have imagined just what a nightmare it would become once the birds started throwing the stones back! And so, as soon as I was able, I threw the gear and bait into the motor and travelled the twenty minutes to the lake. It was heaven, not having to drive for a couple of hours, and all I could think about was chilling out in a swim with not a care in the world. Two things happened that were just about to make this impossible, and the first of those was that the most productive swim on the lake was free. Secondly, I bumped into one of the regulars who waved a red flag in front of this old bull's face. He said that I should avoid the thick clawing silt that was in the distant channel between the two islands and that I should use very little bait. Well, I ask you, what would you have done? As soon as I was on my own, I unleashed the marker, and in no time at all had found the silt at about 70 yards. The area was big enough for me to invest all three of my hookbaits in, which just left me the task of loading as much bait into one spot as I could... Nice! An hour or so later the hookbaits were being kept company by a few kilos of 10mm Pulse, and the corresponding Response Pellets. I smiled as I put the first brew on, sure that the carp would agree with my plan.

About an hour later I started to see the first signs of activity over the bait, the odd subsurface roll indicating that something was in the area. An hour after that the carp were leaping all over the bait, and I started to wonder why I had had no action. I had no idea how productive this lake could be, but I was just about to find out. With little wind on the water I was able to watch the carp fizzing away over the bait and, in an effort to get them at it, I put out a couple of spods every so often. They really got in the mood, and the first bite, although I was expecting one, took me completely by surprise. A frantic fight ended when a rather nice common rolled into my net. At 21lb it was a great start to proceedings, and I got a bite about every hour up until darkness fell, at which point I baited up once again and reeled the rods in. Hopefully that would keep them interested until the cameras arrived in the morning.

At first light I repositioned the hookbaits and in short order I had two nice fish in the retainers. Once all the shots had been done for the magazine, I was left to my own devices, and by the following morning, as I packed up, I had landed a further seventeen fish. If I could get this right, the programme the following week would be a winner for sure... At which point the wheels fell off. Jealousy has got to be the worst thing about carp fishing, and more often than not, is the root cause of all the nasty things that happen in this game. I was aware that a few of the locals were not happy about me catching those fish, and were even unhappier that I was going to do some filming there. Not one of the cowards, for that is what they are, said a single thing to me. They just thought the following week would be the ideal time to do some maintenance on the lake, something that wasn't to be done for another month or two, when the lake was shut down. Charming! All of which left me in a bit of a pickle.

I was desperate to get my new mission off the ground, but I had agreed to do the filming, so that is what I would do. As luck would have it Ben Lofting, who runs Cleverley Mere, was in the throes of taking over a lake, Boyton Cross, from a local club that had been suffering in the present economic climate. It wasn't the day-ticket water I was looking for, but in every other respect it was perfect. Three hours after talking to Ben, I arrived in Essex with a plan. I would spend the night at Cleverley, and the two days either side of that would be spent at Boyton trying to find out what was what. Boyton looked fantastic, and as the club that ran it before had put massive restrictions on the amount of bait that could be used, I guessed I should feed them. So I did! I didn't fish at Boyton, and nor did I cast out at Cleverley, but spent as much time looking as I could. Unbelievably, as I was mooching around Cleverley, I came across my target. In the back of a small bay Hendrix was sunning herself above an open sandy area in the early-spring sunshine. Huge and black as your hat, I told her I would be seeing her sometime soon... I just didn't realise at that moment just how soon that would be.

**Filming at Boyton Cross before the hunt for Hendrix began.**

With some difficulty I put Cleverley to the back of my mind, and, after briefing the film crew, I concentrated on getting the programme done. With all the gear packed I set off, after first ensuring that I had loaded my floater gear. The plan was not for big fish, but to have some fun, and I was just about to get a whole lot of that! The lake was incredibly deep, but I did find a slightly shallower feature which I baited rather heavily. Once that was done, I strolled around with John Dunford and his camera, catching a few off the top. It was great fun, the action came thick and fast, and eventually I retired to my swim. Once the hookbaits were out there, things got even more frantic. In the end, I landed 15 fish for the camera, and by around 10.00 in the evening, I decided enough was enough. We had more than we needed to create a spell-binding programme, and I could not have been happier as I packed away. I really didn't want any distractions when I started the hunt for Hendrix, and to that end I did two more features for the magazines.

With that lot out of the way, I started my motor at around 4.00 in the morning one Tuesday in April 2009, and headed east. I arrived at Cleverley just before dawn the day after the Easter Bank Holiday and, as normal, did a couple of laps of the lake. The first thing that became very obvious, after relieving regulars Dan and Paul of some tea, was that all the fish seemed to be in front of one swim, the Second Point. It was occupied by a fellow called Rob Willingham, and once I had seen some activity in his swim, I wandered over for a chat. He had landed a 22lb mirror and a 35lb common and, even better than that, for me at least, he was leaving later that day. Top man! He landed a 17lb common a little later and was soon throwing his gear onto his barrow. It transpired that Rob had been on the lake for four years and had only one fish left to catch, Hendrix. Lightheartedly I said I would tell him how much it weighed in the morning. Dream on Chilly!

My gear was just behind him, and soon enough I was on my own readying the rods.

***All ready to rock and roll on the Second Point at Cleverley.***

For the first time in a few years I was using a new bait from Mainline. Kev (Knight) hadn't pressured me into it, but during a conversation the New Grange was mentioned, so I decided that it was about the right time to change things. Ironically, what this meant was that at no time have I ever cast out the biggest-selling boilie of all time, the Cell. As far as I knew, because the New Grange was nowhere near being in the shops yet, I would be one of the first to use it on this lake, and I kind of liked the thought of that. Rob had been fishing in close during his session, and as much as that is where I initially thought I should position my rods, I wasn't really happy with the idea. The opposite bank was lined with some marvellous overhanging trees at 60 yards, and my first cast in anger into the lake went right into a gap, landing with a donk in about 8ft of water. That, as they say, would do for me. I put the line in the clip, and after one more confirmatory cast, I connected my normal bottom bait rig, armed with a PVA Bag of New Grange, and at the first time of asking it landed bang on the money. The rod was baited with 10 PVA bags of the same make-up, a tactic that had worked everywhere I had used it, so why not there? I put all three rods on the treeline, and once I was happy I spent the rest of the day chatting to a few of the regulars who came to visit. It was a great place, with great people, and once again I was happy with life.

As the sun fell from the sky I started to get a few liners, and as I sat gazing across the lake, the odd carp started to show, too. I was far too excited to sleep properly and at first light I sat on my bedchair sipping a brew. It was a glorious morning and I was just thinking that the only thing that could make it any better was a carp, when the bobbin on the rod that I had made my first cast, pulled up tight. It looked exactly like all the other liners I had received, and when the bobbin fell slowly back to the ground, that's what I thought it was. A second later, my brew went flying as the bobbin cracked into the rod and the line pinged from the clip. At first I thought I was playing a tench, as all I could feel was a bit of feeble headshaking coming down the line. I reeled the fish quite forcefully towards me until it was about halfway across, at which point it woke up, and the rod was nearly torn from my hands. It obviously felt the other end of the lake was a better place to be... This was probably a carp then! For a while we battled in the open water, until it kited hard to the right and straight into the weedy bay. All I could do was kick off my shoes and wade out beyond the trees that mark the entrance. I held the rod as far out as I could and worked the fish towards me, at which point I realised my landing net was back on dry land on the other side of my rods. And while I went to get it, the fish headed back farther into the bay. By now I had got the message; this was a good fish.

Still up to my waist in the lake, I managed to get the fish out into the open water, and for the first time it hit the surface. It looked big, and by keeping the pressure on I had it moving towards the net. At which point it righted itself and exposed the most enormous set of black shoulders... Surely not? With a huge sigh of relief she was in the bottom of my net, and I

*Hendrix at 44lb in all her glory.*

peered down on her. She looked familiar, but I couldn't allow myself to believe it just yet. I left her in the net and prepared the weighing equipment, and the mat. With everything ready to rock and roll, I bit through the line and rolled the net down to the fish. My God, it felt and looked heavy. As I sorted out the mesh, the dark and rather unmistakable scaly flanks of Hendrix were exposed, and I rocked back on my heels; what an absolutely stunning carp. She had last been out at 45+, but I guess the harsh winter we had endured had taken its toll and I recorded a weight of 44lb exactly... Oh Chilly, you lucky, lucky man!! I slipped her into a sack, making sure she was comfortable and safe, and stared at my phone. First up, of course, was Lynn who was thrilled, and because I was, and still am to be honest, hopeless with anything technical, I rang Mike Kavanagh by mistake. That said, he agreed to be with me within fifteen minutes and I could not have been more pleased to share such a moment with such a great man. He arrived just as Bailiff Nick did, so I had a couple of great guys on hand to do the pictures. With a little time to actually look and appreciate what I had caught she took my breath away; she really is a spectacular carp. As soon as I could I held her in the lake for a moment before she powered away. Incredible, absolutely incredible!

Once I was on my own I had time to reflect. Very often I have to catch just about everything in the lake to get to where I want to be. On this occasion, however, I had landed the fish I most wanted to catch with my first cast. I shook my head in disbelief. I also couldn't help thinking of Rob, from whom I had taken over the swim, and silently wished he would be the next to catch her. The great thing about catching this particular target was that there was still one other fish in the lake that was considerably bigger, and I could spend some time there and try to catch it. I sat down with a celebratory brew and wondered if lightning could strike twice... Well it's always good to dream.

As much as the capture of Hendrix had my fires well and truly blazing, I wasn't too sure that I wanted to stay on Cleverley in the short term. My next trip to the lake was clouded by my indecisions, and whilst I was wandering around I bumped into Rob Willingham, who warmly shook my hand whilst I apologised for being a jammy git. He was as determined as ever to land the last piece of his Cleverley jigsaw, and I left him buzzing because he had fish all around him. Neither of us could have ever guessed, but he would be buzzing a whole lot more the next day. I ended up in the same swim from which I had landed my prize the week before, but I couldn't settle. A 17lb common saved the blank, and on my final morning I was given a good reminder to find another lake to fish. Rob had landed the biggest fish in the lake at 50lb 12oz, and I could not have been happier for him. As I was pondering what to do next, my phone rang and I had to go to a meeting to pick up a load of tackle, then some bait, which was going to be a little difficult with a car already full of my gear. I rang a mate of mine, Darren, to see if I could leave my gear with him and pick it up the following Monday. He readily agreed and whilst we talked, he told me of a lake he had been fishing. It all sounded like damn good fun, and got even more interesting when he said the average size of the fish was around 32lb. I was surprised, therefore, that I had never heard of Fryerning Fisheries, but I could never have imagined just how quickly I would be fishing there. Darren gave me a ring and said he would meet me at Fryerning, so I could retrieve my gear, and that Chris, the lake's owner, had invited me along for a chat. As long as I ticked the right boxes, it looked as if I had a new lake to fish, and I really couldn't wait.

I arrived the following Monday morning, after first meeting Darren on the A12. In no time at all we were driving through the middle of nowhere, and even passed the best road sign I have ever seen – 'Ducks Crossing'... priceless! I think I knew then I would like it, and when I first set eyes on the place, it just confirmed my thoughts. I met up with Chris and we chatted for ages. Ironically, as carp anglers often do, others had told me that I would never get on with him, but nothing could have been further from the truth. Some, well in fact a lot of people, just don't like those who say it how it is, preferring to dance around the handbags all the time. I, and just as importantly Chris, aren't like that; it's either black or it's white and there are no other options. Obviously we talked about the lake, and what he had achieved there was incredible. It all started 25 years before, when he set out to create the 18-acre lake by damming a small stream that ran through his property. He had made mistakes, which he readily told me about, but ultimately I believe he has created a brilliant English carp fishery. Supported by his son, Charlie, who

*Checking out the lake from the Millstone Swim.*

at the time was 18 years old, I think the future for the fishery is very bright indeed. All of which meant that I was itching to get the rods out, which is exactly what I did.

All the time we had been chatting I was watching carp after carp show to the right of an island, at the far north-easterly end of the lake. As quickly as possible I was wheeling my barrow into the swim that covered the activity. I had no intention of targeting individual fish, but I am only human, and after looking at the pictures which adorned the walls of his cabin, I had selected a 'most wanted', a common called Luke's which hadn't been out for a few years, and was expected to be massive, certainly well in excess of 40lb. As much as I tried to push that thought to the back of my mind, it was difficult, as everyone I bumped into mentioned that fish. For now though, I just needed to get angling.

There were two things I had to get my head around first. The lake is bereft of features, apart from an island, a shallow end, and a deep end. It reminded me of Mercers Park, and I knew I would have to get to work with the marker rod. It is the tiniest of details in these circumstances that can make all the difference. Secondly, the lake was full of crayfish, something that I had never had to angle around before. Interestingly, Chris had deliberately introduced these creatures to his lake, the thinking behind which was that the carp would get massive as they munched their way through them. I have no idea if the plan worked, but after I had left the lake, I heard he was trying to eliminate the Turkish Long Clawed critters. We live and learn. Darren had sorted me out with some wide diameter, clear shrink-tubing, and although it looked horrible, I guessed it would do the trick. Once I had encased the hookbaits I positioned them; one at 80 yards, one at about 90 and the third about 100 yards along the back of the island. I put a few spods of 15mm New Grange around each hookbait, then put my house up and enjoyed my first brew on the lake. An old buddy from Horton, Simon Marris, turned up a little later, and we nattered into the darkness. He fished down to my right, so at least I had someone who knew a little about the place. I had seen a few more fish show at range, but by the time I got my head down all the activity had stopped. I woke before first light and started looking all over again, and was still staring when Simon joined me a little later. As we chatted I got a stuttery take on the rod behind the island, and as soon as I had the rod in hand I could tell it wasn't a big fish. After pumping it all the way in I scooped it up in my net. Simon burst out laughing, because I had only gone and bagged the only bloody bream that resided in Fryerning! The capture, however, was probably the biggest confidence booster I could have got. I released the fish, and although the crayfish had mullered the hookbait, it still popped up when I tested it in the margin. All I needed to do now was catch a carp.

Over the next day or so I moved four times, and whilst I was doing a recce for yet another move, I spied a few carp in the shallow bay behind the island. As nonchalantly as possible, I raced back to my motor and grabbed a couple of stalking rods. Within half an hour I was ready to rock and roll, and lowered two rigs armed with a small bag of crushed and whole boilies onto two clear spots either side of an emerging lily bed. The traps were only a couple of feet from the bank, so I ensured the line was completely slack, switched the buzzers on and retreated a long way back from the edge. I really needed a brew, but before the kettle could boil one of the rods roared into life. I raced down the bank and lifted into the fish, which was to my left, travelling at speed, with half its back out of the water. It was a good fish, but just as I thought I was getting the upper hand, the bloody hook fell out. Now, I have my own reasons for hating barbless hooks, but right then I had never hated them so much! Still, them's the rules and, although this was a bit of a blow, I would have to persevere with them. I was quietly telling another member my tales of woe a few minutes later, when the other rod decided to come to the party. I was taking no prisoners this time, and within a couple of minutes I had a nice-looking linear in the net. I smiled the smile of a contented man as I held the 31lb 4oz cracker up for the cameras. What a great way to open my account. I was going to like it there, for sure!

The following day I had arranged to do a segment for Sky Sports' *Tight Lines* about floater fishing. Everything, of course, depended on the weather, so you will understand my disappointment when I woke that day to heavily laden skies and drizzle. I was going to do the piece up at Boyton Cross, and that is where I met up with Gemma, and Simon the cameraman. I walked down to the lake and couldn't see a single fish anywhere, and I ended up just as gloomy as the weather. With my head in my hands I didn't know what to do, but when Gemma said it really didn't matter if I caught one off the top or the bottom, I picked up my phone and rang Chris at Fryerning. I asked if it would be okay to do a bit of stalking on his Car Park Lake, to which he readily agreed. Thirty minutes later we pulled up beside the little lake and as always I went off for a recce. There was bugger all to go on, apart from a few bubbles in the first part of the lake I looked at, so that would do for me. As quietly as possible I got two traps set in the margin, and sat back and prayed for the bite I was sure would never come. There was a lot of stuff to do for the camera to support the piece and eventually I got that out of the way, but still no bite, and no signs of carp. I wandered down the lake a little to investigate what I was sure was some carp movement, when all of a sudden the first rod I had ever cast into this lake broke the gloomy silence. We battled away for an age, and not once did the fish make life easy for me. However, with a little patience I was soon lifting the net around a lovely-looking common. At 23lb 12oz I held her up for the camera, and that, as the 'luvvies' would say, was a wrap. A great couple of days for sure, and I just couldn't wait to get back.

It is not very often that I know where I am headed on a lake before I even get there,

*A cracking 31lb 4oz linear, what a way to open my account.*

*Fryernings's Car Park Lake saved my bacon on Tight Lines.*

***At 33lb 12oz I couldn't have been more pleased.***

but with the weatherman forecasting a warm south-westerly breeze I just couldn't think of fishing anywhere else but the bay at the back of the island. It's all well and good catching carp from open water but, for me, there is no better way to angle than stalking. I had a bit of work to do with David Little for the upcoming Fox DVD, which meant I spent the whole time in front of the camera looking over it at the far end of the lake. I just couldn't wait to get up to the bay, and a couple of hours later I was practically running, with my barrow, to get there. It was some time before I found anything, but as the sun got higher towards midday, more and more fish arrived. Eventually, I found two small areas that several carp were visiting, and got a couple of traps set. All that was left to do was dress back from the water and wait. The bloody coots were busy, so much so that I was sure they would ruin my efforts, but I needn't have worried. Forty-five minutes later it appeared the carp were hungrier than the birds because one of the rods was howling for my attention. With bow waves creasing the water all over the bay, I tried to regain some semblance of control. In shallow water the fish had no depth to play with and the only thing he could do was run away from me at a hundred miles an hour. It was a very spectacular scrap, but after much huffing and puffing I led a good fish into my net. At 33lb 12oz I could not have been more chuffed, and full of confidence I set out to catch another. However, the fish had other ideas and although I investigated much of the lake, no more bites came my way.

The following Tuesday I was back for more, and stood by the lake at first light. It was absolutely freezing in the stiff easterly wind, and all I could think was that if I were a carp I would be on the back of it. I wrapped up warm then barrowed my gear to the far end, and sat on the millstone from which the swim gets its name. Over the next two hours I saw six fish, and all of them had shown in roughly the same area. When I hadn't seen anything for some time I decided to investigate the spot. It was a fair old way out, probably about 120

***Not as big as everyone expected. Luke's Common at 38lb 12oz.***

yards, and straightaway I found what appeared to be some old and very deep tyre tracks. In a relatively featureless lake this was as good as it gets. Indeed, a while later Chris came round for a chat, and I mentioned what I had found. In the time since the lake had been dug, no one had ever noticed them, and he said that is exactly what I had found. I was doing something right then! A couple of hours later I had two hookbaits nestling in the ruts, and scattered about 4 kilos of 15mm New Grange and Response Pellets around them. A couple of fish showed as the darkness settled over the lake and I went to sleep full of confidence.

I woke around 4.00 in the morning and sat with a brew, cursing my rods for not producing a bite. It wasn't their fault, of course, but why blame yourself when you can blame someone, or something else, eh? Feeling a little deflated I put the kettle on once again, and as I did so one of the rods blistered off. On and on the fish ran, and there was nothing I could do to stop it. It turned eventually, and I managed to get into my chest waders at last. The swim was very shallow immediately in front of it, and the netting would have to be a fair way out, if I got that far of course. The fight went on forever, but I got it within netting range and eventually into my outstretched net. It was a good common, that much I could see, but it wasn't until Chris and Charlie arrived that I found out which one! Luke's Common spun the scales round to 38lb 12oz, not as big as most expected, but her size was irrelevant to me, considering the length of time she had been getting away with it. Another target quickly achieved, I was certainly on something of a roll, and after a quick trip to the shops I was once again set up as before. The day and night followed the same pattern, until an hour after first light when the baited area produced another bite. This fish argued about having its picture taken for a few minutes, but after the battle the day before, it was something of a lightweight affair. To that end I was soon gazing at a nice mirror resting in the bottom of my net. At 31lb 4oz she was the final confidence booster. The crayfish weren't a problem, the lack of features

*At 31lb 4oz she was the final confidence booster.*

I could get around, I could catch carp, and that would do for me! There were a whole host of carp-angling-related commitments I had to take care of before I could get back, but I got all that out of the way as quickly as I could, and soon enough was on my way back to Fryerning.

What follows is the spookiest fishing story I have ever witnessed, and I have heard a few over the years, I can tell you. For around three years we had been the proud owners of a guinea pig, and not just any old guinea pig, oh no! A few years before, Lynn's hairdresser had told us about a long-haired albino guinea pig that was going to be destroyed if the shop it was in couldn't find a home for it. It is the law evidently; be sold or die! Now, nothing dies in Lynn's world, and a few days later, and £500 light, I arrived home with all the trimmings necessary to look after little Monty. Basically, he took over Lynn's life, and the pair of them were almost joined at the hip. And what strange little creatures guinea pigs are. They belong to a family of animals called cavies, and work remarkably like a cow, in that they have two stomachs. In those stomachs lives bacteria, and it becomes necessary to feed the bacteria, not the animal. To that end, only grass and dandelion leaves will do, and I had lost count of the amount of piss-taking I had to endure around many of the lakes I fished, as I collected the relevant leaves. If only Monty knew! The problem was that guinea pigs are short on longevity, and as I set off for my next Fryerning trip, little Monty was not

*At 36lb 12oz she almost stopped me thinking about Monty.*

well at all. I am lucky in that one of my friends is a vet, and Andy Bradnock is a renowned expert in cavies. He is also a very good carp angler, but it was his guinea-pig-nursing skills that I needed this time around. With Andy on standby, I tried to keep my mind on the fishing. I had a very uneventful night on the fishing front, but things seemed to be getting worse for little Monty. Andy had already given him something that we hoped would ease things a little, and was due back that day to assess the situation. To be honest, I was tempted to go home, but Lynn insisted that I stay, and that all would be fine. I crossed my fingers and hoped for the best, and to try to take my mind off things, I went for a look around. Convinced I could find something to fish for in the warming weather, I peered over some marginal reeds and nearly swallowed my tongue. There at my feet was the biggest fish in the pond, and right next to it was a fish called the Pig. Either of them would do, and although the Pig isn't exactly a good-looking fish, I really wanted to catch her.

Some fifteen minutes later I had lowered a rig into position, and with the line slackened off I moved back a fair way from the water's edge, behind the reeds. As I waited, Lynn informed me that Andy was inbound with a little more medication, so I crossed a few more things other than my fingers and tried to concentrate on catching a carp. It seemed to work a treat, as a few minutes later the rod heaved round and the spool was a blur. The emerging weed caused a few problems, as did a small set of pads, but eventually I won the day, and was soon staring down at the unmistakable bulk of the Pig. Thankfully, a couple of guys spotted the action and came round to assist. At 36lb 12oz she almost stopped me thinking about Monty, but as soon as I slipped her back I was on the phone to Lynn again. He had received an injection and was fast asleep on her lap. Only time would tell, but other than that we simply didn't know what would happen. Again Lynn insisted I stay, and as soon as I started looking again, I spotted a cloudy area on the other side of the bay. It was obvious

*A farewell gift from Monty, a 31lb 4oz ghostie.*

the fish had been feeding there, and in no time at all I had a trap set no more than 2ft from the bank. I leant back on the fence some 10 yards behind the rod, but was soon running for cover. The biggest swarm of bees I had ever seen came over my head, and I had visions of being stung to death. It took several minutes for them to clear off, before I could get back in position. A fellow member, Jason, had crept up to me and whilst we were discussing tactics the rod pulled round in the reeds and a huge bow wave sped across the shallow bay. The fight was spectacular, and took my breath away as I tried to get the fish into the net. The water was so clouded up by now, that even as I drew it over the net cord, I couldn't see it properly. That said, it did look incredibly pale, and fairly big. At that very moment my phone started ringing in my pocket. It was Lynn, so I handed the net to Jason. Lynn was in tears; Monty had passed away only seconds before, just as I was playing and landing probably the only white albino carp I will ever catch! I would like to think that the little fellow had sent me a farewell present as he made his way to the great dandelion field in the sky. It was all a bit upsetting, so forgive me if I don't look best pleased in the picture. After some time, and once I had my composure back, Jason helped me record a weight of 31lb 4oz and I held the strange creature up for the cameras. It was only a couple of hours later when the carp started to spawn, and the last thing they need is uncaring anglers fishing for them, especially when you consider they only get one chance to get laid in a twelve-month period!

I always seem to get a little lost at this time of year, invariably not knowing what to do with myself. You see, once the fish have spawned they will invariably be down in weight, and probably bearing the scale and body damage that a prolonged leg-over (or should that be fin?) can cause. Do I want to catch a target when they are in that condition? If I am honest, I would rather they were left well alone to recover, and to that end I normally flit around from water to water trying to have a little fun. This was the situation I found myself in now, and for the next couple of weeks I again tried to get a few things out of the way. The two most important things, however, were the Fish with the Stars event at Chilham Mill, and a concert at Brixham Academy to see my favourite band, Lynyrd Skynyrd. The second of those events was an amazing occasion, being with Lynn, Keith Jenkins, Rob Hughes and Richard Stangroom, singing to the greatest rock and roll anthem, *Free Bird*, was simply incredible. I managed to return to Fryerning, but spent my time stalking and surface fishing around the Valley Lake. No monsters, but for the majority of my fishing that isn't what drives me. It was fun, and at the end of the day that is all I really need.

# Chapter Eight
# Common Phenomenon

I made a return to Cleverley Mere

I really couldn't make my mind up what to do with myself. The annual spawning seemed to have lasted forever on a lot of the lakes I was interested in, and that made me wonder what the hell to do. Buoyed by the capture of Ringo, at well over 50lb by my old mate Milky, I decided that I would make a return to Cleverley Mere. The lake had been closed down whilst the carp got their once-a-year sex-fest out of the way, which I wasn't too bothered about. If they were down in weight then I wasn't that concerned; I truly liked the place and the people fishing there. It was nice that the fish had got on with their business undisturbed, just the way it should be, but I wanted to fish, so with my gear packed I set off for Essex one warm and overcast morning. Upon my arrival I wasn't surprised to see the lake less busy than it had been. Be that as it may, all the more popular swims were taken. However, with everyone sound asleep, I crept around a little as the light filled the sky. There seemed to be some activity in most of the areas I visited, but one spot, as it always did, seemed to hold the majority of the fish. It was a swim called the Bowls, and I had spotted several fish head and shoulder in it on my way round to investigate. As luck would have it, the occupant was just about to pack up after a blank overnighter, which had me thinking for a fraction of a second before depositing my bucket in the swim. Well, it would have been rude not to!

I sat for a while watching the water, and noting the two spots where a couple of fish had showed. The problem was the weed. At the time it wouldn't cause too many problems, but in a few short weeks it would make several areas impossible to fish. Within an hour I was angling, but had discounted the popular spots because of the dense weed. The three rods were fished almost directly out in front of the swim at about 15 yards, and the three PVA bags of 10 and 15mm boilies came to rest just over the top of a huge bank of Canadian pondweed. I baited each rod with about ten PVA bags of the same, and sat back to take it all in. The line bites started just after dark, but I didn't get a bite until around 2.00 in the morning. The weed caused problems, as I knew it would, but eventually I had an upper-double common in the net. It seems that every campaign I have ever undertaken starts with one of these fish, but at the very least I was catching. I landed a few more commons of similar size, and even had to take to the boat at one point, to rescue a 20lb common from the weed. The action carried on the same throughout the next day or so, and I left wondering just how many mid-doubles to low-20 commons there were in there.

Unfortunately, things weren't about to get any less frustrating. Four days later I was opening the gate just before first light. Milky was fishing from the point where I had landed Hendrix earlier in the year, and it was in the bay to his right that I spotted several fish. For much of the previous session I had been trickling a handful of bait into the bay. It seemed to me like they wanted some more of the same, and with several good fish in attendance, I set out to get a couple of traps in position. I am not the most patient of men, and couldn't help having a sneaky peek every so often. The odd big fish was very evident in the area, but things had changed dramatically when I looked for the third time. Probably every big fish in the lake was drifting around the bait, and some were feeding. They all had a go and I couldn't, for the life of me, understand why I hadn't had a bite. Eventually, they drifted away from the spot, coming to rest behind a large ball of weed some 5 yards from the bait. I lifted the rig out and could find no reason here for the lack of action, and within a minute had attached another PVA bag and tried to reposition the rod. What happened next was simply amazing. I rather clumsily lowered the bag down, and as I did so a huge common came round the weed, and seemed to zero in on my efforts. It slowed and looked as if it was going to, and probably would, eat the entire bag. That was until a much smaller common raced up to the rig and engulfed the lot. I hadn't even spotted a fish that small, but yet again, I was playing one. I rebaited the spot and retired to Milky's swim for a brew. Jon Bones was coming to

*The boat came in very handy with all the weed in the lake.*

*I should never have been surprised to see a 25lb common in my net.*

do some pictures for my *Total Carp* piece and planned to fish the bay to his right. I very rarely have company when I am fishing, and I was looking forward to a bit of a social that evening. Just after Jon arrived I decided to reposition the rod in the bay and in short order I was playing a fish. It was a little fraught in the tight foliage, but eventually I landed a 25lb 2oz common for the camera. However, as this was about the tenth common of this size over the past two sessions, I couldn't help wondering where all the big fat mirrors were.

Jon and I left for Boyton Cross in the morning, and had a hugely frustrating time trying to get a bite off the top. The weather was cold, overcast and thoroughly miserable, to be honest, but with the *Total Carp* camera there I was determined to get one. Thankfully, with a huge amount of cussing and swearing, I managed to bag one. Yes you've guessed it, a 21lb common! Back at Cleverley, I should never have been surprised that the only bite of the night brought another 25lb common. I suppose I could have been forgiven for being a little frustrated at the situation, considering the number of large mirrors the lake held, but the truth was, I was getting an inordinate amount of bites from this tricky lake, so I was just thankful for that. One great thing that did happen on the trip was the arrival of Rob Willingham, to complete the final part of his Cleverley jigsaw. He turned up the following morning at around 8.00 a.m., and he quickly spotted some fish a little farther up the lake mooching around on the top. In short order he had a hookbait in position and it didn't take long to get a bite. A short while later he was staring down on the immense bulk of Hendrix! Rather marvellously he was totally blown away, and I couldn't have been happier for him. I had my usual little flurry of bronze commons, and on the drive home, instead of trying to find a way of sorting the common problem out, I was thinking of my short holiday in the West Country, and a little time with my parents – although that turned out to be full of fishy surprises, too.

Lynn had got me a backstage pass to Plymouth Aquarium, at where I was supposed to dive with the sharks. However, they had put a new feature in their tank and it had upset the toothy devils a little. I wouldn't be diving, but at the end of the tour I would be feeding them instead. If you ever get the chance to do such a thing, grab it with both hands, because you won't be disappointed. Every aspect was intriguing, but I must admit I was keen to feed the sharks most of all, and that nearly ended in disaster. We sat on the concrete side of the massive pool, and, along with gazing at the sharks, I could even see the faces of the public looking through the convex window about 10ft below the surface. Then the girl we were with loaded a few mackerel and a couple of squid onto a plastic pole and held it just below the surface. One of the sand sharks casually swam up, and stripped it off in the blink of an eye. Would I like a go? Oh, yes please! How hard could it possibly be? I threaded four mackerel on the pole with some more squid and lowered it over the side. Lynn watched casually from my left, leant up against a massive concrete column, and eventually it seemed as if one of the sharks was coming for dinner. It increased speed and in the blink of an eye clamped its jaws over the stick and swam off with a mighty sweep of its tail. I forgot to let go, and was dragged savagely to my left, and crashed into Lynn. I wasn't letting go, no matter how much the girl screamed at me to do so, and probably a microsecond before I disappeared from view, it let go. Lynn was in fits of laughter, which I couldn't help joining in with, but the girl was almost in tears. I don't think she was looking forward to removing my remains from the tank, but I hadn't had that much excitement in a long time. A fantastic day!

I returned to the real world to find that the weather in Essex had been horribly hot and humid, not what we think of as ideal fishing conditions. However, some of the country's biggest and most famous carp had been caught during that time, which just goes to show, as much as we think we know everything about carp fishing, we actually know bugger all.

It was now the height of summer, and very often at this time of year I am at my busiest with other commitments that take me away from the fishing I want to do. I did manage a quick trip to Cleverley, but the commons still wouldn't leave me alone. Come the second morning, after landing four more of them to 23lb, I decided that I needed a change of venue for a while, and I had just the place in mind. Before that though, there were a couple of things to take care of, the first of which I was looking forward to hugely. Steve Cole at Fox wanted us to test various bits of kit in extreme circumstances, and there was only one place we were going to be able to do that. We were off to Brighton again, with skipper Paul on Brighton Diver 2, and for the first time I would be going fishing with Bob Nudd. He really is one of the nicest blokes I have met in this fishing game, and I was looking forward to a day out with him. We were also going to make a programme with *Fishing.TV*, which just added a bit more spice to proceedings. We steamed out around 13 miles into the English Channel, and for the rest of the day Bob and I winched up countless cod from around 200ft of water. It was great fun, especially as I did all my fishing with carp-fishing tackle. We had tested the gear to destruction, made a great programme and, best of all, I had spent the day shooting the breeze with Bob. And it doesn't get much better than that. However, on the way home I decided I wanted to catch a mirror, and Ashmead in Somerset still held a great many of those I wished to catch. Top of my wish list was a mirror called Moonscale, and whilst I thought of her and the tranquil environment she lived in, I had one more weekend of madness at Cudmore Fisheries. It was a match-fishing environment really, but I still managed to sell out of books, which was nice, and on the drive home I just couldn't wait to point my car towards the south-west early the next morning. I had a couple of weeks before some more madness would keep me away from my fishing, and I only hoped I could take advantage of the few days I would spend at Ashmead.

As soon as I was home I sorted out the gear, and as knackered as I was, set the alarm for

3.30 a.m., early for sure, but one of the most fantastic times at Ashmead was when the light was filling the sky, and I wanted to be there to see it. The drive took a couple of hours, and after locking the gate I stared across the part of the lake I could see for ages. It is so special being there it very often took me time to get going, but eventually I got on my toes and went in search of a mirror carp. Having only fished the lake in winter, I was amazed at how beautiful the place looked in all her summer glory. I was even more amazed at the number of fish I found. The problem, if I could call it that, was most of the fish I saw were small commons... and I had a good idea what was just about to happen! As luck would have it, there was only one other guy fishing the lake, Simon, and he had just landed Single Scale at a post-spawning weight of 51lb 8oz. My timing, therefore, was perfect, because she was the last carp I would ever want to see in the bottom of my landing net again. After a bit of hopping from one

*Fox sea fishing with carp gear, once again.*

foot to the other, I settled in a swim that covered a fair bit of water. I had only just got the third rod in position and baited with a scattering of 15mm boilies when the first rod was away. Yep, you've guessed it, a 12lb common! It's impossible for me to moan about these carp because they are the future of the venue, but he did swim away with a bit of a flea in his ear. He didn't pass on my stern words to his mates, because by early evening I was three more little commons to the good. The fish did get bigger though, and just after darkness fell, I landed a common of 23lb. The night brought more small commons, and the rudd started to become a real problem. The lake was full of the little red-finned devils, which simply attacked your hookbait until the hook found purchase in some part of their anatomy. It was a ruddy nightmare to say the least!

By first light I was desperate to move, but had seen and heard several good fish boom out in the night so I just had to stay, and mighty glad I was about that. One small common around lunchtime had me doubting the wisdom of my decision, but just as I was once again thinking of a move, one of the rods howled for my attention. This, I convinced myself, was no small common and as the battle raged on, the more convinced I became that it was a mirror. Soon enough I heaved the fish over the net cord and there lay a cracking 28lb 4oz mirror by the name of Black Eye. The mirror drought had ended, and with one of Ashmead's original carp... perfect!

My return the following week only resulted in another beating by the little commons. Maybe it was the August doldrums, but I simply couldn't get any of the bigger fish to feed, despite the fact that I had found them just about everywhere I looked. I was desperate to carry on, but my life is rarely that simple. The following week I had to attend the Fox Fishing Experience at Willow Park, just up the road from my Aldershot home, which was a lot more

*A cracking 28lb 4oz mirror called Black Eye.*

interesting than I thought it would be. And once I had finished there, I jumped in my motor and headed off to Oxfordshire for the Tony Parsons Memorial. I loved this event (as it was back then) as much for the excitement of watching the young kids catching carp, as it was the chance to catch up with other people I hadn't seen in ages, probably since the last event at Linear. I had a wonderful, if not knackering time, but of course there is no peace for the wicked, is there? I had a night at home before heading to Yateley the following day for the Stoney & Friends do. At the time Allan and his cohorts had raised over £300,000 and much of the reason for being there was to celebrate Allan's efforts. I shared the event with Tim Paisley, and again it was just nice to catch up, although we didn't land a carp. We never seem to have much luck doing that, and at the end we promised we would try harder the following year.

By the time it was all over I was shattered and decided there was only one place I could get the peace and quiet I needed, and that was Ashmead. I spent the Monday catching up with some admin (not my strongest point) and early the next morning I was tearing up the tarmac on the southbound A303. My mate Simon was once again the only angler on the lake, and I set off for a nose around. Unbelievably, the first fish I found was Single Scale, sunning herself in one of the narrow channels that form the outer reaches of the lake. Further inspection revealed that just about every big fish in there was doing exactly the same thing, and as the second-biggest mirror, Moonscale, was in there I needed to set up nearby. I also discovered a huge black common, one that I had seen in the winter, and one that some thought was a figment of my imagination. It wasn't, and I was pleased that a couple of the lads saw it a little later in the day. They were as amazed as me: it truly is a monster.

Eventually I set up about 40 yards from the fish at the other end of the channel, and with them so far from me, I could take my time and get things right. It was a fifty-fifty bet, and I was sure if they turned my way, I would get a bite. The channel was weedy, but there

**All the big fish were sunning themselves in a narrow channel.**

were plenty of clear sandy spots to go at, and eventually I had two rods fishing. Both were my normal bottom bait setups armed with a PVA bag of crushed and whole New Grange boilies. I also placed several PVA bags of the same around each one of the traps. It looked the nuts, and as soon as I had slackened off the line I moved back to my bedchair. The day was roasting and I managed to get badly burnt, but I didn't want to put up a brolly because I was on top of the spots. I was able to sneak up every now and again to check on the fish, and as the light fell from the sky, they were all still in situ. As I got my head down, I hoped they would come my way. I was woken at 2.00 a.m. by a big fish booming out in the area of one of the hookbaits. Confidence was high, but, with some difficulty because of the sunburn on my back, I managed to doze off. At 4.30 the farthest rod was away. My passage to the rod was difficult in the dark and, standing on shaky legs that had a million nettle stings, I picked up the rod. The first thing the fish did was swim into the nearest bit of weed, so it was a while before I could get it moving. And every time I did it would simply tear back in. This went on for about ten minutes, and I couldn't help wondering when the hook was going to come out. Its power was shocking; at no time did I ever feel in control, and fifteen minutes later it was stuck fast in a massive ball of Canadian. With no ambient light – Ashmead is so dark – and the thick cloud cover only compounding the problem, in the end I climbed up the steep bank and put the rod down, ensuring the freespool was engaged, trotted back to my bedchair and switched on my headtorch. With the red filter on, I could make a little more sense of the situation. Another five minutes passed before I had the fish moving again, but it only left me feeling more out of control than before. What the hell was I playing? With the fish now charging up and down the middle of the channel I slipped the net over the marginal weed and decided that I needed to be in the margins myself. Unbeknown to me it was 4ft deep, and literally took my breath away as I sank down. The fish made a mad dash for the weed to my

*Moonscale completely spawned-out at 38lb 12oz.*

right, and again it was stalemate. I then did something I have never done before, and that was grab the line. Thankfully, things started to move very slowly and I could soon see the lead. I thought for a moment that the fish may be gone, but in a spectacular shower of weed and water the line was ripped from my grasp. We carried out this manoeuvre several times before I had the fish ready for the net. I was up to my chest in the water, not an ideal place from which to land a carp, but somehow I managed to scoop it up, along with a great big wad of weed.

It took a while to get out of the water, and I couldn't help laughing at my predicament. At first I thought it was Single Scale again, and I felt a little crestfallen until I cleared some weed and found out that I had landed the second-biggest fish in the lake, Moonscale! The incredibly long fish was completely spawned-out and spun the scales to 38lb 12oz. Simon and a mate of his arrived in my plot at first light and we got the pictures done. The weight was immaterial; it was a fish that I had wanted to catch and that was all that mattered to me. On the drive home, I thought long and hard about my fishing. My problem now was that I had landed the lake's two biggest occupants, and although it made me sick to my stomach, my time at Ashmead was coming to an end. I would turn my attention back to Cleverley the following week; there were plenty of big mirrors in there that had avoided my traps and I was keen to set the record straight.

With that in mind I set off the following Monday, Essex-bound. I had been giving the 'common' problem some thought. The New Grange was getting me an inordinate amount of bites, mostly commons, but of course I had landed the odd good mirror on it, too. It had nothing to do with bait, and I could only think that it was something to do with the way I was fishing it. The PVA bag trick had worked well for me, and over the four years I had been using that tactic it had accounted for some excellent captures. I came to the conclusion that on this trip I would introduce bait via a spod or catapult, thus spreading

*A beautiful dark 24lb common, but where were the damn mirrors?*

it all out a little more. Well it sounded like a plan to me, but, in good old military parlance, "No plan survives first contact with the enemy". On my arrival one of my favourite swims was free; it is very central to the lake and I had landed the majority of my fish from that area. Knowing it as I do, it was a simple case of positioning three hookbaits and baiting up with a scattering of 10 and 15mm New Grange. The weed was certainly getting worse, but for now I was happy, and with the lines slackened off slightly, I fired up the kettle.

The first 24 hours were slow, and unusually for these fish, they refused to show. I didn't get any action until first light on the second morning, when one of the rods screamed for my attention. The angry fish took full advantage of just about every weedbed between me and it, but eventually I had a huge ball of weed heading towards the net and I hoped it contained a carp. Convinced it was a mirror, I tore the weed away from the fish in the margins. I was truly amazed when I uncovered a small section of common-carp scales, and for a minute or two I felt a little glum. That was until I uncovered a beautiful dark common of 24lb. It was a cracker and I was still catching, I reminded myself. I had one more small common before it was time to leave, and couldn't help smiling at the thought of my friend Dave Lane fishing there over the next couple of days. What happened when he got there amazed me. He caught carp, as I knew he would, but the fish he landed were all mirrors! I was even further from understanding what I was doing differently, and it didn't get any better on the next trip either. With Dave's jibes about Essex commons ringing in my ears, I set out once again at the start of the following week.

The lake was fairly busy and as I completed my first lap, I could see that all the likely areas were covered. I really needed to wake someone and get a cup of tea over which I could ponder. Sean Leverett seemed the obvious choice, and we were soon sharing a brew. He was in the most popular swim, but it never did much for me. In saying that, I had seen a few fish to his left and, in time-honoured tradition, I said I would move in once he was

*At least the commons got bigger. 32lb.*

gone early the next morning. I set up to his right and with Jon Bones inbound to do some pictures for my *Total Carp* piece, I settled down to wait. I only fished one rod that night, and when Jon arrived I got a bite. The weed was a problem, and I was concerned about letting a carp fall off while I was doing a feature, when eventually all became solid. Sean arrived to generally take the piss, but he did help me out, and eventually he slid the net under a huge ball of weed. He had glimpsed the light orange flank of what he thought was a fish called Tango, a 40lb ghost common that resided in Cleverley. I wasn't about to argue because I had seen what he'd seen, but they aren't really the kind of fish I want to see swimming around in our waters. However, he was a difficult fish to catch and I was just happy about that, until Sean got the lot on the mat and removed some more of the weed. "Sorry," he said, "it's Baby Tango." We all fell about the place laughing, because there on the mat was the little ghostie, all 18lb of him! Sean was away shortly after and I moved down to that swim. One spot required me to wade along the margin to get a hookbait on it, and with much huffing and puffing I eventually got it sorted. I just hoped the carp would appreciate my efforts.

The night was deathly quiet, nothing seemed to stir, and I was sipping my second brew as dawn broke. I nearly jumped out of my skin, when, with no preemptive bleeps, the rod I had waded out ripped off. The weed was a problem, as I knew it would be, and Milky,

*Gazing across the remarkable Wellington Country Park.*

who was fishing up to my right, volunteered to get the boat. It wasn't needed in the end, because I managed to get the fish moving my way. I heaved a big ball of weed over the net cord, along with what appeared to be a much bigger common than of late. At 32lb she was definitely that and I was truly chuffed, but where the bloody hell were the mirror carp?

The rest of the session came and went and once I was on the road home I decided that I would make my first recce mission to a lake I had just acquired a ticket for. For the life of me I cannot remember exactly how the situation came about, but I was contacted by a guy whose friend was selling his Wellington Country Park ticket. I wasn't sure I really wanted to fish the place, to be honest, but eventually I parted with £750, and a while later the ticket arrived at my house, along with the rule book. Number one on the list of things to adhere to was: 'Tickets are not transferable'! Seemed I had broken a rule before I had even started, and I could have no idea things were not going to end on a very nice note, either. That was yet to come; for now, though, I was happy to make a few new discoveries on my carp-fishing travels. Now, as much as there have been a million articles written about the place, I knew very little about it. In many respects that is how I like things to be, simply because I won't be working to, or influenced by, any preconceived ideas. As normal, it was an hour before first light that I turned up the following Monday, and, rather surprisingly, there was only one other angler on the lake. I had done a couple of laps before I saw my first fish show, and as that was the only bit of action, I guessed I ought to set up in a swim that covered the area. The lake was far weedier than expected, but eventually my float settled over a clear strip at around 70 yards. It was big enough to accommodate all three of my rods, and once I had scattered a kilo or two of 15mm'ers over the traps I sat back full of confidence... What could possibly go wrong?

A big south-westerly kicked in later, and I spent the entire time removing weed from my line. Thankfully, it stopped before dark and I settled down to a very good night's kip. Awake before first light, I sat and watched the water. I had had no encouragement so far, but was suitably buoyed when a big fish boomed out to the right of the baited area. Forty–five minutes later the right-hand rod was away. Let the games begin! The first fish from any new water is exciting, as they all should be, and with the weed causing no end of problems the fight became very exciting indeed. That said, I was soon guiding a massive ball of the green stuff into the net, and there right in the middle of it was a common! At 25lb I couldn't have been too disappointed could I? It was my first Welly fish, and once it was back home I sorted out the swim and settled down once again. The night produced two more fish, unbelievably both commons, of 14 and 16lb. It was hard to get my head around the common phenomenon, but I had gotten bites at the first time of asking, so I was happy with that. A young bailiff came round a little later, just as I was packing up, and when I told him what I had caught he told me that there weren't many of them in the lake, and hadn't I been lucky! He missed out on a brew; lucky, my arse! I was keen to get back, and one of the nicer aspects of fishing at the Country Park was that it is only twenty minutes from my house. It was a breath of fresh air, considering the amount of travelling I had been doing of late for my fishing.

I was staring at the alarm clock when it made its first bleep, but it didn't get to the second before I had silenced it and in short order I was gazing around Welly once again. There were a lot more anglers on than the previous week, but I was determined to take my time. That was until I came to a swim called the Sluices. The occupant was asleep, but I couldn't help noticing that the front of the swim was decorated with a retaining sling. Interesting! I sat in the swim next door, a swim that covered a completely different part of the lake, and was pleasantly surprised to see a fish show at around 80 yards. If all else failed, I would set up there and see what I could glean from Jason, the successful angler next door. Thankfully, he was soon awake, and I was into his tea supplies with gusto. The retainer contained a mid-30 mirror

*It was hard to believe my first fish was a 25lb common.*

and as we waited for better light for the pictures, he got another bite. After a short tussle, a pretty 30 slipped into the net, and once all the pictures were done I raced to my car for my gear. Now this was the Welly I had been told about, and I was looking forward to bagging a mirror or two. I could never have imagined just how frustrating the next two weeks would be!

I set up and had a feel around with the marker, finding myself an interesting feature at around 70 yards. It was a very dominant area in a relatively featureless lake, and it certainly didn't get any alarm bells ringing. A couple of hours later my boilie concoction was spodded out, and I sat and chatted with my neighbour for a while. You meet so many different people on the bank, but Jason was one of the 'liveliest' I have ever bumped into, although I suppose that any man who drinks twenty cans of Red Bull a day and stuffs his face with Haribo sweets is going to be a bit lively. Bonkers just about sums him up, and although I had done nothing to warrant it, I felt completely shattered by the time I was on my own. As bonkers as I may have thought he was, he did land another good mirror that night. By morning I was feeling a little out of it, and was no nearer getting a bite for myself. The regulars I had bumped into had said that one of the best times for a bite was between 9.00 and 11.00 a.m., so I was a little surprised to find myself playing a carp at 5.00 in the morning. From the off something was wrong; there was the most horrible grating on the line. The fish was on for no more than a minute before the line fell slack. The line was so chewed up that I could only guess that mussels were the culprits. It wasn't the first time I had lost a carp, and it most certainly wouldn't be the last, but I was truly gutted. There were two RAF Regiment guys fishing the lake at the time, Glenn and Reg, and it was nice to just have a little military input, but carp were still being caught around the lake, and I wasn't catching any of them. At that point I started running around like a headless chicken. The situation changed how I fished, and for a week or so I really couldn't make any sense of it all. I even lost another fish in very similar circumstances to the

*The Wellington mission didn't get off to the best of starts.*

previous one that fell off. I moved and found a small bay full of veritable monsters. This was the moment I was waiting for, especially as the swim that covered it was rarely fished. I took my time, and as quietly as possible I got three traps set. With the carp still in attendance I tried to settle down. I say 'tried' because it's not very often I am totally and utterly convinced I am going to get a bite. That was until around 3.00 in the morning when I woke to what sounded like a lead landing in my swim, a fact that was confirmed when two of my rods were wiped out by the ignorant moron on the far bank. Angling etiquette is something that seems alien to a lot of carp anglers, and these two northern anglers proved that point very nicely indeed. I say northern simply because that is where they were from, but this particular moronic behavior is just as prevalent in the south, too. All that was needed was a little bit of thought on their part, but no, my chance had been ruined. There was no point in me arguing, I don't go angling for that, so I simply packed up and headed home... gutted once more.

I was prowling the banks again at the start of the following week, determined to get even with the Wellington carp, but it didn't exactly turn out that way. I came to a swim on a point and decided that was where I would angle for a while. I'm not sure why I chose it; it just felt right, I suppose. The problem there was that the weed was ten times worse than the rest of the lake. The balmy September weather had seen a massive increase in the flossy green weed that was such a problem, and I was just about to get a real beating. Several fish came adrift over the next 36 hours. They simply got bogged down in the weed and fell off. There was nothing I could do, and to add salt to the wound, a couple of good fish were caught from other areas. I felt so out of luck that I was sure if I had found a good branch from which to hang myself, the bloody thing would have snapped!

The following week was the turning point, although it was eventually sorted out for reasons that had very little to do with carp fishing. Once again I was at the lake early the next Monday morning, and spotted several fish at range in front of the swim I had been in the week before. I rushed back to my car and got my gear into the swim, and with that done I decided to have a mooch around before I set up. Nothing else caught my eye so I headed back to my swim, noticing that the surface weed had all but disappeared. Just maybe I would get a chance to land a fish this time around, though, of course, I had to hook one first. It wasn't until 3.00 a.m. that I got my first occurrence. With weed all over the line and far more of it down towards the fish, I simply concentrated on pumping it all toward me. The difference this time was that as I waded out I could see the fish was still on. I set about trying to remove weed from the line, all the time watching the tail of a big fish waving in the weed some way beyond. There was tons of the stuff, and by the time I had what I thought was a carp in the net, it had already made its escape. I sank to my knees and held my head in my hands. What in God's name had I done to deserve this? A lad called Dean turned up later and asked if I was moving, which I told him I was, in the morning. He would fish far up to my right and move in once the swim was free. And that night I eventually landed a carp; it was a common of course, but it was a carp, and at 17lb I thought he was the greatest carp I had ever caught. Dean arrived as I was playing another, and as I lifted the net around the little 17lb mirror, I could not have been happier. That was until he told me he had simply launched out a couple of single hookbaits, and landed a 45lb mirror sometime in the night. How's your luck, eh? I drove home happy, however, because I was sure the wheels of fortune were turning in my favour.

On the drive home I got a call from Jenks to say his daughter, Christine, had just given birth to her second baby. He informed me that once again, at one minute past ten, I had become a stand-in grandfather to her daughter, Willow. The rest of the drive was done with a huge smile on my face, and I couldn't help thinking that there are so many things in life more important than me catching a carp. It's not often I go into many details about my fishing with

*Willow at 43lb 6oz. Things were starting to change.*

Lynn and, as buoyed as I was about the birth of Willow, my frustration was simmering just below the surface. As astute as ever, she said that I was probably not giving the lake the respect it deserved and removing my head from my bottom and fishing for myself was the only way to resolve the problem. For the first time in a few weeks I looked at the fishing with renewed vigour. I could never have imagined just how much influence those two comments would have. The first thing to do was air-dry a few kilos of boilies, and dust off the throwing stick. Now, I have a problem with throwing sticks, because many years ago I received a brutal injury to my right wrist. This means that the use of one of these tools is a very painful experience, but I was determined this was how I would be doing things from now on. The other problem was the gulls, of course. Never believe for one second that they don't get every single boilie, because they bloody well do. To that end, all my baiting up would have to be done after dark, which isn't the best scenario, but it would have to do. Loaded up with bait, and with a completely different attitude, I arrived at the lake. I didn't care who had caught what and I wasn't about to stop for a chat, I was going to find some fish to fish for. After an hour or two I noticed a boat being launched and once I arrived in the swim, I found out a great young lad called George had landed a personal best 43lb mirror. It was a very special moment, but as we sorted the pictures out, I saw a fish show up the far end of the lake, and shortly after George's fish had swum off, another showed in the same area. I said my 'well dones' and rushed up the track with my barrow, and on arrival yet another fish boshed out. I always harp on about reconnaissance, because it is hugely important, and because I had investigated this swim before, my diary told me all I needed to know. There was a long silty strip at 75 yards, and I got three Pineapple pop-ups in position along its 15-yard length. All I had to do now was wait for darkness and then spend a couple of painful hours baiting it. Troy and Neil, two lovely guys who worked on the estate, came round a little later for a chat and wished me luck. I told them to get around early if they wanted to see the fish I was going to land. Who needs luck?

At 4.26 a.m. I was woken by an alarm. The trouble was, it was over the other side of the lake. As I watched the guy's headtorch dance around I made a brew. Oh why wasn't it me? I sat staring accusingly at my rods, when the middle bobbin pulled up tight and dropped back slightly. In the blink of an eye the line pinged from the clip and the buzzer howled. From the get-go it was obviously a big fish, and for the first time at Welly I didn't have to worry about the weed. On and on the fight raged, until eventually it rolled some 20 yards out. In my pants once again, I marched out into the lake throwing the net in front of me, and I nearly swallowed my tongue when a big mirror rolled just out of reach, but it was another five minutes before I was able to steer her into the outstretched net. 'Light My Fire!!' I took a moment or two to get my breath back before sorting things out. She looked big, and at 43lb 6oz she was. Knowing that Troy and Neil would be around in an hour I slipped her into a sack and she came to rest a few yards out. The time for pictures came and I was very interested in the fact that no one knew the fish. She looked amazing, with a few noticeable scale clusters, so I was a little surprised. A 40-pounder with no name; how fantastic was that? However, that was about to change. I am not normally into naming fish, having only done it once before, but as I sat on my own shortly after, I couldn't help thinking of three-day-old Willow and the part she had played in my new-found confidence. And so for the rest of her days that is the name this fish will carry. Interestingly, a funny thing happened a few days later, once I had emailed the pictures to Carp-Talk. Paddy Webb rang me, which is a very rare occurrence, and said that he would like to congratulate me and the photographer for getting the only picture of a Wellington Park carp that looked interesting! As it happens, I tend to agree.

Having caught my first big fish from the lake, I wasn't about to move, but I was keen to look at the areas I had yet to investigate. To that end I did one more night in the swim, which reminded me that no matter what I did, I was going to catch little commons. Two more of the lively little chaps came to visit me during darkness, so by first light all of my gear was on the barrow and I was off, and eventually I arrived at the most popular swim on the lake. I had tried not to fish it too much because there was only one area to fish safely, and I don't really want to fish as everyone else does. In saying that, several fish showed a long way out from that swim, but even retrieving a lead from that area resulted in pumping in what felt like a small van! I set up as best I could, but nothing happened until the wee small hours. I heard several good fish crashing out in the bay behind me, Bramble Bay to be exact. This just happened to be the final area I needed to investigate, so by mid-morning I was wheeling the barrow the 150 yards to a small point that would give me a good view of the bay. I was amazed to see the water looking very muddy. The fish had obviously been there for some time, and I cursed myself for not being brave enough to move in the rain during the night. It was late evening before I had set three traps, and by the time it was dark I was in the land of Nod – but not for long. At 8.30 p.m. I was once again very much awake as a fish raced across the shallow bay. His initial run seemed to knock the stuffing out of him, and soon enough I was sorting out a dumpy 26lb mirror. A guy had moved into the swim I left earlier in the day, and I thought I would ask him to do a picture for me. On waking the bloke I was shocked by his reaction. I should never have woken him to do the pictures of a 'pasty' (his words not mine). He was deadly serious, which left me wondering what the hell was going on with carp fishing. Truly sad, and his efforts with the camera reflected perfectly what a dick he was. Be that as it may, and luckily for him, I was buzzing. I had now fished most areas of the lake with a modicum of success in the swims I had fished. At long last, I felt like I was ready for the winter ahead. The fact that the lake was a little trickier than I had thought just added to the excitement.

*At 37lb 2oz he needed his picture taken.*

At home the next day I once again got a load of boilies in the air-dry bags; one thing was for sure, they would be seeing plenty of those. Again, I was early to rise the following Monday morning and soon enough I had seen two groups of fish. One was in the popular Hole in the Bush Swim, and the other was in front of the swim from which I had landed the 43. Not wanting to do the same as everyone else, I pushed the barrow into the swim that I now knew as The Reeds, and straight away a fish showed exactly where my middle rod would end up. Game on! I didn't want to disturb the fish, so got myself set up first, and changed my rigs. A rig change is a big thing for me, but I felt the stiff link pop-ups would give me a better chance. I have absolutely no idea why, which is the funny side of the story. The activity died down later, and at long last the three hookbaits were fishing, all on the same patch of silt in around 5ft of water. The baiting up would again be done after dark, and with that sorted I gazed across the pond, more than happy with my efforts. The only problem now was the weed that was continually breaking off in huge clumps, and drifting around the lake. Indeed, every now and again it changed some of the areas, and as the wind blew I had to keep removing it from my line. With around 5 kilos of 15 and 18mm baits scattered around the hookbaits, it may seem that it would take a while for the carp to get through it all, but I have never found that to be the case. I believe many would be very surprised if they knew just how much food a carp can eat, and how quickly! To that end, just as I was settling down, the bobbin on the middle rod dropped to the deck and then smashed into the rod. As soon as the rod was in hand I heard the fish hit the surface, and expected all hell to break loose. Nothing happened at all, actually, and I simply reeled the fish into the net. As wholly unspectacular as the fight was, there lay a good mirror in the folds of my net, and at 37lb 2oz he needed his picture taken. A neighbour duly did the honours, and I punched the air as the fish waddled off.

The rest of the night was uneventful, and I spent much of the following day just wandering

**The Clean Fish at 45lb 2oz.**

about and investigating certain areas with a rod. I saw nothing to act upon, so arrived back in my plot around mid-afternoon and repositioned the hookbaits. With that done I received a call from DHP's Jon Bones. He wanted to come down to do the pictures for my next technical piece, to which I readily agreed. He would be down very early in the morning, and I promised to have a monster for his perusal. After saying something as stupid as that, you can't help thinking you may just have put a hex on the whole damn thing. That said, as the night wore on, I received more and more liners, and the odd fish boomed out in the darkness. It was incredibly hard to sleep but eventually I drifted off, and the next thing I knew I was scrambling for the rods. The bite was incredibly fast, so fast in fact that as I picked up the rod I braced myself for the battle that would surely follow, but nothing really happened at all. Apart from the odd headshake I simply reeled the fish towards me. Sometimes when you are playing a carp you actually want a bit of a scrap, but when I saw the size of the fish I was playing I thanked the Lord it hadn't taken a single inch of line. I thanked him a whole lot more when it rolled into my net. It was 5.00 a.m. and with Jon inbound I decided to sack the fish; he was going to see a monster after all! At 45lb 2oz she was my biggest Welly fish so far, and I giggled to myself as I made sure she was safe and secure in her black mesh overcoat. Jon arrived and, I hope, was suitably impressed with my efforts. And when the light was good enough, she posed for her picture. A special fish indeed. Interestingly, she was called the Clean Fish, and had been expected to be the lake's next 50-pounder, but having to deal with some horrible injuries inflicted on her by a guy who was unbelievably still a member, she had probably used all her energy to repair herself. Whatever, she looked fine as she swam strongly away, and I spent the rest of the day with a cheesy grin on my face, wondering if life really was simply all about being lucky, rather than good.

To be honest there is little point in trying to tell you anything about my fishing for a while, because it fizzled out to nothing. However, every cloud has a silver lining and all that, and as I turned up for another session at Welly I realised I was out of breath as I pushed my barrow to a distant swim. It was the first time in my life I had struggled to get where I wanted to be, in good order. I felt as if I was the unhealthiest human on the planet, and what do you think I did about it? I put the barrow down halfway to my destination, leant against a tree and sparked up a Benson. Brilliant! As I stubbed the cigarette and lifted my barrow to complete the rest of the journey, I realised it was about time I gave up the cigarettes. That was the last time I thought about it for a while; there was fishing to be done, and of course that takes precedence over everything... doesn't it? At the time, I was smoking around three packets of 24 Royals, which constitutes 72 fags a day, and for the next couple of days I tried to keep up the quota. It wasn't until the following week as I settled down for the second night that the non-smoking thing came to mind again. As normal, I had sparked up a ciggy and rang Lynn. It was 7.05 p.m. on 12th October 2009, and I told her I would ring if I landed a monster, and put the phone down. The next thing was to stub the dog end out and at that moment I knew I would never smoke another cigarette as long as I lived. I even reached into my kit and destroyed the other three packets. I must admit, when I did that I wondered if I had not been a bit presumptuous, but I am proud to say that from then on I have never smoked another one of those smelly, horrible and expensive things again. The amazing thing is, why the bloody hell didn't I do it thirty years ago? I don't think it made too much difference to the physical side of life, but when ten months later I counted up the money that I had squirrelled away during that time, I was shocked to count in excess of £6,000. How much had I spent in my life? I was 49 at the time and had been puffing away since I was 11. It hurts to even think about it!

Welly had shut up shop, and I was looking for a change of scenery, so headed to Ashmead the following week. I wasn't expecting too much action, but it is a place where I can think, and in the main that revolved around where I should spend the winter. Writing a diary, as I had been doing for eight years, means that you have to think long and hard about the waters you fish, and winter venues can be the most important. I could have had no idea how close the answer was. The previous weeks had been filled with a whole host of aggravating administrative things, and I proverbially dumped all my angst on the A303 as I roared south. The lake was empty on my arrival and I wandered around just soaking up the atmosphere. I was clearly looking for fish, and I couldn't believe what I found on the little island from which I had had so much success before. The water looked remarkably like pea soup, and it was obvious where the carp had been feeding. Evidently, nothing had been out for ages, and as I could find no evidence that anyone had fished up this end for some time, it appeared they had sought refuge in that area. One nice thing had happened since I was last there, the bridge had been completed and I simply pushed my barrow over it. Nice! I sat watching the water, and it became obvious the fish had stopped feeding. Mark rang to say he would be down to do some work on the trees that had been affected in the wind, and I promised a brew was always available. That just left me to get three traps set, and I did much as I had always done in this swim. Then Mark arrived, and over a brew we put the troubles of the world to rights. He went off and started slashing away with a chainsaw. The noise concerned me a little, but I tried to ignore it. Then a fellow member arrived with his dogs, and, with my head in my hands, I started to wonder if all the commotion was just a little too much for this intimate corner of the lake, which just goes to show how little I know about carp fishing. With the noise as loud as it could be, one of the bobbins lifted savagely and the buzzer howled. The weed was still quite thick and the fish got bogged down for a minute or two. I couldn't help smiling as the fish kicked away from the weed, in an environment that sounded more like a battle scene, and with several kilos of bait to get through, I had

*At 32lb 8oz Opal Fruit was a great welcome home.*

hooked a carp, and a very special one too. I lifted the mesh around it and the guy I was with recognised it as Opal Fruit. At 32lb 8oz she made a great 'welcome home' present, and once the pictures were done, which Mark had come round for, we talked some more. I love how fish get their names, and this one was no different. An Opal Fruit, as some may remember, was a very English sweet, until one day an American company bought the firm that made them. They changed the name to Starburst, which just happened to be the name that someone wanted to give this fish many years before. Mark wasn't having any of that American-influence stuff on his lake, and the pair decided the carp would be called Opal Fruit, which is just about the best story of a carp's name I have ever heard! I landed another small common, and that was my lot for this trip. However, as I took one last walk around, I peered over the otter fencing at the three small lakes on the other side, and realised how little I knew about the place. As it turned out I would be spending the rest of the winter there.

Ash Fisheries was run by the farmer, Pat, whose land surrounds Ashmead, and unbeknown to me the waters contain a lot of carp. I asked some questions and was invited down the following week, and from a half-frozen lake I landed 17 carp. It was ridiculous fishing and all my winter was spent there, when the conditions allowed (which wasn't very often). The carp were very obliging, and got even more so when I decided to use maggots for a time. I even managed to do another instalment of *Chilly on Carp* there with cameraman John Dunford from *Fishing.TV*. It was great fun and I enjoyed myself immensely, and it also helped me sustain my *Advanced Carp Fishing* diary. But, of course, there were plenty of other things to take care of. Fox had booked a stand at just about every show that winter, so I was pretty busy with that, and *Light My Fire* was selling so well I had a few book signings to do, and it was whilst I was at one of those that I met an old friend. We had fished together in the 1980s, and he went by the name of Paul Bennett. He was involved in the

*Lynn and John Nettles. It is amazing where carp fishing can take you!*

production of TV programmes and films, and I could never have imagined what would come out of me seeing him again. Lynn's favourite programme is *Midsomer Murders*, and he was now working on that. He would see if he could get us some extras' work one day, but to be honest, I really didn't give it any more thought. That was until he gave me a call and said that Lynn and I could come up and be part of the proceedings. It was something I will never be able to thank him for enough, and we even got to meet the star of the show, John Nettles. I was just relieved that he didn't remember me. You see, back in the late-'70s and early-'80s I spent a great deal of time on Jersey, and one night in the pub that they used to use in the Bergerac show, I offered him out. That, as they say, is another story, so let's move swiftly on! Things with *Midsomer* would get a whole lot better, but more of that later.

As the country recovered from one of its most savage winters, I decided that it was time to get reacquainted with Wellington Country Park. The first couple of sessions were a complete dead loss. I didn't see a single thing on either 48-hour trip. In fact it wasn't until after the Carpin' On show in Essex that the worm began to turn. I landed a small common on my next trip, and although it may not fit in with the 'seal clubbing' that I had been told to expect by those, incidentally, who didn't fish the lake, it was just about the first fish of the year from Welly. I was chuffed anyway, but I couldn't get back for a couple of weeks, and still the fishing was slow. The weather was so good that I left home early the next Sunday, something I normally don't do. I was excited, and eventually arrived with my barrow in a swim called Laurie's. Within half an hour I had seen several fish at distance, just to the right of an

*It was an immaculate mirror of 39lb 9oz.*

island. That would do for me, and after a couple of exploratory casts, I realised that I would have to be fishing a spot at around 130 yards' range to get myself in the ball game. Three stiff link pop-ups came to rest out there, and for the rest of the day I warmed up my right arm ready for the night-time boilie assault with the throwing stick. I delivered 5 kilos of New Grange to the area, and settled down for the night. It was too settled for my liking because by the morning, although plenty of fish had showed over the bait, I hadn't received a single bleep. I went for a walk and decided that I would fish my hookbaits a little farther out than the bait and see if it would make a difference. I have no idea why I came to that decision, but at least I was trying to be a bit proactive. Twenty minutes after returning I had repositioned the hookbaits and had a chat with a couple of lads, Phil and his son Tom, who had come down from Yorkshire to fish. But the talking didn't last long. One of the rods chirped into life and I, quite correctly as it happens, assumed that that was a bite. Unfortunately, the fish had picked up the other two lines and it was an age before I could get it anywhere near the net. Of course, being a country park, a large crowd had gathered to watch the entertainment. I had to wade out farther and farther but at long last the fish lay in the net. At which point a lovely ripple of applause rang out, and I did my best to take a bow. The members of the crowd were impressed, and, at 32lb 6oz so was I. With the pictures done, and I was on my own again, I sorted out the carnage. It really was a mess, which eventually would only be sorted by respooling my reels, and an hour later I was back in the ball game. What a palaver that was!

I sat on my bedchair and was just about to check the pictures on my camera, when the

*I wasn't sure if it was a common or a ghostie at the time.*

same bobbin made a repeat performance. It was flying by the time I picked up the rod, and nothing I did made a blind bit of difference. Once I had what I thought was control, I got my chesties on and marched out into the lake. The powerful fish made life as difficult as possible, but with a large slice of patience I eventually led it into the net. "Light My Fire!" It was an immaculate mirror of 39lb 9oz and, not surprisingly, all thoughts of a shitty winter and giving up smoking were banished to the back of my mind. Spring was most definitely in the air, and I was having fun. The rods were recast, I settled down for the night, and I was still settled at first light the next morning. The smile was still there, though, and as I sipped my second brew of the day one of the rods made me smile even more. Battle was joined as I watched the sun come up over the island to my left; it really was one of those mornings that make carp fishing so special. Of course, it was a whole lot better because I was playing a carp, and after a short battle I was able to lead the fish into the net. She was one of the weirdest-looking fish I had ever seen. Not only was she a peculiar shape, but she really couldn't decide if she was a common or a ghostie. At 33lb 5oz I was happy, and at the end of the day that's all that really matters. Twenty-four hours later I packed my gear away, still smiling inanely and probably the happiest man on the planet. God, I love carp fishing!

As much as fishing can be terribly unpredictable, so can all the things that surround it. The carp, the people who fish for them, and the venues that we visit are all so different and I guess that, at the end of the day, is why I love carp fishing so much. How boring would it be if we could predict everything that will happen? I for one would be looking for something else to do, if that were the case. Amongst all of that, and not wishing to go into too many details, Lynn had had another stroke, and at the time it was thought this would lead to a much more complicated scenario. When this kind of thing happens to Lynn, and she has suffered countless extremely worrying situations, I tend to lose it a little. I don't mean I hit the bottle, or anything selfishly crass like that, but I can never seem to get a handle on anything until I am sure I am in control of what is going on. She was keen, once she could speak, for me to carry on with my fishing as best I could. So that is what I did, and with her being looked after, I tried to get my head back in the ball game. I returned to the same swim I had caught from a couple of weeks before. I took over from one of the regulars who had fished it a little differently than me, and had blanked. I got myself sorted and the rods were back on the same spots within the hour. I even managed to get a couple of kilos of 18mm'ers out via the stick during the day; the gulls were obviously having an away day somewhere else. All that was left to do was wonder how big and how many I was going to catch. I didn't have to worry too much about losing any sleep because the first bite came at around 7.30 the next morning. It was an angry fish, for sure, but eventually I managed to get him into the net, with a little help from a guy called Matt. At 29lb I was chuffed to pieces, and although I am not that keen on catching ghosties, I couldn't help but smile. A 23lb common the following morning was to complete my action on this session, and although I could never have imagined it at the time, this would be the last carp I would ever catch from Wellington.

For some while a marker float had been cut off and was bobbing around in one of the popular swims. The bailiffs had been asked countless times if they could remove it, but nothing was done. It was a safety hazard for the carp, and when I next arrived I decided that I would go out in the boat and remove it. I had moved half my gear down to where the boat was and went to get the rest. When I returned, much of it was missing, and from what had disappeared, I could tell a carp angler was involved. I was fuming, and had to go home to re-equip myself. An hour later I returned, no happier I might add, but I had moved my gear into the swim I wanted to be in and put the bits and pieces in the boat, removed the marker and line, and then dropped off the stuff from the boat. Onboard, amongst other bits and pieces, was a bucket of 18mm boilies. The last one had been nicked, and once I had got rid of the float and around 80 yards of line I couldn't resist throwing two handfuls of 18mm boilies over the side. I was all sorted and fishing an hour after, although the baiting up would have to wait until later, of course. An hour after that, the management arrived. First thing they said was that I was never going to get banned, and they wouldn't tell me who had said it (although I now know), but it had been reported that I had deposited two buckets of bait from the boat. I was so shocked, and showed them the only bucket in my swim that was full to the brim with bait. Actually, the management were very nice about it all and told me not to worry. But I did. So many anglers slagged Welly off at the time, and I defended not only the fish, but the anglers who fished for them, and yet at least two of them had tried to get me banned. I was mortified and could no longer think of staying there fishing amongst cowards and low life like these. I decided that in the morning I would go round and speak to everyone, which I did, but not one of the snivelling little pricks would admit to it. I had paid my money for the next year, and decided I wanted it back, so on the way home the next day I called into the office. I reminded them that there were far worse things going on at that lake; chiefly amongst those was a person claiming invalidity benefit. Were they seriously telling me that a bloke who can push a fully-laden barrow around a lake for a mile or so, can't do an honest day's work? Yet no one complained, even though most on the syndicate paid taxes that supported his fishing. I was disgusted, and, sadly, it was over.

A chance conversation with a friend a couple of days later lifted my spirits a little, as it gave me a chance to fish a private syndicate, one I had wanted a ticket to fish for ages. It involved a little messing around but eventually I had the key, and a couple of days after that I swung open the gate. Then, once it was shut, I felt as if I had shut out the world. I walked for an age until I

*I forgot the cowards when this 43lb 2oz mirror ended up in my net.*

at last saw a fish, and a very big one, too. It was in the centre of the largest part of the lake, and two minutes later a couple of his mates had made their presence known as well. The marker came to rest in a gully between two gravel bars and I decided to invest all three hookbaits there, along with a few kilos of boilies. At long last I felt comfortable with life, and sat contentedly by my rods. It always amazes me how frustrating carp fishing can be, but just as quickly it can take all that frustration away. All I needed now was a big fat mirror and, to be honest, I didn't have long to wait. Two hours after the bait went in, one of the rods was bouncing in the rests and I settled down to a rather normal sort of battle to begin with. That was until it kited round to my left, and got hung up in some overhanging branches. Six times I waded out to try to get the fish moving, and on my last attempt she swam into the open water. As she did so, I noticed that she was absolutely massive! I could hear the clutch purring away back in the swim, so ran round and once again leant into the fish. Thankfully, we argued about her going in my net a bit more normally from then on, and I steered her into the mesh some time later. At 43lb 2oz she was truly a monster, and I simply let the aggro caused by a few cowardly wankers wash away. Carp fishing, and more importantly, a carp, had come to the rescue of my sanity once again, and I will never be able to thank that wonderful fish enough. It was time to move on, to where I had no idea, but that is what makes life so exciting for me... the unpredictability of it all.

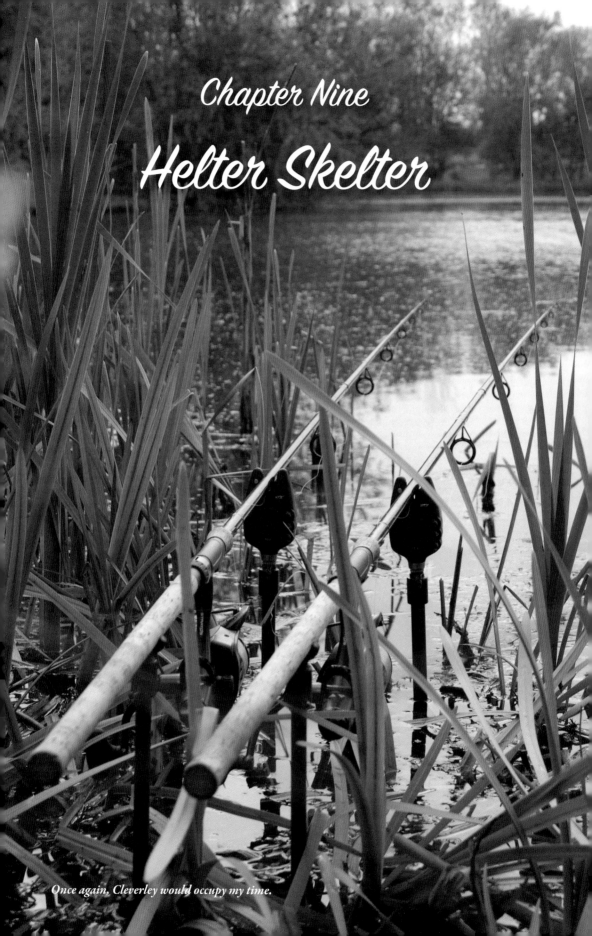

# Chapter Nine
## Helter Skelter

*Once again, Cleverley would occupy my time.*

I sat at the private lake and pondered my future. Wellington was over, unfortunately. I had, of course, got my money back, but what next? From memory, what follows is a bit of a mish-mash of waters, tackle and tactics. There are so many big fish around these days, and as I have said before, I don't just want to catch a carp simply because it's big. For me that's a meaningless pursuit to undertake; at the very least the fish I want to catch aren't ones that are spread all over the papers from one week to the next (although I have had my share of those), and hopefully the waters I fish are a little less busy. I also want them to mean something to me, which unfortunately isn't always possible. And of course there is my writing and TV work to consider, which in a roundabout way is why what follows became a tad mad! I really had no idea where to go, but as I stared over the lake the phone rang in my pocket. It was David Hatter from *Fishing.TV* and he wanted to know when we could start filming for the next series of *Chilly On Carp*? To be honest, I hadn't been giving that a lot of thought. The Wellington thing had been hacking me off, for sure, but the situation with Lynn had made me very afraid, more afraid than I had been in a long, long time. Ironically, just as I was trying to sort my fishing life out, her consultants gave us the news we had been praying for. Things, whilst still being very worrying, were not as bad as first expected. We could look to the future with renewed hope, and long may that continue!

With all that running around in my brain, I assured David I would sort out a venue and get back to him ASAP. The problem was, I had absolutely no idea where to go, as I sat gazing at my phone. Oddly enough, it was that very device that gave me the answers a little while later. It was a friend of mine, and during the conversation he suggested a lake that might just fit the bill for the TV programme. All it took was a couple of phone calls, and it was sorted. The next day I found myself wandering around a cracking 10-acre lake, somewhere in the northern hemisphere. There were a couple of anglers fishing at the far end of the lake, and I wanted to be careful not to get in their way, or upset them. They were fishing in the teeth of a horrible north-easterly wind, and I was sure the carp would have backed away from that. I ended up at the car park end, and if I was a carp that is exactly where I would want to be. And, as it happens, that is where I spotted a few fish. I had to be very careful at this point, because I would never have a swim shut down and baited for me in order to get a programme or article done. These things should be done on everyone else's terms, but very rarely are. To that end, I needed to keep my activities away from any prying eyes.

I found a nice silty gully surrounded by weed at around 60 yards, towards an out-of-bounds bank. However, I could bait up from that bank, from where the marker was about 40 yards out. Boilies at catapult range – my favourite. I went round and fired out 5 kilos of 14 and 18mm New Grange boilies, and smiled contentedly as I put the lid back on the bucket, and, undetected, made good my escape. I would be back on Sunday to put a little more in, and arrive on the Monday to get the show on the road. I got sussed out on the second baiting mission, damn it, and I could only hope that no one would take advantage of my efforts. It may surprise a lot of people, but this filming thingy is not as cut and dried as you would think. For a kick off, it costs a whole heap of money to have a few people on the bank for a couple of days, and my fishing time can be very restricted. You see, there is so much stuff to do to the camera around the lake, and that is time when your rods are not in the water. All in all, I reckoned I would have hookbaits in the water for around 24 hours of the following 48. No pressure there then! John Dunford and his crew would be with me around midday, and this would give me a chance to get sorted after my early-morning arrival.

I hate doing programmes that are scripted, and much prefer to do things on the run; I think it comes across so much better. With everyone in situ, we got the filming started, and once the casting and baiting up was done, all I had to do was pray. The only action over the

**At 38lb 10oz she was more than I could have asked for.**

next few hours was John deleting the card on the HD cameras that are always locked on the rods. Those false takes that infect so many carp programmes look so damn cheesy. We had been giggling about them, when out of the blue one of the bobbins cracked into the rod and the buzzer sang its tune, at which point, with a couple of cameras stuck in your face, the praying becomes a little more intense. There is also the task of trying to talk the viewer through the fight, making out that you are confidently enjoying yourself, which of course you are not! All you want to do is plead with the fish not to fall off, but as calmly as I could, I led her towards the net. The relief was huge, but I couldn't help thinking it was the ugliest carp I had ever seen. She got all my thanks, though, over and over again, and once she was back home I got the rod back in the ball game. With loads of stuff to talk to the camera about, we carried on with that, until it was too dark to film, when I could get my head down.

The night was quiet, but minutes after John had set up the cameras on the rods next morning, one of them burst into life. This fish felt different; heavy and slow as she plodded around at range, giving the impression of being a big fish. Nothing she did made me change my mind, and as cool as I tried to be, when she hit the surface I nearly swallowed my tongue. Once I had lifted the mesh of the net around her, I heaved a sigh of relief, and at 38b 10oz she was more than I could have asked for. The programme was in the bag really, so we spent the rest of the day doing all the other stuff I needed to do around the lake. The rods went back out as the light was fading from the sky, and we agreed that one more fish would make it a truly spectacular show. By around 9.00 a.m. the next morning we were all starting to make excuses. We had plenty of footage, a couple of good fish, and all was well with the world. Well no, it wasn't actually, I wanted another fish, and as I stared accusingly at the rods one of the bobbins rose steadily. I was on it in a flash, and the rod hooped over in a satisfying curve. Again, the carp did little to make me think it was anything but a big one,

***This 40lb 2oz mirror made a truly dramatic end to the programme.***

and I swore just a little when a hoofing great carp broke the surface just beyond the net. Once in the mesh, the 40lb 2oz mirror made a truly dramatic end to the programme. Luck, or good skills, I have absolutely no idea, but I will take this carp fishing any way I can!

So, with programme two in the proverbial bag, it was time to decide what I wanted to do with my own fishing. With the weather getting warmer there was only one place to think about such things. As soon as I was home I uncovered the Harley-Davidson, and, with Lynn on the back, I set out to ponder, whilst catching loads of flies in my teeth! I was amazed that I hadn't thought of it sooner, but Cleverley Mere suddenly became the place to be. I had been fortunate the previous year to catch Hendrix, the one I went there for in the first place, on my first night at the lake. However, he was not the biggest fish in there; that honour fell to one called Ringo, and I guessed I ought to go back and catch it. I had thoroughly enjoyed myself there, and the majority of the anglers were great, so the choice was an easy one. I gave lake owner Ben Lofting a buzz, and it was all sorted out... Let the fun begin!

Before that could go ahead, I had to attend to one very important task that had been given to me by Fox. They don't ask me for much, but when they do, it's normally something incredible. This was no different. They wanted me to catch a couple of carp to show some people, and what people they turned out to be! ITV were making a series of programmes to be aired during the coverage of the 2010 World Cup, and each would feature one of the team telling the world about what they did outside of football. The interviewer was to be none other than James Corden, and the interviewee was the England captain, John Terry. Wow! It was going to be my job to catch one or two carp that the guys could talk about, the only problem being that I would be on a lake where the retention of fish was banned. That said, and although I felt it was a bit of a tall order, the management was cool with holding a fish for a short while. The main men were due to arrive at 6.00 p.m., so I didn't start fishing

*It was a day that will live long in my memory.*

until midday. I was as shocked as anyone to see a 32lb mirror in my net just a few minutes later. I felt it was too long to retain it, so let him swim away, thinking I had just let the only chance I would have disappear into the depths. I still have no idea what I had stepped in that day, but some time later I landed a 20lb common, followed minutes later by another 32lb mirror. This one I retained, because I wasn't sure how long this lucky streak was going to last.

People were starting to arrive by that time, so I guessed the fish wouldn't have to hang around in a sack for too long. I have absolutely no idea how anyone can have all that crap going on in their lives on a daily basis, but what happened that evening left me speechless on many levels. It was as if the circus was in town! James was the first to arrive, and he was such a brilliant bloke to chat to, and hilarious beyond belief. He had even written a lovely note to Lynn in the most amazing handwriting after hearing she was ill, something which I will never forget, and neither will Lynn. With all the 'luvvies' in situ, JT was the last to arrive, along with agent, Paul Nicolls. I felt a bit sorry for John as he got out of his motor; he was simply swamped by people wanting to pat his back and shake his hand. I just sat at the back of my motor and let the mayhem continue, and eventually John got away from the scrum and we chatted for a while. You can quite simply forget everything that every sports writer has ever written about him; he is a genuine bloke who, like the majority of us, loves his wife, his family and his country. The interview only enhanced what I felt initially, and I am sure went a long way to showing people that what you read in the gossip columns is rarely the truth. Although the fish never got his moment of fame, I did put him on the mat, and once again JT showed what a great bloke he is. They asked if he would lift it up, and talk about it. He said he would, if he had caught it, but not today. Top man! James, however, was fascinated by the carp's mouth, but I guess I should keep quiet about what he said it could be used for. It had been a huge day for me and it will live long in my memory, but let's not mention the football, eh?

**At 30lb 5oz she made a great end to my first session back.**

The next thing on my to-do list, although (one) I never thought I would get that far, and (two) it isn't something I want to talk about too much, was that I had turned 50. I remember as a young man looking at people of that age and wondering why they weren't dead! The miracle, of course, is that I was actually still alive; I have danced with the Devil far too often. In all honesty, I shouldn't be here, but I am and all I have to do is live my life with the same gusto that I always have, and I will be happy. The main thing was that as I swung my legs off my bedchair that morning, I couldn't help feeling turning 50 was a bit overrated. I was fishing, and until the day the good Lord wants to issue me with a harp instead of a carp, then I will continue to do so. A quick inventory established that I could remember my name, I wasn't dribbling down my chin, and there wasn't a Zimmer frame where my barrow once stood. So to that end, the following week I loaded an air-dry bag filled with 10 and 15mm boillies into my car and sped off, Essex-bound. The lake itself wasn't too busy, and the first thing I noticed was Dave Lane's truck. I found him in his plot on the far side of the lake and, straight away, I had to laugh. Some things never change, and the lunatic had gear everywhere, along with talking about fishing seventeen different ways all at once. I calmed him down enough to make us both a brew or two before I decided that I ought to go and find some carp for myself. As I walked away I realised this would be the first time we had fished the same water for around four years. The next few weeks would certainly be interesting! Eventually I arrived at a swim that has a track record for producing the big mirror, and surprisingly it was empty. Now I was in a bit of a dilemma. I don't usually choose a swim because of its record, but prefer to fish a swim that has fish in it. (Call me old-fashioned if you will.) However, I trotted down to the left of the swim and gazed at the water I would be fishing, and there at my feet was Ringo herself. The Bowls it would be then! It was still relatively weedy but soon enough, through having a cast around with a lead, I had three areas to go at. Hooklinks and PVA bags were attached,

*Fish like this, to me at least, are very special.*

and after a bit of huffing and puffing I was in the ball game. Come on Ringo, light my fire!

As per usual I was awake before first light, and wondering why I hadn't heard a thing, or received a single bleep. I was still feeling puzzled when one of the rods ripped off an hour or so later. It immediately got stuck in weed, and from the off I knew I would need a boat. Milky was fishing the next swim down, and was soon paddling his way towards me with the lake boat. I put my life jacket on and reeled myself very carefully to the fish. As per normal I got the fish moving straight away, and soon enough it was in the net. The beautiful scattered-scaled mirror made a great start to part two of my Cleverley mission, and once the fish was back home I went for a wander round to the bank where I had seen Ringo the day before. It seemed silly to make life difficult and not fish the area from the swim itself, so with my barrow parked in the swim, I moved my gear round there. Now it was just a simple task to lower the baits into the edge. Sorted! The fish just swam over the top of my traps for the next 20 hours until one of them put me out of my misery. It was one of the lake's original mirrors, no monster at 19lb, but he meant the world to me. I redid the rods, but it wasn't until first light that once again I was called to arms. The fish didn't do a great deal and simply chugged around for a few minutes until I bundled an obviously-good common into the net. At 30lb 5oz she made a great end to my first session back.

I was desperate to return as soon as possible, but the carp started to spawn a couple of days after I had left. The break gave me a chance to catch up on all the things that carp fishing makes me forget, but soon enough I got the nod that it would be opening up again. The next couple of sessions were rather painful experiences, really, because they simply refused to eat. I suspected that they hadn't finished getting laid, and was sure they would do it again soon. The tench, however, made a meal (excuse the pun) out of it, and I landed more than forty of the red-eyed monsters. I was losing the will to live, but eventually the carp started to play ball. I

*The massive ghostie, Tango, weighed 43lb 4oz.*

had set myself up in the area of most activity one Monday morning, and sorted things out as quickly as I could. The carp came to the party eventually, and at 5.00 a.m. I had my first visitor in the shape of a 23lb common. A mirror of 28lb 12oz followed shortly after, and now we were fishing! The night brought four fish, both commons and mirrors to 24lb 12oz, and I was left wondering if it could get any better, but it did. The following day was hot and humid, and it didn't surprise me that I had no further action until 6.30 the next morning. The battle was breathtaking, as was the fish, the second-biggest original mirror at 28lb 4oz. Fish like that, to me at least, are so special and I really didn't believe it could get any better than that... but it did.

I sorted the rods out later in the day, and whilst the sun threatened to fry my brain, I tried to keep cool. I never expected a carp at all, so you will understand why I nearly had a heart attack when one of the rods roared for my attention. A chunky little 23lb mirror was soon powering off back home, and an hour later I was watching a very spawned-out and battered common of 27lb 12oz doing the same. I got my head down as soon as it had cooled down a little, but not for long. At 11.00 p.m. I was standing in the darkness wondering if I had overcast the spot earlier in the day, and hooked a car on the nearby A12. The fight was fast and furious and the fish felt big, too. I would like to claim I had control of the fish, but it was the weed, not me, that stopped it. I pulled a little more than I would have liked, but the weed started to move, and all I had to do was lift the net around a huge ball of Canadian. I ripped away the weed and there before me lay a huge yellow carp, which decided to go absolutely mental. It was all a little late for that, and the elusive Tango was mine. The massive ghostie weighed 43lb 4oz, and I was blown away by the whole experience. A lad called Rob came round and did some pictures, and I gently sent her on her way. I hadn't even thought about catching her, to be honest, but I'm glad I did. In the morning, as I packed away, the fish started spawning once again, and as I pulled away I could see Tango and all her suitors going at it in one of the bays. Bless her!

*One of the best days I've ever spent on the bank.*

For me, July and August have become my new winters. I always find the fishing to be such a struggle at this time of year. However, in my absence Ringo had been out at 53lb, so all was still to play for. I watched Laney running around the lake for a day or so not catching carp, and smiled as his sweaty mass came into my swim for a brew every now and again. It was hard going, and it wasn't until the following morning, with a lot of help from Dave, that I landed a 30lb 14oz common. The boat battle was just a little fraught, but eventually I had something to smile about. Nothing else occurred and as much as I wanted to get back as soon as possible, I had something that went way beyond catching a carp to do the following week. I don't normally do nervous, but I was going to interview Chris Yates near his Wiltshire home, and I was starting to lose sleep over it all. I have written on countless occasions how Richard Walker shaped my fishing as a young lad, but close on his heels in terms of inspiration is Chris. For me, he is the link between then and now, and never once has he compromised his beliefs. He simply does what he wants and to hell with everyone else... Now I can relate to that!

I spent the night fishing at Ashmead, (one) because it tends to calm me down and (two) Mark Walsingham is very good friends with Chris. Mark said that Chris would be cool talking about anything, and as long as I didn't ask embarrassing questions all would be well with the world. As far as I could tell, if I didn't use such dickhead phrases as, "Well carpy, geeza", all should go according to plan. I even managed to catch three small commons from Ashmead, but when Single Scale glided into my swim I quickly reeled in. The last thing on the planet I wanted was to catch her, and anyway, I needed a good night's sleep. By 7.00 a.m. I was washed, shaved and on my way to Hindon, a place where I learnt many of my fishing skills as a child. I spent a while checking out some of the river stretches I fished way back then, before arriving in the hotel car park where the rendezvous was to take place. Then Chris arrived. It's not often that within a few seconds of meeting someone, I know I will get on like a house on

**This 31lb Boyton Cross mirror was just the pick-me-up I needed.**

fire with that person, but this was one of those moments. I should never have been worried, but strangely, I was glad I was. The lake was secret, and stunning; everything you would want from a lake as a backdrop for a chat with Chris. And boy, did we chat. We covered his youth and his fishing beginnings, his life as a young adult, and Redmire, of course. But it was when he told of things he had never spoken of to anyone that it got really interesting. We had it all on film for *Fishing.TV* and I can never quite tell you how proud of that episode I am.

Not sure of how things were going at Cleverley, I spent a little time at Boyton Cross, another water on the Cleverley ticket. I had done some filming there the year before, and was keen to have another go. The first day the action was thick and fast; nothing big, but all about what fishing should be, fun. That was until the next morning when I hooked a bit of an animal. I was expecting maybe a 24-pounder to be my biggest fish, but the mirror in my net was certainly bigger than that, and at 31lb he was. Summertime is a constant concern for me, in that the carp have spawned and I worry about fishing for them, especially the bigger, older fish. But this was just the pick-me-up I needed. I stayed at Boyton for a few weeks, and thoroughly enjoyed the fishing, using just about every tactic in the book. I even managed a segment for *Tight Lines* there, catching the most spectacular linear whilst doing so. Although I had lost touch with my own fishing a little, everything was going really well.

Saying that I had lost touch with my own fishing is a bit misleading really. I still had fish I wanted to catch, but my life in carp fishing is so much more than catching the fish I desire. I find the thought of sitting on the same water year after year, chasing the same fish, a rather boring thing to do. Fair play to those who do, of course, it just doesn't appeal to me. Carp fishing covers a million different scenarios, and I will do my damnedest to experience as many of those as I can before I spin off my mortal coil. I write a diary, and have been doing so since 2002, so that is very much the theme that dominates my life. Winters can be the worst time of all, because the fishing can be so hard. Very often I am running around like a headless chicken trying to get a fish that would help to illuminate an otherwise boring article. It's not everyone's cup of tea, for sure, but then how boring would life be if we all wanted the same things from it? To that end, I have had to select much of what will, and has been, written in this tome, leaving out some waters, and their fish. There isn't room for all of it, unfortunately, and if I said it as it happened on the odd occasion, you, the reader, would probably end up not only being confused but also feeling a little travel sick! I mentioned just now that winter can be the worst time of all for a diary writer, but the warmer months can have their moments too, as I was just about to find out.

I was keen to get back to Cleverley, and hoped the fish had recovered from the rigours of spawning. I was just writing my diary on the Sunday, trying to clear the decks before resuming the campaign, when my phone rang. It was Derek Ritchie, who had been at Cleverley for a day or two, and whilst he had been walking around that morning he had come across the body of the big girl, Ringo. I was crestfallen; my target for the year was no more, and with nothing else to turn to, I stared at the computer screen for inspiration. There was nothing to be found there, so the phone received a bit of abuse over the next hour or so. That didn't bring any joy either, so the only thing to do was ready my gear for the next instalment of *Chilly On Carp 2*. I was off to the Warwickshire Avon to make the second episode, and I was overly excited about this trip because I was yet to pop my cherry as a river carper. The target-less world was pushed to the back of my mind; I wanted nothing to get in the way of my first river fish. The following week I was racing up the M40 and, at the prearranged services, met up with cameraman John Dunford. He had arranged to meet up with a fellow by the name of Andy, who had a lot of experience on the river. I was keen to have a chat with him, but I wanted what happened on film to be based on my choices, and my efforts. As it happens, things turned out rather well. Andy gave us a couple of options, but one absolutely screamed carp. It was the outside of a gentle bend in the river, into the centre of which ran a small drainage channel, and it was covered in lilies. In short order I had three spots where I could present a bait. Once I had positioned the bottom bait rigs with the PVA bags attached, I sprinkled a handful of the 10 and 15mm boillies over the top, and all that was left to do was sit down and wait. And it didn't take too long. The only problem was that within an hour I had let two carp get away without having their picture taken, the lilies having ruined both of my chances. What the hell did I have to do to land a carp from this river? Keep persevering was the answer to that question, and just as the light was fading I landed my first-ever river carp. What made it all the more fitting was that it was probably the same size as the first carp I ever saw in the water way back when I was 16. In the scheme of things, a 10lb carp isn't going to set any records, but that lovely little fish certainly lit my fires. I caught more the next day, and I cannot even begin to tell you how exciting the whole thing was. The biggest shock of all was the boat traffic, which consisted mainly of school kids trying to drown themselves in my swim, and a traveller chap

***As it happened, things turned out rather well on the Warwickshire Avon.***

who obviously got his rocks off doing doughnuts in his little outboard motor-powered boat. Charming! I even had a visit from the Army in the form of a remedial PT class, during which the instructor bellowed across the river for an hour or so. It made a fantastic programme, one I am very proud of, and all done in the shadow of Warwick Castle: Middle England at its finest.

All of which got me no closer to finding a carp to fish for. All I could think of doing was going to one place that has very often sorted my head out in times of crisis, Sandhurst

*I eventually heaved a stunning common of 34lb 5oz into the net.*

Lake at Yateley. It hasn't always been kind to me on the carp-catching front, and it most certainly wouldn't be quiet, but it was all I had for now. So at the next opportunity for a spot of angling, I fitted my gumshield and crash helmet, sorted out my gear and headed off. I ended up in a swim called the Pipes, and as normal, I sent two PVA bags sailing out into the lake at around 80 yards. (I can never seem to find a reason to change things that have always worked wherever I go.) A 28lb mirror during the night led me a merry old dance for ages, and I was chuffed to nuts to see him swim off strongly after a couple of pictures. The following day began very quietly, apart from my phone. By mid-morning I had received a few calls from friends about new waters, and by lunchtime I had a couple of choices. One was a very private estate lake, and the other was a small day ticket water that had a 50-pounder in it. As it happens, I spent the next few months fishing them, only to find out that the lakes had been stocked with big foreign fish, both from very dodgy sources. I no longer care what people fish for in this county, each to his own and all that, but this was not for me. For a while I wasted my time, and that period certainly won't get covered here. We all make mistakes, but it is how you learn from those mistakes that is important. The Sandhurst sabbatical was completed in the most spectacular way when I hooked an absolute animal. For around half an hour I played the fish until eventually I heaved a stunning common of 34lb 5oz into my net. It seemed to clear my mind, and I was sure I had found a place to be. Unbeknown to me, however, I would be spending some time in the wilderness.

I had more filming to do across the Channel at Abbey Lakes in France, and as much as it was a nice distraction, I am not that keen on fishing abroad. Again, don't mistake that for a criticism, I have a huge amount of respect for many anglers who spend much of their time on foreign soil. One such example would be Andy Chambers' experiences and captures on the mighty Orient, probably the only lake I have a wish to fish on the

**Hunts Corner in all its winter glory.**

Continent. There is also the fact that Lynn is not well, and I have severe reservations about leaving her for long periods. I have, on occasion, done so, but I spent much of my time away worrying about her, and when that happens I really can't see the point of going. I would never let the most important person in my life suffer simply because I want to catch carp, and that's all there is to it, really. Eventually, when a couple of worthies told me about the waters I was fishing, I was once again targetless. I tried to fish at Boyton Cross, but Ben had changed the fishing to days only for the winter.

As much as I tried, it was hard work staying in Essex when I had to pack up at last light, and sleep outside the farmer's land, only to return at first light. I gave that up as a bad job after only a couple of sessions, and as I nearly always do, headed off to Linear. I had absolutely no idea which lake I was going to fish, but the first visit would be a recce, and there was the added bonus that John Dunford and I were going to film a couple of TV interviews with Gary 'Milky' Lowe and Ian Russell, who were fishing on Manor. I hadn't cast a rod into that particular lake for around 14 years, and I was kind of excited about doing so. However, once the filming was over I wanted to move on and Ian suggested Hunts Corner. I could find no reason to disagree, and after a visit to the local shops, I went for a look around. The carp seemed to be in the first swim I came to, and although I normally hate car park swims, what was a man supposed to do? Armed with a healthy supply of 10 and 15mm New Grange, I set out to fish the way I always do. All three rods were fished in a line at around 50 yards, and each hookbait carried a bag of the boilie concoction. About half an hour later I had spodded out about a kilo of boilies and Response Pellets, which may seem a lot for winter, especially when everyone tells you that you have to nick a bite. I have no wish to nick a bite; I want to nick loads of bites, thank you very much! And contrary to those who think a little differently to me, it didn't take me long to get one.

I was taken completely by surprise and was in a bit of a panic as I lifted into the fish. This is something I love, and if that feeling ever leaves me, then the rods will gather dust in the shed. We danced the dance for a few minutes, but soon enough I lifted the net around a cracking-looking mirror of 28lb 12oz. I couldn't have asked for a better start to proceedings. I ended up with 17 fish on that 48-hour trip, and by the time I returned home I had decided on a plan. I am not the world's greatest maggot fisherman, but for some reason that was what I was going to use next time out. I relieved Will Raison (Gold Valley is only round the corner from me) of a gallon of maggots on the Sunday, and by 7.00 the next morning I was waiting for the bailiff to open the gates at Linear. This was going to be a recce for a bit of filming I was going to do the following week, and we wanted it to centre on maggot fishing. The weather was awful; high pressure with a horrible easterly wind, and fog... Yuk! That said, I found where I needed to be, and set out to introduce a few pints of red maggots. The rigs, armed with a PVA bag of the same, were dispatched to the target, the edge of a large weedbed at around 50 yards' range. It all looked so good, and it looked even better when I was playing a carp about an hour later. Sooner than expected a 25lb mirror lay on my mat, and at that moment, I decided I would do the filming there. I left the following day having landed seven fish, the pick of the bunch, whilst not the biggest, being a fantastic dark linear of 23lb 4oz. She made me happy, as they all did, and I can see no reason to go fishing if they don't.

The following week I was once again prowling the banks of Hunts Corner, only this time I would have John Dunford for company again. I had also visited Gold Valley the day before for another gallon of their finest red maggots as the programme was all about fishing with the little critters. I skidded to a halt in the car park and set off with my gear, and thankfully I only bumped into two other anglers. They were fishing on the back of the wind at the far end of the lake, which just left me to secure the swim I had angled from the week before. A

***At 25lb it was as good a start as I could have hoped for.***

lovely south-westerly was trickling into the area, and for now it felt reasonably warm. Rather pleasingly, three fish showed as I was gazing across the lake and in no time at all I was set up and had baited with about 4 kilos of the 'germs'. I didn't cast out because the cameras were still on the M4, and to catch one before they arrived would be a bit of a waste. We had two nights ahead of us, and as I sat and waited for John's arrival, I noticed that two of the baited areas already had a few bubbles popping on the surface. It was looking good, and looked even better when John got one of the HD cameras locked on the rods after I had positioned them. At that time of year, early November, it is very important to utilise all the hours of daylight, so as soon as he was ready we started doing some pieces to the camera. We got one little segment done without too much bother, then decided to break for a brew, and as we did so, one of the rods chirped into life. A little over an hour and I was playing a carp, how cool is that! A twitchy ten minutes followed, enhanced, I suspect, by my nervousness, but it didn't fall off and a rather good mirror was soon lying on the mat. It had fallen to the tactics which I had just been explaining to the camera; the maggot trap had worked. Basically, my simple little maggot rig was armed with a large PVA bag of the same, and cast to a silty area 40 yards out. I had baited with around eight similar bags, which were catapulted into position. At 25lb it was as good a start as I could have hoped for, but as is the way of these things, fate and the weather decided to intervene. We were buzzing, but over a brew we listened to the radio telling us that England was soon going to become the new North Pole. It was a little depressing and got a touch more so when two anglers set up in the swims opposite me. They were quite within their rights, of course, but it would obviously interfere with my angling. That is carp fishing, but I must say, by the morning I was wishing I was doing anything but. The margins were covered in ice, and the temperature had fallen below zero; it was time to run for home, and that is exactly what we did. We arranged to do a second half to the programme at some

***I had been inducted into the Carp Fishing Hall of Fame. A very proud moment.***

stage, but neither of us could ever have imagined it would be over a month before the weather eased up. This is when Lynn decided that it was time to get the whole bungalow decorated.

Not being able to go fishing very often brings into stark reality the things that I have spent the last 12 months trying to avoid. A case in point would be something called decorating, or anything to do with... um... err... IYD, I think it's called. I was never put on this Earth to do such things, and to be honest the thought made me feel a little nauseous and dizzy. The first 'immediate action' was to desperately find somewhere, anywhere, to go fishing. When that ruse failed, I had to find someone who could carry out these heinous tasks. Luckily, I have a friend called Barry Cole, and he knows about such things, so after assisting him in the paint-buying, I was sure I was free of the labours. No, I was recruited to help, but that wasn't part of the plan, either. In the end the best thing is to simply break something, so I did. I was immediately excused YDI for the rest of the month... I love it when a plan comes together! There was, of course, the odd carp-related thing to do, and the most important was the Sandown Winter Show. Shortly before, I had been contacted by Simon Crow at Carp-Talk, who informed me that I had been inducted into the Carp Fishing Hall of Fame. I was to be the 27th inductee, and I cannot even begin to tell you how proud that made me. Being placed alongside some of the anglers who have shaped me as a carp fisher is incredible, although I would like to point out that I feel I am in no way as worthy as they are. Carp fishing has been so good to me, and I always find it a real pleasure to put as much as I can back into this marvellous pastime of ours. I believe humbled is the word. Interestingly, there were a few derogatory remarks about the award. No names, no pack drill of course, but I found it ironic when a few of those detractors were later inducted, and it then became the best thing ever!

It wasn't until 2011 was under way that I could get out fishing once again. I had had a little flutter on a local river, but that was just a glorious waste of time. We had the rest of the maggot programme to film, but the most important thing to consider was my Carp Diary. Although you don't make much money out of such things, the diary is the epicentre of what I do, and to that end can very much dominate my life. This winter was no exception, and all I wanted to do was illustrate my articles with a carp or two. Once again I turned my attention to Ash Fisheries, the lakes next door to Ashmead. The original fish in those lakes were related to the fish next door, but the lakes were a little bit overstocked, if I was honest. Be that as it may, it was great winter fishing, and I wanted to take as much advantage of that as I could. There was also the wonderful nature of all that surrounds this part of the world, especially the local hunt when they came through on a couple of occasions. Even though the lakes had only just thawed out, I was keen to get going and the first thing was to do the filming. I was confident, but still wondered if the water would be wobbly as I raced past Stonehenge, but I need not have worried. There before me, as I pulled through the gate, was a nice ripple on the water, and as the cameras weren't going to be with me until 8.00 the following morning, I could take my time. With it being such a small water, it was easy to think all you had to do was lob the rigs out anywhere. But small-water fishing is rarely that easy, and it is from very specific areas that you are going to get bites.

As I walked the lake I was distracted by the hunt coming by, and couldn't help but laugh. The main man was discussing where he thought the fox was, and all around him were agreeing with what he said. I was amazed, and almost tempted to tell them the error of their ways. I didn't of course, and doffed my cap to the fox that was sitting on a hill gazing down rather calmly at the chaos below him! Once the hunt and hounds had gone on their merry way, he simply trotted off! It was great to see, but I needed to concentrate on what I was there to do. I found three tiny little spots that seemed perfect, baited them up, and eventually I was ready to rock and roll. I try to be disciplined, but very often the child in me won't allow it, and a few minutes after a good fish had boshed out over one of the spots I had a rig there. I giggled like a kid until I drifted off to dream of *Thomas the Tank Engine*. I did remonstrate with myself an hour later as I slipped an upper-double mirror back to his home. He would have been perfect for the filming, but it was far too early to sack him up. It went a little quiet after that, but at 7.00 a.m. I got another chance, and the resulting 22lb mirror came to rest in a sack. He made a great start to the filming, and without going into all the details, I stacked up a fair few more fish. It was great fishing, and a great start to the year. It was so good in fact that I rang DHP and asked if they could come down and do the pictures for my next technical piece, which they did, and all was well with the world. I had started off the year well, and hoped I could carry that on.

The weather didn't get much warmer over the next few weeks and I continued fishing Ash, catching plenty of fish and enjoying myself. But it wasn't too long before I needed to get away for a change of scenery, the only problem being that I had absolutely no idea where to go. It was situation normal for me, and over the next few weeks I just fished wherever took my fancy. Sandhurst was visited, rather unsuccessfully, and 24 hours later I was wracking my brains once again. Hunts Corner got a visit or two, but that became a little predictable, and all I could think of was a trip to a syndicate water that I'd had an invite to for some time. I wasn't a member, but it just seemed the right place to try to get my head into gear. Not knowing the water, I really didn't think I would be catching anything, but that wasn't the point of being there, really. The weather was just about as bad as it can get, and even the two pike anglers I bumped into said that the toothy ones weren't up for it. I had a couple of rods on a little bait, and a single rod roving around, although I never once cast at anything; it really was that lifeless. I woke on the second morning and was just about to accept the inevitable blank, when one of the bobbins pulled up tight and stayed there. At which point

*At 35lb she made the last few weeks a passing memory.*

the rod was in my hand, and rather pleasingly arched over with a carp hanging on the end. The fight was anything but spectacular to begin with, and all the fish did was plod around for a few minutes. All of a sudden, though, the rod was nearly ripped from my hands and I marvelled at just how out of control I was. It's what I love most about hooking a fish, but at some point you have to gain the upper hand. This was obviously a good fish, and large inky swirls appeared as I drew it towards the net. It simply gave up in the end, and rolled into the net with no bother. She was dark and hugely impressive in her full winter colours, and at 35lb she made the previous few weeks of my life a passing memory. Once she was home I asked if I could have another session some time, and I got my wish a little sooner than I thought.

I messed around at Boyton for a few days and generally got my magazine life sorted out, before getting permission to fish the syndicate lake once again. The hour-long journey one Tuesday morning was uneventful, and the lake was devoid of anglers. It was a perfect start to any session, and after a look around I came to a small open channel behind an island. I was gobsmacked when I peeked over the low-lying foliage to see a squadron of carp, and some of them were monsters. One area in particular caught my eye, a small silty patch near a rather nasty snag. I knew I would fish it, but made the decision to only do so in the daylight hours. I just couldn't risk it in the dark, and, more importantly, couldn't risk the fish's safety. So a good night's kip and maybe I'd land a chunk in the day... sorted! It was just a case of lowering my two PVA bag rigs into position once the fish had turned their backs, and with that done, I settled down to wait. Which didn't take long. The first fish swam out of the channel when hooked, and as I played it, I couldn't help hoping that any more fish I hooked would do the same. Dream on boy! Without fuss I managed to get this one in the net fairly quickly, and at 31lb the leather made a great start to things. As much as I was there to chill, it was difficult not to get caught up in the exciting

*The stunning beast was a little bigger than the last one, at 31lb 10oz.*

fishing, and by nightfall I had landed several others, topped by a rather rotund mirror of 39lb 12oz. I'm not really supposed to write about this lake, and in any case, it wasn't somewhere I could spend my time, but saying that, it certainly sorted my head out!

I had procured a ticket for the Essex Manor, and that was the next place to visit. However, to cut a short story even shorter, I hated the place. It was nothing to do with the people, they were great, it was just that I didn't feel comfortable there. To that end I decided I would return to the little Estate Lake at Melchbourne, and continue my search for some of the uncaught fish. There was also the fact that it now contained an upper-40 common, and who wouldn't want to catch one of those? As it happens, that mission ended a lot quicker than I would have liked. No, I didn't catch a 45+ common, because I had already caught it twice without realising! I had wanted to go there and then, but I had a DVD to do for DHP in conjunction with Fox. It was all about PVA, and I was going to film it with Tom Maker at Linear Fisheries' Hunts Corner. The subsequent story is out there on disc, so I won't go into details here, but one brilliant story that came out of the session for me was the capture of one of the lake's originals. I had seen pictures of this particular fish in magazine articles over the years, and always thought how nice it would be to catch it one day. Well, the second day of filming saw me draw that spectacular 29lb 2oz mirror into my net, and I cannot even begin to tell you how pleased I was.

With the weather becoming more and more spring-like, it was time for me to head towards Northampton next time around, and as I drove around the big house the following Monday morning I once again stopped at the top of the hill to gaze upon the lake. It really is the most perfect place to while away a couple of days, and soon enough I was on the prowl. It was midday before I saw anything, which happened to be two good mirrors feeding in the shallow arm. Try as I may I couldn't get a bite; they really are the most arrogant carp I have ever fished for, which just makes the fishing that much more exciting. I moved a dozen times that day, and just as I was about to set up for the night, I spotted a movement out of the corner of my eye. A tail pattern creased the surface only inches from the bank, and once the fish had moved off the spot for the tenth time, I lowered a rig into the muddy cloud. Slackening off the line I retreated a tactical bound of about 10 yards, and waited. The freespool hissed and the water erupted a minute later as an angry fish bow-waved out of the shallow area. Shallow-water battles are always fraught affairs, and this was no different, but soon enough a shockingly handsome mirror lay in the net. At a little over 21lb he made a great start to yet another Estate Lake campaign. With the help of the Estate manager, Tye, I landed another fish of similar size early the following day. I was on my own for a while before the first visitor arrived. He had landed the big common at 45lb+ a few weeks before, and I can only think he had come down to rub my nose in the fact. I believe he wanted me to be jealous, but I had to tell him, once I had seen the pictures, that I had already caught it. Twice in fact! I thought the big common was another fish to be honest, and didn't realise until that point that our paths had crossed. I reckon he was more gutted than I was when I told him, and I believe he went away and amended his Facebook page, that had originally said, "I am the guy who caught the big common that Ian Chillcott couldn't." How friggin' sad is that?

Anyway, my next visitor had come to fish, and I was having a walk around while he was setting up. As I passed I commented on his strange bobbins that gripped his line by a clip on the side of them. Evidently they were all the rage, and the only thing to use when slack line fishing. No names to protect the guilty here, of course, but I did smile to myself as I wandered back to my gear. He was fishing one side of an island in a slightly deeper part of the lake, and I wished him luck. The night was quiet, but I was awake well before light, sipping a brew and soaking up the atmosphere. I did try to get some more sleep but a howling buzzer wouldn't allow that. In the bright moonlight I was able to watch the fish charging around in the shallow water. Even the tail vortex that broke the surface and swirled the mist around above it was breathtaking, but at long last the broad shoulders of a mirror were visible at the bottom of my net. She looked magnificent on the mat, weighing 29lb 4oz, her massive golden scales picked out by the full moon. I wanted a picture and decided to put her in a sack for an hour or so, before asking the bobbin man down the way to do the honours. I didn't recast the rod, and hoped that the other rod was still in the ball game. I was just about to have a cuppa, when I noticed a swirl over the other hookbait. Before I could consider the possibility that the fish were back, the rod tore off at a frightening pace. I was almost scared to pick it up, but I did, of course, and it made little difference to the fish. Patience and pressure soon took its toll, and after a while I scooped it into the net. The stunning beast was a little bigger than the last, at 31lb 10oz, and completed an incredible brace. All I had to do now was get matey to take some pictures. With no rods in the water I wandered down to him, and straight away noticed that the line from the right-hand rod was pointing to the other side of the island he was fishing. I

**Lynn and me with the new Barnaby, Neil Dudgeon.**

*I really don't think my time at Melchbourne could have ended any better.*

coughed, and he said hello. I asked if anything had happened, to which he replied that he had had a single bleep at around 1.00 in the morning. I couldn't help but tell him about the line, and he rather sheepishly tried to sort things out. He couldn't of course, and all was lost. Amazing what a load of bullshit marketing can do, eh? With the pictures done, I was away a little later. I would be back next week, but knowing I had caught the biggest fish in the lake (not at 40lb+ I might add), I decided that it would be for the last time. However, there was one more surprise in store.

Before I could get back there Lynn and I had one rather pleasant thing to do, and that was being extras on *Midsomer Murders* once again. It was a brilliant day out, and we even got to meet the new Inspector Barnaby, Neil Dudgeon. The start of the next week saw me heading north one last time. I spent about 24 hours not knowing what to do, and not being able to find anything to fish for, but eventually it was the bream that gave the game away. It was around midday when I spotted some activity in the only large weedy area of the lake. I legged it down and discovered a herd of bream having the once-a-year sexfest. And it got a whole lot more interesting when I saw a few carp drifting in and out of the area. They were feeding, and with the bream's activity covering my actions I fired out four pouches of 10mm boilies. It took about fifteen minutes to sort out a couple of rods, but soon enough two of my bag rigs were in the area of most activity. And it didn't take long to get a bite. From the get-go it was obviously a big fish; it just plodded around ignoring my efforts to have my picture taken with her. However, a bit of weed stopped her in her tracks, and once it had covered her eyes I simply led her into the net. I was chuffed to bits, but lying in the net was probably the one carp I never wanted to catch again from there. It was the mirror from the cover of *Light My Fire*, and I was a little gutted. For me, it took something away from that first meeting. However, just as I finally knew my time at this lake was over, the other alarm burst into life. Now this fish really went mad, and the more I pulled the madder she got. The weed once again slowed her progress and eventually there on my mat lay the most spectacular common. I had two regulars with me at the time and neither they nor anyone else had ever seen this fish, all 29lb 2oz of her. I never like to leave any lake with a cloud over my head, and as AC/DC's *Highway to Hell* made my ears bleed on the way home, I really didn't believe things could have ended any better.

# Chapter Ten
## Shoot to Thrill

*I was off to the USA for the World Carp Cup.*

I am always amazed at how the hand of fate can play such a big part in our lives. The previous few months had been filled with me running around like a rabid dog, not knowing from one day to the next where I would be going, and ensuring I fulfilled my commitments for the magazines. In that sentence it can appear like I wasn't enjoying myself, but I was, and even though I had found nowhere to really lay my hat I was just happy to have the life that I was living. However, although for a short while it didn't seem as if I would, I could never have imagined where I would end up, or indeed how I even got there. But isn't it the total unpredictability of it all that makes life so interesting? I had recently been to an Airborne reunion, and while I love meeting people for whom I have so much respect, I don't want to dwell on what I had been doing twenty years previously. I've done that, got the T-shirt, and moved on. I would rather think about what I am going to do tomorrow, and how I am going to do it. It had been 11 years since I had left the Army, and the crazy thing was that none of my plans had worked out as I expected. I often shake my head and wonder, 'How the hell did that happen?' And do you know what; I wouldn't have it any other way. For one, it keeps me on my toes, but most of all, it makes life so damn entertaining!

With the Essex Manor being a non-starter for me, I was once again wandering around searching for clues, and I was driving home one day, when I received a call from Mick Brais at Sky Sports' *Tight Lines*. They wanted me to do a segment for an upcoming programme, and my old buddy Dave Lane would be in the studio. I couldn't say no, of course, but where the hell was I going to go? Fate, bless her, was just about to deal me another favourable hand. I had been talking to a friend of mine from Worthing, Ian Stevens, about my dilemma and he appeared to have the perfect answer. He was the head bailiff on a lake called Patching Pond. The first thing, as always, was to ask about its history. By the time he had finished I was open-mouthed; if you wanted history then this was it... and then some! The venue is the oldest man-made lake in the country, which in itself is awesome, but it had been mentioned in the Domesday Book, and ultimately stocked a couple of times by Donald Leney. I got so keen to find out more that I eventually discovered that there are two Domesday Books, one big and one small, but maybe that's a story for another time. Ian sorted me out a ticket, and a date was set the following week for me to visit and do the filming. It may seem a little crazy to fish a lake I had never heard of, let alone seen, but that level of a challenge is like a red rag to a bull for me; I was so excited.

I drove to Patching the following Sunday with my hair on fire, met up with Ian, and went for a good look around. It was an incredible place of around six acres, and very shallow. Couple that with shady bays and loads of lily beds, and I couldn't have thought of a better place to do a bit of filming. I baited the odd spot and eventually drifted off to sleep, before the cameras arrived in the morning. I hadn't fished, of course, but was keen to get going once we had chatted about the programme. To be honest, the day turned into a bit of a nightmare, and I was worried I had wasted everyone's time. That was until I arrived back at the swim I had slept in, and noticed a little movement under a tree some twenty yards to the right. In no time at all I had a bag of small New Grange boilies positioned as near to the movement as I dared, and sat back to wait. After some time I needed a pee, and as I was doing so the buzzer howled. As fast as I could I got to the rod, and the fun began. It wasn't a big fish, that much was obvious, but once it was on the mat I could just make out a small blue tattoo spot on its belly. That meant that the 11lb mirror was one of the originals that were stocked by Donald himself, and at around 51 years old he became one of the most special fish I have ever caught! Patching really is an incredible place, and I would certainly be back, but the drive home was just about to change everything.

I was bombing down the A27 towards Portsmouth when I glimpsed a speedboat tearing

*At 30lb 12oz she was a great way to get off the mark at Westhampnett.*

around a lake, with a waterskier in tow. I realised that I was looking at Westhampnett, somewhere I had driven past a few times but had never given it a second thought. I dredged my memory banks and remembered that it had some good fish in it. Most pleasing of all, though, was that I already had a ticket for it in my pocket, because the water belonged to CEMEX Angling. Right there and then I made the decision to go and have a look the following Sunday. A little more homework revealed that there was little known about the place, and that just made it all the more important for me to fish there. I wouldn't be fishing for fish that are paraded every week in the papers, and this in itself made writing about it better for me, and, more importantly, the reader. I went down with Lynn on the Sunday for a look-see, and, most pleasing of all, I didn't see another angler. I made the decision to fish there for the next month, starting the following day, and see if I had found the next leg of my journey. I had one more ace up my sleeve, and he went by the name of Duncan Charman. Duncan is well known in the specimen world, and had spent a fair bit of time at the lake chasing bream and perch. Living about half a mile from me meant that we were soon sharing a brew in my kitchen. He drew a marvellous little map, and passed on what he knew about the carp fishing. He also mentioned that there could possibly be four or five fish over 40lb, which all meant that as soon as he had left I was sorting out the bait and tackle for an early start the next morning.

The lake is around 40 acres, and roughly a figure-of-eight shape, then, as I pulled up to the gate, I saw several carp leaping. I could only see one angler, and as soon as I saw movement in his bivvy, I made my way around to him. His name was Steve, and he happened to be a firefighter. He had also fished a few of the non-publicity big-fish waters that I would love to fish, but never could. The conversation was easy, and he even told me which swim I needed to fish, The Banker. And, as the saying goes, that would do for me! I found a strip of silt at around 80 yards, and within a couple of hours discovered the lunacy of listening to a bream

*A truly handsome carp of 31lb 14oz.*

angler. There were boilies in the mix, but I had gone heavily with Duncan's recommendation, and added a healthy amount of chopped tigers and hemp along with loads of pellets. The bloody bream loved it, and by morning all that I owned had a thin coating of bream slime over it. Why didn't I just go in with my "Oh so predictable, boring boilie, why don't you do something else?" approach that has worked on every water I have ever fished? I did have to chuckle when Duncan told me his best bream from there was 16lb+, and I had to tell him I had landed a brace of 17s. The fireman was off later, and as he had had a couple of carp in the night, I guessed it may be considered a little rude if I didn't move in there after him... so I did! I sifted through my 'bream bait' bucket and removed all the boilies, which were destined to find their way to a spot at 100 yards. All three hookbaits were spread along it, and as I got about halfway through lacing the spot with boilies, one of the rods ripped off. The fish fought hard and deep, and it was a while before it came anywhere near the net. I could see something strange about it as I drew it over the net cord, but it wasn't until I had it on the mat that I could see most of its right-hand flank was pitch black. She looked huge but had obviously spawned-out; however, the needle settled at 30lb 12oz and it was a fantastic way to get off the mark. I found out all about that fish a little later. She had been out at over 37lb previously, but most interesting was how she came to have the black scarring on her flank. When she was being held in a stock pond before coming to Westhampnett, she jumped out and landed on a sheet of black polythene. In the heat of the day it was roasting hot and it had melted into her side. Remarkable fish, carp, don't you think?

I landed a further ten carp that trip, all of them males, with the next biggest at 22lb. I had no idea it would be that productive, but I liked it there a lot and couldn't wait to get back. I arrived the following Monday and started catching from the off, the boilie-only approach, as it always does, working a treat. Four fish up to 27lb 2oz was great, but the big south-westerly winds coming in fresh off the sea were causing havoc with the weed. I was constantly removing great swathes of it from my line, and the session turned into something of a nightmare. The next session was exactly the same, although I once again worked my way around the weed as best I could. It wasn't until the second morning that I got some action, and straight away I thought I had hooked a monster. The fight went on for over half an hour, but eventually I led her into the net, along with a large amount of eelgrass. She looked huge, but again the spawning had left her very empty, although I could never complain about a 33lb mirror, could I? I walked around the lake with a rod, doing a little more homework if you like, until I arrived back at my plot and got the rods back in the game. It was around 3.00 in the afternoon, as I read a book, when I got myself another bite. This fish gave up the ghost almost straight away, and as I held the 27lb 12oz mirror in the net one of the other rods joined the party. If you will excuse the pun, this was a completely different kettle of fish. Even at range it continually flat-rodded me, and that is pretty much how the whole fight went. When I eventually got it in the net all became clear; the tail was enormous and almost looked like it didn't belong to this carp. Again it looked like one of the originals, a truly handsome carp of 31lb 14oz. It was right then that I decided I had, at last, found somewhere I wanted to be.

Coastal waters can be a tad difficult to fish if you are relying on the weatherman to point you in the right direction. I have already mentioned the wind strength when it was coming off the sea, but I was amazed just how wrong the television and radio were in predicting the weather on the south coast. I was fed up with even listening to forecasts in the end, because they never seemed to get it right. I began to wonder if I could be a weather forecaster, because the job was obviously so easy. All I would need to do is wake up around 4.30 a.m. and, over a cup of tea, make up my prediction that would constitute just about every kind of weather imaginable. After I had rung through the information to whoever required my guesswork, I could climb back into bed and sleep until it was time to come up with another load of bovine manure 24 hours later. I gave up in the end and just went with what my eyes told me from day to day, and anyway, angling pressure, I feel, has far more influence on carp than the weather. Thankfully, Westhampnett didn't receive that much pressure at the time and all I had to do was find the carp. Simples! It became obvious very early on that casting to the long-range spots I had found was the answer, in the short term. Hell, it might even be the answer all the time I was there, but for now I was happy that I could catch from those areas. It was just a question of how much the wind hindered my ability to reach and fish accurately at ranges that made things a little harder than I think they should have been. That said, and amongst whittling effigies of weathermen to stick baiting needles in, I did start to consistently catch from the lake. I very often have to think of my writing when I select a water, but on this occasion I had done nothing of the sort. I just wanted a relatively unknown water to spend some time on chasing a few good fish, but I had killed two birds with one stone there, and my next session proved the point very well indeed. I had been writing a series called the Chillcott Files in ACF'S sister magazine *Total Carp*, in which I would describe to the reader how to go about certain things. The next month I would go on the bank and prove it. This time, however, I had written about catching bigger carp, and the last thing the editor said as I wrote down the date the photographer would be with me was, "All you have to do now is catch a big one." Easier said than done!

With catching four carp the previous week, I was kind of excited and confident about the session, which isn't always the case. I arrived on the Sunday and spent an age looking for signs. The carp, bless 'em, gave the game away and looked as if they were still in the same area as the week before. Indeed, even my marker and spod rods were still clipped up to the subtle feature that I was fishing to, which meant I could set a trap for a monster with the minimum of disturbance. The wind was due to stay in a south-westerly direction, and once I had positioned the hookbaits and baited up, I breathed a huge sigh of relief and sat down for a brew. It had been hard work, even with the wind in my favour, and I could only imagine that it would be almost impossible if the wind changed – which, contrary to what the imbecilic weather fellow had said, it did about four hours later. I wasn't pleased and my angst was compounded still further by the strong northerly wind bringing with it huge rafts of eelgrass. It wiped out my lines on countless occasions, which meant I was constantly recasting every half hour or so. It increased in strength, too, and it became harder and harder to get the hookbaits back in position. I cracked-off once (which I hate), I trod on my spod reel, breaking the bail arm, and bent the bail arm on another, along with a few other tackle-destroying disasters, all of which meant that Coco the Clown had to go home at 5.30 in the morning for fresh supplies. Of course, that included rush hour, and it was over three hours before I strode, rather disgustedly, back into my swim. To say that I was in a bad mood wouldn't be too much of a gross understatement, but I had to get my head back in the game so as to not waste everyone's time and effort.

By 9.00 a.m. I was sitting drinking a brew, wondering if the repositioning of the rods was good enough, but knowing it was the best I could do. Again I had to spend my time getting weed off the line, but eventually it started to ease off, and for the first time in a couple of days I could relax a little. It wasn't until the next morning that I was woken by an angry buzzer, but the little common wasn't exactly what the feature required, and I slipped him back home. I lost what felt like a good fish (don't they all when they fall off?) and as I swung the empty hook to hand I thought I may as well go home. But just as I was losing the will to live, the photographer, Jason Umney, arrived and at long last I had someone to tell my tales of woe to. As I waited for him to walk round I sat on the opposite side of the point I was fishing, and, unbelievably, spotted a couple of fish crash out in the waves. It looked as if I would have to move into a swim I had never fished before, which probably wasn't the best scenario on which to base the capture of a big fish, if I was honest. With Jason's help I moved over and within minutes had found a lovely silty trench surrounded by weed. At 75 yards it was just what the doctor ordered, and for the next hour I let 'em have a bit of bait... as I do. Aided by a northerly wind that should never have been blowing, I finally positioned the hookbaits

*At 36lb 8oz she was the icing on the cake.*

at around 1.30 p.m. We got on with the technical pictures and were just taking a break for a brew when one of the rods – cast at the church spire and which I had christened the God rod – chirped into life. I probably played that fish a lot harder than I should, but I wanted to keep it out of the weed, which worked out just fine in the end. I held it in the net whilst we discussed the pictures, when one of the other rods interrupted the debate. From the off it felt a bigger fish, and it did nothing to make me feel any different during the fight. Eventually, as Jason clicked away, I heaved a rather larger carp over the net cord. The first fish was a 22lb 4oz mirror, and the second took the scales round to 33lb 13oz. The article was complete at that point, but Jason could stay until the following morning, so I told him I would get a bigger one, which I did at around 6.00 a.m. I had just lost another fish in the weed, and as I was about to javelin the rod onto the A27, one of the other rods came to the party. With Jason clicking away, I concentrated on the job in hand. All went a little quiet when we got our first look at the fish. It was big for sure, and once in the net we could see just how big. At 36lb 8oz she was the icing on the cake and, with the pressure now well and truly off, I enjoyed the next couple of hours, landing two more mirrors of 24lb 6oz and 28lb 10oz.

Westy was turning out to be a really special water. At the very least I had found a home for a while, and I was enjoying life on the bank a little more than I had for a few months. Several more 20s graced my net before I headed for home, and on that drive I organised another feature the following week with a great photographer, Pat MacInnes. It wasn't actually that

*A cracking Stoney & Friends 28lb 7oz mirror.*

important to catch a carp this time around, but, as normal, I couldn't help myself. I arrived 24 hours before Pat would be with me, and, fishing in exactly the same way, I landed three lovely fish in the day, but when I woke in the morning I stared accusingly at the rods. Pat was running a little late, and I worried about catching, but I should never have doubted my luck. At around 8.00 a.m. I was playing a fish, and a good one too by the feel of it. It hit the surface and stayed there the whole fight, but, nervous though I was, I soon had a rather large and good-looking fish in my net. I retained it for a short while waiting for Pat, and soon enough I was posing behind a 35lb 2oz mirror. I could not have been happier with life at that moment and a couple more fish came my way before I left the following day. It was turning out to be a great summer, but as always the carp had other ideas and the fishing slowed dramatically. I ended up in danger of disappearing up my own backside trying to keep things going, and although I did land a couple more over the next two weeks, I was never in control. It was August, and there were a couple of other things that would undoubtedly distract me.

First up was the Stoney & Friends do at Yateley. Then there was also the fact that Fox was going to be able to provide all their anglers for a series Rob Hughes had organised for Sky. I reckoned I had the perfect place for that. Yateley first... I would be sharing my time there with Tim Paisley, as I normally do, only this time we had agreed that maybe it was time we caught a carp or two. We fished along the Works Bank and in true Chillcott fashion I decided to fish two rods on the same spot and let 'em have some New Grange, enough in fact for breakfast, dinner and tea. Several of the locals told me I had it all wrong, and a blank was on the cards. I wasn't too bothered about the fishing, but was bothered about the fact that Tim had invited me some time before to fish as part of the Angling Publications team, in the upcoming World Championships on the mighty St Lawrence River in upstate New York in the good old US of A. Now that was something to look forward to, especially as I would be partnered with Lee 'Action' Jackson, and we needed to discuss a few things. The evenings at these events at Yateley have become legendary and that evening was no different, but the following morning was a subdued event... until I got a bite of course. The fish got stuck in the weed and, whilst trying to remain cool, which I most certainly wasn't, I called for the boat. It wasn't needed in the end, and after it visited a few more weedbeds, Tom Duncan-Dunlop scooped up my prize. It was a cracking mirror of 28lb 7oz and I like to think of it as a bit of a team effort. Tim and I had both caught during the events before, but never when we had fished together. Fishing with Tim is a very rare and special time for me, but at that particular event we can both reflect on how horribly cancer has affected both our lives.

Next up was the MNDA event at Linear Fisheries, and I used it, as normal, to chill out for a couple of days. In reality all I was thinking about was getting back on the trail of a Westy 40-pounder, and sorting out the venue for the filming I mentioned earlier. I had half a mind to do the filming on Westy, but due to the erratic nature of TV work, that would have to wait. It also seemed I was concentrating so much on the American trip that I kind of took my mind off the fishing at Westy. I had probably become a bit blasé about it all, and that is a sure-fire way of messing everything up! I landed several fish over the next few weeks, topped by a glorious 30lb 12oz common, but it was the World Championships that were taking up every waking moment, and to that end I wrapped up my fishing at Westy the week before we left. She would still be there when I got home, I assured myself.

When we set out on any adventure, we all have dreams and aspirations about the outcome. It is those dreams that drive us on and I cannot imagine a life without them, but what happens when those dreams come true? I could have had no idea what was about to happen when I boarded the Canadian Airways flight to Montreal on September 21st alongside the rest of the Carpworld team, a team that consisted of: Tim Paisley and Steve Briggs, John Lilley and Paul Musson, Lee Jackson and me, along with Tom Duncan-Dunlop and George Csonka. The last pair weren't actually part of the team (three pairs were all that was needed), but they were funded and sponsored from the same sources. We were excited, truly excited, and knew that should one of us get in a 'going' swim then we could win the World Championships. As with any match-fishing event, luck plays a huge part in the form of a drawbag, from which you randomly pick your peg. It has no bearing on things, no matter how much experience you have, if you select somewhere with no fish; you can't catch 'em if they ain't there. For the moment though, I had to contend with flying to Canada, and you can never imagine just how much I hated that. It may surprise some of you, because I am an ex-paratrooper, but I much prefer to jump out of a plane than land in the bloody thing! So, as my white-knuckled hands gripped the seat handles, I tried to take my mind off things by thinking about how it all began. It was the year before when Tim had asked me if I wanted to be part of the Carpworld team for the event. It took about one nanosecond before I nearly bit his hand off at the shoulder. All that was left to do was decide who my partner would be. As it happens the answer was readily at hand a month or so later, when Tim was fishing in France with Lee Jackson. I received a text after they had been there a day or two, and it was a text that would kick-start one of the most amazing experiences of my life. "How about you and me doing the World Cup?", asked Lee. "Oh yes indeed," I replied, and from that moment on the game was definitely afoot.

I rarely go abroad for my fishing because I don't like to leave Lynn on her own for

*Lee and I probably needed a little help!*

long. Without going into details, she doesn't like me talking about her illnesses, she is very poorly, and needs care much of the time I'm away for any length of time. I took care of that first and foremost, then turned my attention to the fishing. Being a consultant for Fox and Mainline meant that I was at the heart of negotiations about the tackle and bait that would be sent to upstate New York. In the end, both companies went way beyond the call of duty, and, in no small way, were responsible for the way things eventually turned out. Before I forget I would just like to thank them all over again, which sounds so inadequate for such a financial and logistical endeavour. Anyway, knowing that we had a massive pallet of bait and essential items such as brollies, bedchairs, hooks and leads amongst a whole host of other vital components, left me with just my personal kit to sort out. Tackle-wise I wanted to put some new reels and rods through the rigours of the match, because they really wouldn't come under that much pounding in any other environment. I wanted to fish much as I do everywhere I go, but of course I had to up the breaking strain of my main line and hooklinks. After chucking in a few changes of clothing and my iPod I was ready to rock and roll. We met up at Heathrow in the early morning and suffered the annoying process of getting rod tubes and sports bags onto the flight. With an extortionate amount of money removed from our wallets to get it all onboard, all I had left to think about was the flight, which mercifully went by without a hitch... or an explosion... or a door dropping off... or engine failure... or...

It was early afternoon when we arrived in Montreal, and we quickly got the hire trucks sorted out. An uneventful two-hour journey found us turning into American Carp Adventures Lake View Motel, at Massena, New York State. Owned and run by Jerry and Marcy Laramay, it would be our home for the next 12 days. It was truly awesome and I cannot say enough about the brilliant accommodation and the way we were received. It made the start of the journey just the jump-off point we needed. After a night of 'getting to know you' kind of thing, the morning was all about sorting the pallet out that had arrived via US customs. It was then

**Some of the team even did a recce of the river through an underwater camera.**

that all the lads could see what Mainline and Fox had done for us, and it took a good while to sort out what was what. Jerry also had the gear on hand to prepare the maize and seed mix, which would form a large part of our baiting strategy. In all, each pair would have four large buckets of the particle mix, about 80 kilos, and around 30 kilos of Plum boilies, big yellow baits that looked to be exactly what we should be using. It looked like a ridiculous amount of bait, even to me, and I could never have imagined sending out for a resupply... but we did!

Jacko had a little ace up his sleeve, and over the next four days we spent much of our time and money on trying to get it sorted out. Grits were the things we were after, a cereal product that is infinitely more popular in the southern states than it is in the north of the country, where we were. However, we did amass about 15kg of the stuff and the plan was to mix it with liquidised corn to form groundbait balls. The preparation was going well, but our collective consumption of red wine and beer defied belief. We did it for England of course, and we made a sterling effort to drink the place dry! It is interesting, because now Jacko no longer drinks at all, not a drop, and I have limited my drinking to the odd glass of red every now and again. Maybe we took the socialising too far, eh? For two days we busied ourselves with recceing the river. On one particular day half our party went out in Jerry's boat equipped with a remarkable underwater camera. They said it was very interesting, but the one thing that stuck in everyone's mind was that any carp they had seen all appeared to be in 25ft of water. We met up every evening and before we decided where we were going to go that night, we talked tactics. It was interesting for me to listen to others' ideas, and very quickly I felt more a part of a team than I had in years. On the day of the draw we all got together one last time, and talked again of swim choice. It was noticeable that no one wanted to fish in any of the swims in the town of Ogdensburg,

**As a team we gathered for the draw.**

something that was to be very interesting over the next few days. Most of us chose the same swims in our top ten, and once the lists had been written up, it was off to the draw.

Each pair had to draw two swim numbers, and then they had a few seconds to decide which one they wanted. It was a tediously long process, but just about as fair as these things can get, and then Jacko and I took to the stage. You can never know about these things, but I have a feeling that selecting swim number 59 had little to do with the outcome. It was a swim in a narrow shipping channel, probably 250 yards wide, for a starter, and was in the middle of five other tightly packed swims. We were sure that we could catch carp from it, but neither of us were under any illusion about winning the damn thing from there!

The following morning we all went about sorting and loading the gear. Jacko and I were the last to leave Lake View, and remarkably it was the first time that we were quiet in each other's company. Like any other intense period, it is very often a time to collect your thoughts, and run things through your mind. In essence it was time to stiffen up the sinews, and summon up the blood. The trouble was that neither Jacko nor I had any idea just how much stiffening and summoning we would have to do over the next five days! The man-made island that ran for about half a mile in front of us formed the very channel in which we would be fishing. Knowing that it would be crowded was bad enough prior to the event, but seeing how near our neighbours were when we arrived was like a kick in the bollocks. There was one other problem that wasn't so obvious at first, and that was how narrow the channel was, and the impact ocean-going ships would have on us whilst they passed through. As the ships passed, the water level would drop by around 7-8ft, and that would expose any fish you had sacked and leave them thrashing around on the rocks. Regularly, one of us would have to hold the sacks aloft and I did it once with fifteen fish. It got so bad in the end that we had to ask for a marshal to be

***It took some time, but eventually we got into some kind of rhythm.***

with us 24/7 to save the carp any injury. Crazy! Secondly, the bait was washed for miles down the river, so could end up anywhere, and the rods would all be wiped out. And so it was, after each ship came by, we would have to rebait and recast the rods, in addition to looking after the sacked fish. It only added to the harshness of the job in hand. Looking back, of course, it just makes me feel more proud of what we did, but at the time I could think of a million things I would rather be doing. That was to come, but first of all we had to get sorted and get fishing.

Having fished in the 2005 competition on the St Lawrence, my main concern was getting the bait accurately around the hookbaits. The more we could focus the carp's attention on them, the better, but it took some time to get that side of things sorted. We did get a little help from the team upstream to our left. They were baiting up directly on top of their hookbaits and that meant most of what they put in ended up in our swim. As soon as we were angling I decided that I was going to sleep; if it got busy later then I hoped that may take the edge off any fatigue that was sure to set in. I was surprised to get so much shut-eye, to be honest, and the only time I was woken on that first night was when Jacko caught one of the three carp he landed. It was a start, however, and in the morning, Jacko rather magnanimously suggested we should take it in turns on his rods if things continued that way. The suggestion still makes me smile to this day.

Slowly, on the second day, we started to get it right. A small gap in the island was the line of sight we had to introduce bait for Jacko's rods, and mine was a large tree a little to the right. It is the same in all types of carp angling, whether you are fishing for naive fish or highly pressured ones; get the bait and baiting right, and all the horseshit that is pumped out by the 'salesmen' becomes completely and utterly irrelevant. Every time we picked up a throwing stick, catapult or spod rod, it didn't take too long for the alarms to start singing their

*Trying to look after sacked fish as a tanker went by.*

tune. It took a little while to get into any sort of rhythm because by mid-afternoon we were either playing a carp, dealing with a carp, or baiting up. And I would love to tell you that we had time to get ourselves into sync, but the carp simply wouldn't let us. One other problem, if you can call it that, was that no carp under 10lb would count in the match, but Jacko and I decided that we would retain everything and let the marshal's scales decide if it counted or not. I lost count of the number of 10lb 2oz commons we weighed in, and we were aware that others were simply throwing back seemingly smaller fish unweighed. That was their loss.

By the morning of day three we were totally in the groove; it was almost robotic, a situation that was aggravated by the fact that we only had about two hours' kip since the first morning – and it wasn't going to get any better. We knew we were amassing a good total, but we had no idea how well things were going because no news was coming our way. Enter Lynn back in the UK. She was able to access a website and update us a lot quicker than the marshals ever could. To our complete surprise we were in fourth spot at the end of day three and, during a rare lull in proceedings, we sat down to discuss tactics. Jacko was sure that we would now win; I had to stop him singing the National Anthem all the time! On the other hand, I was a little more pessimistic. In saying that, I knew all we had to do was carry on as we were, and we would give anyone a run for their money. We also agreed to up the baiting levels – although we would have sold our souls to Satan for some sleep – and the action picked up accordingly. Jacko had even taken to playing his fish from what became known as Jacko's Rock. He would sit there, cross his legs and, as cool as you like, bring the carp to the net. On the other hand I did nothing of the sort, and very soon my feet became a bit of a nightmare. My trainers rubbed and the rocks tore lumps out of them, so much so that at one point I found it hard to even stand up. Be that as it may, we had carp to catch, so that is what we did.

**I even caught a very rare mirror.**

As light filled the sky on day four I well remember playing a fish next to Jacko as he sat on his rock, playing one. We didn't say a word to each other, but there was something that wasn't being said, and as we sorted the fish out on the mat our other rods arched over as two more manic commons raced for freedom. I stood next to him again, and he said, "I'm not sure this is fun anymore." I replied that I totally agreed. Surviving on around five hours sleep in three days was hard, and when you throw in the baiting up, and sorting out the fish, things started to become a little blurred. Lynn's next text, however, gave us just the 'pick-me-up' we needed. We were now in first place, and over 200lb ahead. The only problem was that there were two pegs that didn't seem to want the gap to widen. We laughed and decided that we had to try even harder, and to be honest, I too now believed we could win this thing. I tried to keep things in perspective, but by the morning of day four our lead had increased and it was hard to think of any other outcome. The day was incredible as far as the action went; we even caught a mirror carp each, which is a very rare thing on the St Lawrence. However, the runs dried up mid-afternoon, and we sat and had a bit of a team meeting. The bait was running out and we sent out for a resupply, a message which actually went halfway round the world. We told Lynn, and she told the girls at Angling Publications, who contacted Tim and Briggsy's other halves, Joan and Julie. An hour and a half later those two remarkable ladies turned up with food for us, and a bag or two of corn. There was also the added bonus of Jacko's mate, Benji, arriving from Austria. He would be our runner, and until the end he was a godsend. There were two more things that would have an effect on the immediate future and the first of those was a marvellous piece of angling by Jacko. We hadn't had a bite for a couple of hours, and he felt the carp needed a bit of a jolly up. He went to our big green 4x4 hire car and put the only disc we had with us in the player. It was the *Iron Man* soundtrack, and as Angus strummed the intro to the first track on the disc, *Shoot to Thrill*, both of us got a run. All that was left to do was let AC/DC play us to victory, and it almost happened. The

*Jacko sitting on his rock and playing a carp.*

car battery ran out in the early evening, although we were so knackered we hardly noticed it.

We were making silly mistakes, and we came up with a plan. It was 10.00 p.m. so we would go to our beds and get up at midnight for the final thrust of the last ten hours. I think we both had doubts, but I woke at midnight to hear Jacko sorting his rods. I was

*For me, this picture sums up just how knackering it really was.*

actually unsure what bloody planet I was on, but again the autopilot kicked in and we started catching fish the moment we cast out. It didn't stop until 10 o'clock that morning, when the final hooter sounded. As the light filled the sky our two marshals, Tyler and James, were already congratulating us. They had no official confirmation of course, but they were sure we had won. It was only when James returned from a meeting an hour or so later with instructions to get as many pictures as possible of Jacko and

**We knew we had won!**

me, that we knew for sure we were indeed the World Champions. I cannot even begin to tell you how that felt, and unless you ever experience that situation, you will never really know how close I was to spontaneously combusting right there and then!

For around half an hour Jacko and I didn't speak a word, other than to acknowledge the congratulations of visitors, and there were quite a few of them. We packed the gear into the motor, which thankfully someone had jump-started for us, and eventually set off for the hotel. Again we didn't say a lot, just words of incredulity. However, as we approached our destination Jacko raised the George Cross out of his window. At long last we could think about the celebrations, and Marcy and Jerry laid on the most amazing spread that evening. For now, though, we climbed the stairs to our accommodation and there in the kitchen were the rest of the team. I hadn't given it much thought before, but all of them had experienced similar triumphs, a couple of them on more than one occasion! They were great people to simply sit down and share it all with, but we had to get ourselves to the casino where the final ceremony was to take place – and remember, we hadn't officially been told we were the champions at that point. We drove down in a convoy and arrived at a packed arena that contained anglers from all around the world. It was just great, and one moment that I thought showed how well we had all fished, was when John Lilley and partner Paul Musson went on stage to receive their prize for seventh place. They had done remarkably well from a swim that literally no one fancied. When the time came, we only knew officially that the title was ours when the second-placed team climbed onto the stage, at which point everyone started shaking our hands once again. I stood for just a few seconds and reflected. Match fishing isn't my kind of thing really, but there I was, winning just about the biggest event in the world. I had done so alongside one of the nicest guys I have ever had the pleasure to spend time with, in any walk of life, Lee Jackson. But probably most important of all was the man who made all of that possible. We did the handshake thing, but in the end I gave

*An incredible moment shared and enjoyed with an incredible man!*

Tim Paisley the biggest bear hug I could muster. Here is a man who has changed the very face of carp fishing, and had given me and Lee the chance to feel on top of the world.

Jacko and I shook each other's hands as we started the march to the trophy, and instead of the National Anthem they played AC/DC's *Shoot to Thrill*. It may surprise some of you that I wasn't annoyed about not hearing *God Save the Queen*, but I wasn't. Her Majesty knows what I have done in her name, and for her country, and although she may not be among AC/DC's biggest fans, I couldn't have thought of a better way to share that moment than with the band that in essence, carried us across the line in such fine style. We both held on tight to the trophy and posed for the picture... World Champions, who would have thought it?

# Chapter Eleven
# Wild, Wild West

A stunning Westhampnett sunrise

I was a World Champion, and when the last sentence of this book is written, I will still be a World Champion. The event is planned again, possibly in 2017, and whether I am there with Jacko to defend our title doesn't really matter to me. I had achieved something I never thought I would, I had explored another facet of carp fishing, and I had thoroughly enjoyed it all. I dislike anglers who constantly slag off various branches of our sport, having never experienced that part of the game. It may not be for you, but normally the cowards, for that is what they are, haven't the bottle to stretch themselves outside the comfort zone they have shrouded themselves in. There are a lot of aspects of carp fishing that are incredible things to be a part of, and I have enjoyed all that I have done. Keith Jenkins and I were fourth in the 2003 final at Raduta, Adam Penning and I had a ball on the St Lawrence in 2005, and now Lee and I were celebrating being the 2011 winners. I am not the keenest person when it comes to angling abroad, but I have done it and thoroughly enjoyed every minute of it. I just like to explore the fishing in this country, and as we boarded the flight home I was thinking about what I would be doing during the winter of 2011/12.

Westhampnett was the obvious choice, but a couple of faceless dullards had tried to make life a little difficult for me there. The rest of the syndicate were fantastic, but I neither want, nor need, that kind of jealous crap in my life. I wasn't sure if I was going back at that point, but as a carp-angling diarist I needed to do something. I have a chance to fish a water not far from my home every now and again, and although I am not at liberty to mention it, not if I want to go back anyway, I was desperate to return. It is somewhere that I fish simply to get my mind back into gear. I will never have a ticket, but I can visit as a guest every now and again, and that was where I would go. A week after getting home from America I was packing my car early one Monday morning, and, in a rather excited 'hair on fire' kind of way, I blasted down the last bit of dual carriageway. I locked the gate behind me, and set off for a walk round. It was completely deserted, and as it's a fairly large water the fish can be very hard to locate, so it wasn't until the third lap that something caught my eye. An area of water at around 80 yards in a fairly shallow part of the lake looked a little coloured, but it wasn't until the wind died for a moment that I could see why. The tail of a carp broke the surface, and a line of bubbles almost painted the water white. For fish that rarely give the game away, this was a remarkable display, and I just watched. About ten minutes later I broke out of my trance and ran to the car; I couldn't help feeling I should do a bit of fishing! The water level was very low, and to that end it would make positioning the hookbaits with any kind of subtlety very difficult. It must be something to do with the carp feeling a little vulnerable in shallow water, because it seems that the deeper the water gets we can get away with so much more. Whatever the reason, that is where the carp wanted to be, so that was where I was going to fish, I would just have to pick up the pieces if it all went horribly wrong. An hour later the fish had gone, so I leaded around, discovering a long silty strip in-between two large weedbeds. 30 minutes later three stiff-link pop-ups rested in the silt about 5 yards apart, and 30 minutes after that I had introduced around three kilos of 10 and 15mm New Grange boilies.

With a brew in my hand I sat by the rods thinking that would teach them. I really thought it was the one, but 24 hours later the brew I was holding didn't taste quite so good. Following a quick visit to the shops, I once again walked around the lake, but saw absolutely nothing. It was just a simple case of repositioning the rods in the silt, but I probably did it more in hope than expectation. I kept my eyes on the water, in the main to see if they turned up anywhere else, but after a couple of hours a telltale tail pattern appeared on the spot. As the minutes passed, the water became swathed in great sheets of bubbles, and after swearing and cursing at the rods for the tenth time, I nearly jumped out of my skin when the water erupted and the buzzer sang its tune. Once clear of the weed the fish was

*At 35lb she made the session complete.*

reasonably easy to lead to the net, and at 27lb I couldn't have been happier. I repositioned the rods, and rebaited the area, but it wasn't until the same time the next day that one of them bounced around in the rests, and the line hissed from the reel. This fish followed the same route to the net as the last one, only this one was a little bigger at 34lb 2oz. I chuckled to myself as I did a few self-take shots, but no sooner had I slipped her off the mat than one of the other rods called for my attention. From the off, this felt like a different animal as it exploded through the far weedbed: it took an age to get it into my net, and that did nothing to change its angry attitude. I could see why my arms ached so much; she was very long, with huge fins. At exactly 35lb she made the session complete, and I marvelled at her dark, chestnut flanks. By the time my gear was in the car I had made up my mind what to do with myself, but of course before I could get on with my own fishing I had to take care of a few magazine commitments. I did a couple of trips to Patching Pond once again to sort all that out, and eventually I loaded my car and pointed her south. I was Westhampnett bound.

The lake was practically empty when I gazed across the water, but I did spot a bivvy and hoped it was there that I may just catch up on what had been happening at Westy. I arrived in Alex's plot and was offered a tea, along with a view of some carp on his camera. He had been having a bit of a result of late and had landed a couple of the lake's larger residents. It was great chatting to him, and he made me feel a lot more comfortable about coming back. What I needed to do was go fishing, however, so I bade him farewell and set off to fish a familiar point swim that I had had success from earlier in the year. I even fished three rods on the same feature at around 130 yards, and baited them with a few kilos of my 10 and 15mm boilie concoction. It all looked the nuts, to me at least, and I settled down with a cheesy grin on my face. As always, the carp had other ideas about how

*The Extreme Carping filming went very well indeed.*

good my efforts were, and I was just pondering what I had done wrong around 9.00 the next morning, when I received the only dropback I could remember in the last twenty years. The fish didn't put up a fight at all, and all too soon I had a dumpy fish resting in the bottom of the net. At 24lb 2oz the rotund Simmo made me smile, just as he should do. I stayed another night and landed two more, slightly smaller mirrors. At least the lake was being good to me again, but I still wasn't sure where I wanted to be that winter. The weather was relatively mild, and I thought I may as well carry on as usual until the weather forced me to change direction. That said, there was always the commercial side of what I do that invariably throws many of the plans I have into a cocked hat. For the next month I couldn't get my head into my own fishing, but there was still some fun to be had, though.

For some time Rob Hughes, who had just signed up for Fox, had been doing a deal with Sky to make six carp-fishing programmes. By hook or by crook, probably crook knowing Rob, he had come up with the title *Extreme Carping*, although I could never understand what was extreme about any of it. I'm not sure why, but my programme was going to be the last one filmed, which meant that I would have to tailor my fishing for the cold winter weather. Westhampnett was my first choice, of course, especially because of the size of the fish I would be angling for, and the successes I had enjoyed so far. Unfortunately, as I suspected it would, the weather was about to scupper my plans. On the days I had earmarked for the filming, the wind howled and the rain... well, rained. We wouldn't be able to do the job in those conditions, so the filming was binned. The problem now was that the dates would be further into winter, and the prospect of filming at that time of year takes the challenge-o-meter up a few notches, I can tell you! I had a trump card of course, and that was Patching Pond in West Sussex. We have talked about this lake before, and whilst not housing the

*I was back at Patching to film for Fishing.TV the following week.*

*This 26lb 2oz mirror was a great welcome back to Manor.*

monsters that sadly seem the only thing some anglers find exciting in this day and age, it had some stunning fish, steeped in history. I spoke to Rob and plans were made, and all that was left was for the weather to behave itself. And so it was, one mild day in November, I set out for Patching. I fished the night and retained two of the five carp I landed, one of which was held up in the opening sequence. It was a great way to start the filming and things simply got better and better as the following 24 hours unfolded. I landed a stack of stunning fish to just over 20lb, and even 'lent' Rob one of my spots so he wouldn't go home fishless! At which point I ran for home, although the historic lake still had one more task to fulfil.

The following week I was back at Patching Pond with my old mucker, John Dunford, from *Fishing.TV* to do another instalment of *Chilly on Carp 2*. They had sold Series One to some channel on the Continent, and they wanted Series Two as soon as possible. It had, in fact, to be edited by Christmas so the pressure was on. To make the programme noticeably different to the one I did with Rob, I decided that I would incorporate a more mobile approach and, as it happens, things once again worked out very well indeed. Again, I wanted a fish to open the filming with, but as normal the carp kept me on my toes. It wasn't until early the next day that I got two bites almost simultaneously, and very quickly I had two scaly mirrors to choose from. The fishing and the filming went off remarkably well. The last fish brightened up a very dull and overcast day, in that it was a koi; not what I normally want to catch, but it made me smile. I was also proud, as I am with all the filming I had ever done, that no swims were roped off or baited up for me; the session had represented exactly what the guy on the street has to deal with when he goes fishing. The last thing to do was the Sandown show, which I always enjoy, and that was just about to distract me from finding a home for the winter once again. It looked as if I was off to Linear Fisheries Manor Farm Lake, an old stomping ground from the mid-90s.

*A trip to Linear's B1 and several fish to 26lb as Christmas approached.*

I had been discussing the lake with Ian Russell and we decided that I would travel up for a social, which is all well and good, but socialising very often gets in the way of things that I have to do on the bank. Having around 10-12 nights a month may sound like plenty of time, but with other commitments it can sometimes be tough to get enough material to write about in a diary, and a monthly technical piece. I have no wish to try to make you feel even remotely sorry for me, but you can if you wish! In saying that, I knew it would be fun fishing with Ian, and just maybe I could bag a carp. During the journey all I could think about was the time I had spent fishing Manor in the late-'90s. Reg Bampton, Dave Lane, Keith Jenkins and I had fished two winters there, and rather bizarrely it was only Reg and I who caught carp. I have no idea why; that's just the way it worked out. I was also thinking about the changes that had been made to the water. I had driven past a few times, but had no idea as to the extent of the work, that was until I gazed across the lake for the first time in 13 years. Wow, it was bigger and no longer looked like a working gravel pit, and rather interestingly, had about ten times more carp in than it did back in the day. Ian had told me it had around seven to eight 40s in it at the time, and in reality it would make for a great winter campaign. It's nice to spend time catching up and putting the world to rights, but I had a mind on the fishing too, and unfortunately lost the first fish I hooked in some weed. Don't get mad, get even... so I did. I landed an upper-double the next evening, and the following morning landed a cracking 26lb 2oz mirror. It was a great welcome back, but on the drive home – and I have no idea where in my brain this came from – I decided I wanted to catch a 30-pounder from Hunts Corner, again on the Linear complex.

The following Monday I left with a bucket of maggots and boilies, arriving at Hunts in the most horrible winter weather. Ice covered every puddle, the sky was clear, and there wasn't a breath of wind. For me it doesn't get any worse than that, and 24 hours later I was having a brew with Roy Parsons in my swim, and probably moaning a lot. "Go over to Brasenose," he suggested, and as soon as he had left, I packed up and headed over for a look-see. It isn't the kind of lake that I would personally want to fish regularly, but when you want a bite on a horrible winter's morning there can be few places that are better at producing one. There were a couple of lads in the first two swims, and I believe they had caught something like 70 (yes, 70) carp in the two days they had been there. I wouldn't want to catch 70 carp, but seven would do nicely, and after visiting Lidl up the road, I arrived back armed with around 8 kilos of frozen corn. When in Rome and all that. I fished two hookbaits at around 60 yards, filled it in with little golden nuggets, caught the prerequisite seven carp, and then went home to prepare for Christmas. It was as simple as that really, and I have to say, not very exciting at all.

I visited Patching the next week to get some pictures done for a magazine piece, and on the drive home I decided to take a look at Westhampnett. I hadn't been there for around three months, but the more I stood looking, the more I felt I should be fishing there. It hadn't featured in my thoughts, I believe, because so little was known, or was talked about, its winter form. I wanted to get the year off to a good start, and thinking about the fish I had already caught from there made it an easy choice. There was also the fact that there wasn't a bivvy in sight, so I decided then and there, this is where I would be angling for the foreseeable future. As happy as I was about that, there was still a lot to think about. While the weather was unpredictable, it hadn't been too cold, and I still felt there was a chance of a monster or two. The problem could be the lack of angling pressure, I mused, and the fish may simply have switched off. To that end, I thought it may take a session or two to find the fish and get them in the mood for a bit of a munch.

All those thoughts were going through my mind as I prepared my gear the following Sunday. In the end, though, as I always do, I filled two air-dry bags with 10 and 14mm New Grange boilies, and ensured the bucket had a top-up of the corresponding Response Pellets. I have never believed that carp don't eat in winter, and to that end they would be seeing plenty of bait on this trip, and I would adjust things as I went along. The joy of the situation was that I could have had no idea how well the next few weeks would turn out, and it all started with a Lottery ticket. I have never been a betting man; I just don't do it. However, when the Lottery started Lynn and I did it for one year. We did the same five lines and never won a penny. We gave up, of course, flogging dead horses

*A 39lb chunk and I couldn't have been more pleased.*

ain't my style, but for some reason I bought a tenner's worth of lucky dips the Friday before the Westy return. I really couldn't believe it when we won our money back. It doesn't sound a lot, and it isn't, but it kind of set the scene for the immediate future.

It was freezing as I arrived at the lake and I sat in my car to the right of the ski club, looking down the lake. The fish had always given the game away on previous visits, and I hoped that this time would be no different. Ironically, I hadn't been there more than five minutes before I had seen three carp, and thankfully they were in front of a swim that I was very familiar with. Even as I raced down the A27 bank, I spotted two more fish, and by the time I got to the swim I thought I was just about to burst into flames with excitement. It was certainly good to be back. Westy seemed to have a number of silty trenches running down the middle of the lake, and it was into one of those that I was going to put all three hookbaits at around 120 yards. It took about an hour before I was able to settle down with a brew, after delivering 4 kilos of my boilie and pellet mix. I was confident, I always am, but I wasn't sure if I had done the right thing on this occasion. More often than not I go against the popular concepts in carp fishing, and more often than not they work... go figure, eh!

A few hours later I was in my sleeping bag listening to the football on the radio, when I received a single bleep. The bobbin had risen about an inch or so, and five seconds later it lifted a whole lot more and the buzzer screamed. My first carp of the campaign was a 22lb mirror, and whilst he may not have been the biggest carp I've ever caught, he was the first of the new mission, and on the tactics that everyone keeps telling me will never work at this time of year! It was just before first light when my second customer came to call, and what a strange fish it turned out to be. It looked odd in the water, but it looked positively crazy when on the mat. His massive fins, however, told me why my arms ached so. At 28lb 14oz it proved, to me at least, that they were up for a bit of bait and, of course, I was going to give it to 'em! I stayed where I was, although I saw nothing else that day, and topped up the area with a bit more bait. I couldn't sleep that night for some reason, and as I was warming my hands on yet another brew at 5.30 a.m., I heard a big fish boom out in the darkness. The problem was that it was nowhere near me. Three more crashes had me starting to pack things away, and as soon as I could see them I would move. Around 8.00 a.m. they started showing again in front of a swim on the far side of the 40-acre lake. It wasn't an area I was familiar with, so I would need to take my time. Three-quarters of an hour later I was in the swim with the marker rod in hand. I had seen nothing for a while, so got to work. Yet again it was one of the silty gulleys at around 120 yards that got my attention, and my intention was to fish it in exactly the same way as I had done in the previous swim. I got everything sorted, and the waiting began, until I got some unusual indicator activity on all three rods! I have no idea how the fish did it, but it had wrapped himself, all 8lb of it, around all three lines. Still, from little acorns and all that.

I repositioned the rods and topped the area up with a tad more bait. I often wonder how much that kind of disturbance affects the fishing, and I am pleased to tell you it's not very much. 45 minutes later one of the rods was roaring for my attention, and as soon as I had it in my hand I knew it was a big fish. It did nothing to change my mind for 10 minutes, and as it rolled into the outstretched net I could see it was a bit of a chunk, a 39lb chunk to be exact, and I couldn't have been more pleased. As I sorted that fish out one of the other rods arched over and I was playing another fish. In total contrast this one practically found his own way into the net, but at 27lb 4oz I will take them any way they come. It was a little drizzly at the time, and eventually I had to stop a guy on his way to the local recycling depot to take the pictures for me. God knows what he thought of me, but I nearly swallowed my tongue laughing when I lifted the 39 out of the water. He thought the lake was connected to the nearby sea, because nothing could grow that big in a lake, could it? He did a great job, thankfully, and once again the rods were sorted, and rebaited. The rest of the session brought four more 20s to 26lb, all depositing large amounts of bait on the unhooking mat, before it was time to head for home. And some keep saying that carp don't eat bait in winter, a theory that always puzzles me greatly. I drove home thinking that things couldn't get any better but, as always, life and the carp had other ideas. I had an email from my friend Paul Bennett when I got home. He was the second assistant director of *Midsomer Murders*, which I have already mentioned in this tome. Lynn and I had done several bits as extras in the programme, but this time I was to make my acting debut in an episode called A Rare Bird. All right, it was only three words, but hey, you gotta start somewhere right? I also managed to get my Dodge Truck involved in the filming, which was set for the following Wednesday. Before that, though, I had to get to Westy and keep the ball rolling.

I had walked the lake for hours and had seen nothing, eventually going with the old classic, any swim is as good as the next when you are guessing! It made sense to go in the same swim as the week before; it had been good to me then, and I could only hope that lightning would strike twice. I set up exactly the same, too, but this time I had a bitter easterly wind cutting through me, and it was all I could do to stay warm. It was horrible, and it stayed that way for 36 hours. However, by the end of day two the wind had swung round to a positively balmy south-westerly, and as the temperature rose, so did my confidence. It was day three when the action started, and within an hour of each other I landed two cricket-bat commons. Small fish they may have been, but it was action, and that's what mattered. Again I found it hard to sleep, but eventually drifted off only to be torn from my slumber by a 28lb mirror just before dawn. I recast the rod, and I was loving it. To be honest I could have packed up there and then a very happy man, but the best was yet to come. A couple

***Vern's Fish at 41lb 2oz.***

of bleeps at around 7.30 a.m. had me thinking 'liner', but that was dismissed when the spool became a blur. Even my intervention didn't slow it down, and once again my knees started to shake as I battled with an obviously big carp. Not for one second did that fish take its fin off the pedal; every inch of line was fought for, but eventually it rolled and it looked huge. It dived in the deep margins and for one brief heart-stopping moment became snagged on something. A bit of pressure and a lot of praying soon had it on the move, and I practically heaved it into the landing net. It was Vern's Fish, which was right at the top of my list of must-haves from this remarkable lake. She pulled the scales round to 41lb 2oz, and I took a few minutes to gaze on her broad shoulders as she rested in the net. I needed pictures, of course, and Paul Bennett only lived up the road and was inbound in minutes. One other bonus was that Dan Wildbore, who was working for DHP at the time, was on a lake just up the road. Between them I was left with some fantastic shots for the archives, and we all agreed she looked truly magnificent as she rather elegantly swam quietly home.

I was determined to keep going at Westy, the intention being to fish all the way through until I had caught the fish I wanted to catch, and the week after Vern's fish I was once again prowling the banks. The problem once again was the weather. It was high pressure and clear skies, conditions that never really float my boat, if I'm honest. It is very often the case that your fishing becomes all about guessing, and I hate that. I want to react to what the carp are doing, not cast out and hope for the best. Hope doesn't constitute a plan in my world. I set up, rather predictably, in the swim I fished the previous week and had a few visitors throughout the day. No fish had been caught since I was last there, which sort of confirmed my fears that things were slowing up. I didn't see a thing till later the next day when a small common leapt about 2ft out of the water. To me that's a travelling fish, and

***Tight Lines at Sky with producer Mick Brais and Keith Arthur.***

probably doing so close to the surface. To that end, and probably more to do with keeping my sanity, I put a couple of Zigs out. One of these produced a fish the next day, followed shortly after by one on the bottom-bait rod. The jury is still out on whether I got it right or not, but at least I had tried to be a little more inventive. The next couple of weeks were dire. I caught the odd smaller fish, but not once did I base my fishing on seeing fish. I was getting bored with it, to be honest, and it was only the intervention of others that stopped me going round the bend. A trip to the *Tight Lines* studios at Sky helped, as did a trip to the Five Lakes Carpin' On show, but it wasn't until I was travelling back from Essex that my hopes began to rise. The weather was going to be a little more overcast, and with a touch of rain in the air, instead of frost, I got my gear sorted as soon as I was home.

I arrived at Westy just as the light was starting to appear, and straight away I spotted a couple of fish. Game on! As boring as it sounds, they were once again in the swim that I seemed to have grown roots in over the past few weeks. But if that is where they wanted to be, who was I to argue? Once three hookbaits were cast out the required 120 yards, I got to work with the spod rod, which I probably overdid. I looked at the bucket and realised I had hoofed out over half of its contents, and could only hope the buggers were hungry! And I am delighted to say that they were. One of the local lads walked into my swim as I was playing a carp which didn't feel that big, but I really didn't care; it was a mirror carp of 20lb 5oz and that was what mattered. The lake had been frozen for a few days and this was the first one to come out after the water decided to become wobbly once again. I wanted another, and after repositioning the rod, that's what I got. This time it was an angry mid-double common that was the culprit. Things were coming together nicely. I had to wait until 5.30 the next morning for the next bite, and as I tried to get control I was surprised to realise I had none whatsoever.

*This was the real deal at 36lb 7oz.*

I could make no impression on the fish. Indeed it was fully five minutes before I could get my line marker back on the reel. It didn't give an inch for ages, and I have no idea how long it was until I saw a big fish roll some 20 yards out in the murky light of dawn. It wasn't over then, either, because it hugged the bottom of the marginal shelf for another 10 minutes. I held my breath as it hit the surface for the second time and, fortunately, I was able to scoop up my prize at the first time of asking. It looked huge, as did its tail; no wonder I was knackered. I thought I had already caught the carp known as Big Tail, but evidently that was a different fish. This was the real deal at 36lb 7oz, and another of the lake's originals was crossed off my list.

During the session before this one, a guy had told me that he needed to sell his van, and I don't think for a second he thought he was talking to the person who would ultimately buy it, but he was. The problem with me is that I get so attached to the vehicles I have owned. They end up with names and are, at times, treated better than any human being. I owned a 'T' registration Mondeo Estate; she was blue and went by the name of Rosie. I had owned her for nine years and not a single thing ever went wrong with her – and I mean, not one. I had become attached to her more than any other vehicle, and we blissfully chased carp around from one year to the next. Her crowning glory was an appearance on the BBC's *Countryfile*, when I had to do some fishing for them. She was bought at half the book price all those years before, and I never had to spend a penny on her. I rarely even cleaned the old girl from one year to the next, but on and on she went. Let's be honest here, the best bit of fishing gear you will ever own is a reliable car. However, at 150,000 miles I felt it was time to move on, and I set out to find a replacement. Little did I know that the answer to my problem was at the very lake I was fishing at the time. The day before I landed the 36-pounder I had gone to the bank and drawn out the money, and, best of all, the guy selling

**The last time I ever saw Rosie, the greatest carp wagon ever!**

the van had a family member who could take Rosie on. It was sad saying goodbye, and I can only hope she may still be rollin' along somewhere down on the south coast. Of course there are teething problems with any new motor, and naming this one was the first hurdle to cross. She was the first diesel car I had ever owned, and to remind me to fill her with the right fuel she became known as Daisy. She even has a sports button; how cool is that?

And then the weather got really crappy. I was desperate to continue at Westy, and obviously loaded the van early the next Monday morning. After scraping the ice from the windscreen, I headed off, but it looked and felt horrible when I arrived. The wind was hacking in from the east and chilled me to the bone, and as the warmth left my body, so did my confidence. With nothing to go on, I once again made my best guess and ended up in the same swim as before. I put the rods out, as usual, and baited a bit more lightly this

***The weather got colder and colder and the fishing became impossible.***

time around. God it was cold! Things had gone well up to that point, but it didn't last for long. A fish towing line wiped all the rods out, and once I had repositioned them all, it did the same thing about five minutes later. I retrieved the rig too, which simply defied belief. A lead clip had been superglued to ensure the lead never released, and it was attached to an 8ft length of leadcore! I knew who it belonged to, as well, but I will draw a veil over that part of the story for now, at least. I sat on my bedchair, as one does, with my head in my hands. I thought a little sleep might ease my furrowed brow, and I could have only just nodded off when I received what sounded like a nose-bleeding run. However, a large white and incredibly stupid swan soon had me looking for a suitable branch from which to hang myself. It didn't get any better either; the tufties dived all night long, and the coots picked up the slack once daylight had arrived. And of course the mallards didn't want to be excluded from the 'Let's Play Games with Chilly' party. I had kindly given them the odd boilie the day before, but when the supply dried up they took to flying through my lines to get my attention. I can only think they sat by my bivvy quacking like mad because they had discovered the ultimate way to pass some time. I couldn't wait to go home, and was rather pleased not to have to spend the journey with a smelly wet landing net in my plush new van... NOT!! I needed a change of scenery, and a day or so later I decided I had made the right decision. What followed was about as mad as it gets. I had to produce the pictures for 12 different articles over a three-day period, and I cannot tell you how impossible I thought that was. However, someone told me of a lake in Essex that might just fit the bill. I have to be honest and say I wasn't looking forward to it at all, but I could never have been more wrong.

The following Tuesday I arrived at Bird's Green Fishery, a complex that consisted of three lakes, all about 3 acres. And a bit more insider information – Steve Spurgeon I love you – recommended small baits. To that end I had around 6 kilos of 10mm'ers and pellets. If they wanted little baits they could have them. At certain points over the next three days I had visits from Lewis Porter, Harry Charrington and Pete McKenna from DHP. On the final day I even had the company of *Total Carp* editor Marc Coulson to do the final pieces. It was an incredible session, in which I caught a cartload of carp, but I was well and truly out on my feet by the time I loaded my motor for the journey home. Once there all I could think of doing was putting my feet up for a few days, so that is exactly what I did... until of course it was time to do it all over again – and I couldn't wait! As much as I had spent the previous few weeks in a cosmic hyper loop of frustration, I had enjoyed the madness, but now was the time I needed to change from a lunatic to someone who went, thought and caught himself some carp. I had landed one of my targets from Westhampnett in the shape of Vern's Fish, but the ultimate goal was The Scar, and I was now going to stay until she was mine.

What follows started a few weeks before, when I decided that I needed to be more proactive if I was to get this campaign over and done with in the spring. I needed an area to introduce bait regularly, and eventually, after watching what others were doing, I found the very place. The bay to the left of the ski club was never fished, not whilst I was on the water anyway, and I am not sure that many (if any in fact) knew they could actually fish from the gravel bank. Although I had never set up there, I had managed to stalk the odd fish from the margins, and as the weather was getting just a tad warmer, I reckoned it was time to take advantage of a bit of hard work.

I had been baiting an area before dawn every time I arrived at the lake, and as often as I could, away from prying eyes. But the water levels were dropping and the spot was getting nearer and nearer to the bank. I just hoped it wouldn't bother the carp too much, and fortunately it didn't. As the weather improved, so more anglers started to appear from their winter hibernation, and I started to reel in at night to go round and bait up. It may seem a bit extreme, but I was happy that I wasn't just sitting around hoping for some action. Anyway, yet again I arrived at the start of the week, and after baiting the spot, I set off on my travels. There were a couple of anglers on the lake, and it was interesting to hear only one carp had been landed at the weekend, although it had been very busy. I looked all day until my eyes bled, but it seemed as if the lake refused to wake up. I even thought about going home, and I couldn't even remember a time when I felt like that. The thing was, if I didn't have a bait in the water then I was never going to catch one, so I decided to fish the swim that I had been doing relatively well in. I saw nothing to make me do so, and foolishly thought that if I could set up with the minimum of disturbance then the fish would surely follow. I did land an 8-pounder a little later in the day, which hardly set my world on fire, and it was the third time I had seen that fish in my net. Interestingly, the two swims either side

*Set up in the corner swim I had been baiting.*

of the area I had been baiting started to produce the odd fish. I thought I would go round and check out what was going on, but unfortunately a day angler turned up and went into the swim that covered my prebaiting. I was a bit gutted. Of course he was doing nothing wrong, but I still couldn't look over there in case he capitalised on my cunning plan. It turned out that he was waiting for the swim some 75 yards to his left to become free, and by 10.00 a.m. he made his move. He launched his three single hookbaits out at range and set up camp. By now I was in the opposite corner of the lake being told that the guy there had landed a couple of low-20 mirrors. Then, in the blink of an eye, the guy who had moved the 75 yards had landed mirrors of 38 and 21, and as I walked round to do some pictures for him I spotted several fish in and around my little baited spot. I was going to move there and then, but decided that I wanted my investment to remain a secret for a little longer. Maybe next week? I landed a couple of cricket-bat commons that night, and heard that a 30lb mirror had been caught from elsewhere on the lake. Things had certainly livened up some, and I couldn't help thinking I would teach 'em good when I got back. However, it never actually looked like that would be the case when I returned to the lake the following week.

The weatherman eventually, after weeks of easterly wind purgatory, decided that it was about time we had some westerly winds and rain... lots of rain. It looked so perfect on a computer screen, but in reality it was just about to herald the most uncomfortable 48-hour session I had done in a long time. I arrived just before fist light and, with my waterproofs and wellies on, I set off to find some carp. The one thing that surprised me was that the wind was freezing, and I wasn't sure if the fish would move on it. I looked everywhere, except for the corner where the wind was blowing, which just happened to be the corner I'd been baiting. It was five hours before I decided to look at this area. I was soaked and my cold hands felt like soggy bread. I was miserable, but my mood lightened when a small ghostie launched itself out of the water twice, only yards from my bait. I perked up a little at that point, and a few minutes later I nearly burst into flames when a huge orange mirror rose out of the water and silently slipped back in right over the spot... game on! Within minutes I was in the swim setting up my EVO shelter (rain is the only thing that stops me getting the rods out first), and then dragged the rest of the gear into it. The most important things were the rods, of course, and knowing just how I was going to fish meant that I was in the frame within minutes. Two rods were fished on 'the' spot with a spread of boilies over the top, whilst the third was fished as a single a little further out at around 30 yards. I slackened off the lines and sat back, bursting at the seams with confidence. I let the lines sink for a few minutes before I got up and tried to put the bobbins on, and the line in the clips. I never got that far, because as I grabbed the first bobbin and put it on the line, it was literally ripped from my fingers; I had a bite! From the very beginning the fish showed me no mercy, and with a few obstacles, such as buoys, boats and ski ramps to deal with, the fight was a rather nerve-wracking affair. In the end I slipped the net under an incredibly long mirror, and as he came to rest, a couple of lads arrived to help. It was the first fish one of them had seen from the water, and what an arresting sight he made, all 34lb 10oz of him. I was over the moon and that night I added another of around 20lb. The swim on the other side of the ski club was fished that night, and I couldn't help wondering how many monsters the angler had landed, because I had heard a lot of big fish over that way. From memory he landed a couple of low-20s, but I stayed where I was for now, although the night only produced one 21lb mirror for me. I was just packing things away at first light ready for a move, when I hooked and landed the little ghostie I had seen two days before. Whatever I landed, I still think I would have moved, and an hour later I was set up on the other side of the club building. Interestingly, I had noticed where the guy had been fishing the night before, and couldn't help thinking if he had gone a further 20-30 yards he would have been in the area those big fish had boshed out in. To that end, that is where I concentrated my efforts. Two hookbaits ended up some 140 yards from my swim, and I baited with a couple of kilos of 10 and 15mm boilies. The trap was set; all that was left to do was wait.

Around mid-afternoon I noticed that my phone was running out of gas so, because my van was just behind me, I put it on charge. An hour later I went to get it, but I hadn't gone more than a few paces when the remote let out a single bleep. As I turned, the buzzer went into meltdown and I started a spectacular and very heavy battle. It got a bit frantic when it picked up my other line, and for an age all it would do was hug the base of the marginal shelf at around 10ft deep. A huge orange-bellied mirror eventually rolled on the surface, and

*At 40lb 5oz I could never have been disappointed.*

I rather urgently scooped the net under her. I was thinking mid-40 when I gazed down on her broad shoulders, and didn't think I had it too wrong when she rolled onto her side. The scales told a different story, although at 40lb 5oz I could never have been disappointed, and I was the happiest man on the planet as I told Lynn the good news. A good friend of mine, Hampshire Graham, came over from another lake to do the honours, and as happy as I was with the capture, having Graham around just made it that bit more special.

I was keen to get back to Westy. I was getting into my rhythm, and when I am on a bit of a mission that rhythm becomes just about the most important thing. The bait, and the way in which I was using it, was working brilliantly, so well in fact, that I am sure the carp were starting to talk like they came from Essex, and were swimming around wearing Mainline baseball caps and hoodies. All I had to worry about now was putting everything in the right place. The next session coincided with the water levels being at their lowest, which meant that I could now reach areas that had been out of my casting range. It's quite amazing what can happen when you fish an area that rarely, if ever, gets angled on. However, unbeknown to me, that was still a week away and this session turned into a bit of a damp squib. I had seen nothing and banked my fishing on casting into the unknown areas from a swim I knew fairly well. The conditions seemed great, but as good as they were, little happened until the second evening. I was knocking out the Zs fairly early when all of a sudden I was stumbling down to the rods in a bit of a daze. The fish did very little to begin with, and in no time at all I had it rolling on the surface about 20 yards out. At which point it began to wake up, plodding around the deep margins for ages. It felt and acted like a big fish, and as it rolled into the net I saw nothing to change my mind. It was huge, and I left her in the net whilst I sorted out the mat and a headtorch. I couldn't think which fish it was, and even in the red filter of the light I didn't

*I was staring down on an odd-shaped carp of 31lb 6oz.*

know. It wasn't until I came to unhook her that I realised I had landed the same 40 as the previous week, The Bad Mouthed Orange. Bollocks! As big as she was there was little point in taking pictures, because I had already caught her. As I slipped her back I couldn't help thinking just how much the fish were on the bait, and that all that was left was a date with The Scar.

The session fizzled out after that, but on the journey home I made a few decisions. I would stay on Westy until the end of June, or until the fish spawned, and, just as importantly, I would carry on as before; no need to change a thing. Come the following Monday I was sipping a coffee looking down the lake on the right-hand side of the ski club, and the carp painted the most marvellous picture. Shortly after first light I was marching down the road bank with a fully-laden barrow. I was heading for my favourite swim, The Road Point, but this time I was going to find a spot that probably hadn't ever been fished. The water level made the lake look so incredibly small, and it did mean that my marker came to rest above an interesting silty gulley a very long way out. Again, all I was going to do was present my three New Grange pop-ups some 5 or 6 yards apart along the feature, and then let 'em have some bait, or, rather, lots of bait! Spodding complete, I leant the rod against the nearest tree and smiled contentedly. An hour after the bait introduction I saw the first carp show over it, and by mid-afternoon I had seen many more. All I wanted now was a bite, and that wasn't long coming, either. Whilst not the most spectacular scrap I have ever had, the carp did feel fairly big, and soon enough I was staring down on a strange-shaped carp of 31lb 6oz. The session was off to a fine start. The rod was repositioned and once again I baited up the area. A 25lb common was my next visitor, an hour after the first, and when I thought about catching those two fish so quickly over so much bait, I reckoned this might be one of those very productive sessions.

Midnight saw me get a double take, and that is always a problem. I played one fish

*The fish was called Red Spot and weighed 35lb 14oz.*

for a minute or so and then took up the battle with the other for the same amount of time. It worked too, and very soon I had returned a brace of 24lb mirrors. The rods were put back into the action, and again I baited up the spot with a dozen more spods. After making a brew, I wondered if I could possibly love carp fishing more. Two more mid-20 mirrors completed the night, and as a warm and gloriously sunny day unfolded I decided to go and have a walk. I was on a high, but as I got back towards my van at the back of the ski club, I saw two scruffy little urchins snooping around my Daisy. I have no doubt that drugs were involved, and the chemicals that were obviously coursing through their bodies may have eased the pain a little. Let me explain. As happy as I was, I wasn't about to let this act of vandalism (potential vandalism actually, but you never know) go unpunished. I crept up and hollered at the nearest one, and he told me to fuck off. Nice! His mate was just about to join in when I kicked his buddy in the nether regions. He slumped to the floor, and his mate ran over to, what I assumed, would be help. He had no interest in his mate's injuries, and rifled his pockets, I presume, for their ill-gotten gains. I would have let him run if he hadn't started getting gobby, so he got a bit of a kicking, too. At which point a pair of seventy-something ladies came over with their dogs, and started giving me a roasting for sorting out the thieving little pricks. Go figure, eh? I drove to the shops and parked poor Daisy at the other end of the lake behind a locked gate when I got back.

You just know when things are going well, when all three rods land first time of asking, and there are no hiccups with the spod. I was having a brew, and was as sure as I will ever be that I was about to get a bite. It was 4.00 p.m, and with no preamble, one of the rods ripped off. For some reason I had been staring at the orange pole elastic line markers on my line as I got the take, and could never have realised that I wouldn't see it again for about ten minutes.

The battle raged, and for a long time I never felt like I was dictating proceedings. Even when it got close to shore, I couldn't help thinking it was only there because it wanted to be that close to the bank. However, I must have had some influence because, in spite of my shaking knees, I led her into the net. The fish was called Red Spot, and at 35lb 14oz she really was the icing on the cake. My buddy Hampshire Graham was once again over the road, and arrived within minutes. Boy does he take a good picture! A little later I landed a 28lb mirror, and whilst I tried to sleep the carp wouldn't let me, as several more fish found their way onto my mat. It had been an incredible session, and even the goddamn awful weather that morning couldn't wipe the smile from my face as I packed up. The plan, and the whole campaign, were coming together very nicely indeed. In fact I was loving it there so much that I was thinking that even if I didn't get the one I wanted, I may just come back the following year. I could never have guessed, of course, that my time on Westhampnett was rapidly drawing to a close.

The next couple of weeks were very special for me on two fronts. I will tell you about the first, and that should lead nicely into the second. I was so proud of the way the nation celebrated Her Majesty's 60 years on the throne. As much as this Sceptred Isle is losing a lot of its identity at every turn, she has once again united a country that seems hell-bent on flushing itself down the toilet. I fully appreciate that some of you don't understand why many of us get so excited about this, but I can tell you that during my service to this country, the monarchy, and what it stands for, was never far from my mind. We simply do this sort of thing so much better than anyone else in the world, and for me there is nothing like a little (or in this case, a lot) of pomp and circumstance! There was one very interesting statistic that came out of it all, and that was that in all probability all of you reading this will never again have the chance to celebrate a king or queen who has reigned for 60 years. It was a once-in-a-lifetime experience and, as such, should have been celebrated in just the way it was. God save the Queen! I have met the Queen twice, and twice I was in awe of her; a very special lady who holds a beacon of light for a very special nation.

It all set the scene, and as my rhythm was in full swing, I could see no reason to take my foot off the gas pedal as far as my fishing was concerned. That was the mindset I had as once again I left for Westy. Obviously, I was buoyed by the result the previous week, and I lay staring at my alarm clock for about half an hour before it was due to wake me at 4.00 a.m. Within minutes I was on autopilot heading towards the south coast. A stop for coffee only delayed me for a few minutes, and soon enough I was once again staring at the lake from the ski club. The weather was dark and horrible, but the low air pressure had me smiling at the barometer. If I could get my part of the equation right then there were definitely carp to catch. I only saw one fish, however, right out in no-man's-land, and eventually took the best option I could. I was in the old faithful Road Point Swim minutes later, and sorting the rods out as quickly as I could. Well, I had caught a lot of fish from there the week before, and all I could hope was that the carp hadn't been upset too much by me doing so; only time would tell. I wanted to invest heavily in the bait again, and as soon as the marker hit the clip over the area it didn't take long to once again position the hookbaits and fill it in with the boilies. The water level had certainly risen in the few days I was away, and as much as some speculate that it does the fishery good, I have never been sure if it makes any difference at all. I can think of as many times when it has, as when it hasn't, which means all the bullshit talked about such things is just that, bullshit! I was happy, and at the end of the day, that's all what matters, really. In saying that, the first night was like a ghost town around the lake; it was lifeless. So, come the morning, I set off with a couple of rods, a landing net and an unhooking mat to see if I could find some fish to fish for. As the morning progressed the sun started to shine, and the south-westerly wind began to increase in strength. For once in their very frustrating existence, the

*I was in the old faithful Road Bank Point Swim minutes later.*

carp were doing exactly what I wanted them to do. They were actually mooching around in the corner into which that wind was blowing. Remarkable! In short order I had two traps set in the margins no more than a yard from the bank. I secreted myself behind a tree and waited, and then waited a little more. With so many fish cruising around I could only think that I had got something wrong, so exposed myself (ooh er, missus) a little further from behind my cover to see what was happening. The carp were there, that much was obvious, but the problem was they didn't look like they were ever going to feed. It looked more like they were going to spawn, really. I got quite bold in the end and stood right over them, but they simply followed each other around regardless of my presence. While they weren't actually spawning, it was obvious it wouldn't take too much in the way of sunshine to get them at it.

I returned to my plot and, with the hookbaits back in position, I pondered what I had seen.

***At 35lb 2oz she was the second-biggest common in the lake.***

I cannot fish for carp when they are spawning, I never have, preferring to reel in and leave them to it. I know I've mentioned it before, but if you only got laid once a year you would expect a little bit of undisturbed time to make the most of it, wouldn't you? However, until they started I was determined to keep my pedal to the metal as far as my mission was concerned. Again, the night was very uneventful, although several fish had showed in and around the baited area shortly before first light. I was just watching someone turning up to fish down to my right, when one of the rods roared for my attention. I picked it up and wondered if there was actually anything on the end. I had reeled in maybe 20 yards of line before I felt the faintest of knocks at the rod tip. I could only imagine how big the gudgeon was that I was playing. The guy who had just arrived was making his way towards me as the fish surfaced some 20 yards out, at which stage it must have taken all of two inches of line from my reel. That was as exciting as the fight got, and when it was only inches from the net we both agreed that the common was around 25lb. I made sure the fish was okay and lay the net down in the margin, spending a minute or two rushing around getting the reception area sorted. It was then that I noticed the handle of the net disappearing below the surface; it was just about to be out of reach s when I grabbed it. However, when I was once again in control the fish rolled on its side, and straight away I could see it was a little bigger than we thought. The mid-20 turned into 35lb 2oz, probably the second-biggest common in the lake! We posed in the early-morning mist, before I slipped her home; another of the lake's sought-after residents crossed off my list. I got no more action and was home a little later. If they didn't spawn then I would be back as soon as I could to keep the momentum going. While I was away the bream had decided to spawn, and this in turn had the carp rooting around in the long eelgrass, hoovering up all the eggs. And when I was walking around early the next Monday morning I spotted similar activity. The

*I set up towards the trees on the exposed bar.*

carp made it easy for me to select the area to fish; they were obviously still tearing it up and feasting with gusto. As encouraging as that was, it proved impossible to get a bite, from the carp anyway. The bream had obviously returned and joined in the feast too, so by the end of the first night I was 11 of them to the good... it was time to move. Early that morning, as I was returning yet another slimy little devil, I gazed down the lake and spotted several fish show not far out from the exposed bar. The water levels were still exceptionally low, and the bar separated one part of the lake from another. It was well worth investigating, and I discovered from the two anglers fishing down by the lake's entrance that they had landed a couple of fish. I could have moved in next to them, but as always, I wanted to do my own thing. To that end I pushed my barrow out along the exposed bar, right up to the trees that would normally be the far bank. I didn't want to rush things, so I spent ages just watching. I needed to know where the fish were feeding, and by 3.00 p.m. I had two stiff link pop-ups and 1kg of bait on the two areas of most activity. Not having fished this part of the lake before, I was a little wary. There were supposed to be some snags out in the open water and if that was the case the only way the carp could move towards them was if they ripped the rod off the rest! I set about demolishing a chicken salad and tried to do my crossword, making decent inroads into both, when the rod fished 30 yards to my left heaved round and the buzzer made a few bleeps. I was

*43lb 14oz was the unanimous decision.*

on the rod in a second, but it just wanted to move inexorably toward the supposed snaggy area. Instead of giving line I walked very reluctantly to my left, forgetting, of course, my landing net. Thankfully the two regulars, Jeff and John, who I had spoken to earlier, were making their way towards me, picking up the net and bringing it up to me. I could think of nothing else but that this was a big fish, and when it hit the surface a minute later, I was thinking 'monster', and the old knees started to shake. They became a whole lot shakier when Jeff declared it was The Scar, my ultimate target from Westy, and from then on I shut up completely. It actually didn't take too long before the fish was being guided to the outstretched net, but to me it seemed like an eternity. Once in the net there was only one thing left to do... Light my Fire!

I needed a moment or two to sort myself out and get things ready, so the guys looked after her for a few minutes. Soon enough we weighed her, which I wasn't that bothered about really; I had caught the fish I was there for. I let them read the scales: 43lb 14oz was the unanimous decision, and if they were happy with that, then I was too. John did a great job with the camera, and I watched her swim gracefully away. It was a great moment to share with them but I just wanted to be on my own as I had some thinking to do. I made my celebratory brew, and once again looked across the lake. I had now caught most of the big fish in the lake. There was one bigger common, but as it had only supposedly been caught once before, I guessed it may be a while before we crossed paths. There was also the Muncher, a carp that may have been of comparable size to The Scar, but it was never on my list of must-haves. I knew it was over; another exciting stepping stone on my journey was complete. To stay and catch the same fish over and over? That's just not my scene. It was time to move on once again.

# Thunderstruck

## BERNITHAN COURT FARM

*It was the place I dreamed of as a child.*

As pleased as I was with the outcome at Westhampnett, I could never have realised that my time would be over within nine months. And when you throw in the fact that I had only fished it for around five of those nine months, it means that I had done as well as I possibly could. It was a fantastic result, but I have never been one to rest on my laurels. The problem, once again, was where the hell did I go? I never like to be presumptuous about my fishing, and hadn't even considered where I would like to fish next, which in essence meant that I would be doing what I had always done... making it up as I went along! I started thinking about things on the drive home from Westy, but for the life of me, I couldn't come up with anything. At the time I had a whole host of tickets in my pocket, but most of the big carp those waters contained were the fish that everyone else was fishing for, naturally. And whenever I ask people about carp to target, they normally mention the better-known characters anyway. I certainly don't want to catch fish just because others think that is what I should be doing, and, as I have said before, I don't want to catch a carp simply because it's big; it has to mean something to me. My journey through whatever life has to offer is a personal thing, and so are the carp that I want to chase around. I very often end up wandering in the wilderness for ages, and what follows is very representative of my fishing life, at times. Of course, I could simply tell you about the good times in painful detail, but it's only when you are struggling, either to find somewhere to concentrate your efforts, or just with the fishing, that make any good times so good. To that end let's disappear into 'Chilly World' for a few months and see just how far and wide I travelled to a whole host of different venues. It may seem a bit hectic at times, but it was fun, and that is all I am ever looking for.

By the time I had arrived home my mind was no clearer, but Lynn suggested lobsters and red wine by way of celebration, and who was I to argue?! Come the Sunday evening I prepared my tackle and bait, aiming to leave the house early the next morning, but I still had no idea where I was going. The alarm sounded at 4.00 a.m. and, after a quick brew, I sat in the front of my van, leafing through the CEMEX guide book that was housed in my glove compartment. Eventually, I came across Chigborough; now there was a thought. With no plans to chase a big fish around, why not go and have some fun? I had never been there, and had absolutely no idea about the place, but word on the street was that it could be very productive. That was it then; Chigborough here I come! Those who know me will understand the next bit. Put a rifle, a compass and a map in my hands and I will get you anywhere you want to go on this planet. However, sitting behind and holding on to a steering wheel is a completely different matter. What should have taken me around two hours probably turned into five or six, and without the assistance of my mate Steve Spurgeon, it is highly likely that I would still be driving around the Essex countryside today. I reminded myself to get one of those satellite navi-direction thingy doodah contraptions, but I really didn't want someone talking to me whilst Guns 'N' Roses were making my ears bleed. Steve showed remarkable patience, and I eventually arrived at the gate. The first thing that struck me was just how interesting the place looked, broken up by long channels and islands; it wasn't what I was expecting at all. I even saw a few fish cruising under some overhanging branches as I set out for a lap of the lake. Best of all, though, I bumped into one of the bailiffs, Lawrence, and what a brilliant bloke he turned out to be. He brought me up to speed with the place, and it seemed I had made the right choice in going there. I had already decided which swim I was going to fish; it covered the ends of two channels and, as far as I could see, they were stuffed full of fish. Lawrence rated it, too. He also suggested the carp liked a bit of bait, which meant that in my world my trip to Essex had gotten off to the best of starts.

The lake was incredibly shallow, with an average depth of around 3 to 4 feet. It was there, in the deepest water I could find in the mouths of those channels, that I set two traps at the

*Chigborough was incredible fun.*

bottom of the reed-lined margins. Bait was a no-brainer, as always, and I spread about 2 kilos of 10 and 15mm boilies over both rods, and settled down to wait. There was only one other guy on the lake, and he was fishing way down to my right by the car park. He wandered round a few minutes later to say he had just landed a 20lb mirror, and as soon as he was gone I was playing one of my own. I love reading all this nonsense about just nicking a bite on the most pathetically small amount of bait. It has always been my experience in more heavily-stocked lakes that a fair amount of bait gets you considerably more bites. If one bite is all you want then crack on, but what happened over the next 30 hours left me in little doubt about what catches you the most fish. And of course there are the fish to think about

***31 fish in 36 hours... wow!!***

too; a lot of bait is my way of paying them back for all the pleasure they give me. The first
fish turned out to be a ghostie of around 15lb; he made me smile, as did the next fish, and
what an animal that was. The fish had spawned a few weeks prior to my visit, and this mirror
took full advantage of shedding her burden. I kid you not, that fish fought for the best part
of 20 minutes, and never took a break for a second. Even getting her on the mat made little
difference, and soon enough the 24-pounder was roaring off back home. I liked it there... a lot!

I hadn't expected to be using quite that much bait on this trip, especially as I wasn't sure
where the hell I was going, but I did have a plan to try to make it go a little further. I sat for
ages breaking up about half of my 15mm boilies into quarters, and at the very least I created
four baits out of one; I only hoped the carp would like the deal. The action never stopped,
and I spent the whole time baiting up, redoing my rigs, or simply smiling over a cup of tea.
It really was the kind of fishing that I needed to be doing. The night was a sleepless affair,
and eventually, around 4.00 a.m., I left the rigs in the butt rings. I needed some sleep, and
when I had snoozed for a while I got right back on with it. The fish just kept on coming; no
monsters, but 31 fish to 24lb over that period was amazing. Well for me it was! It isn't the
kind of fishing that I want to do too often, but on the drive home I didn't stop grinning
for a second. The trip, however, was supposed to give me a little time to think about what I
wanted to do next, but I was absolutely no nearer finding a place to be. I needed some time to
think, and had just the place to do it the following week. It may surprise the odd one or two
of you, but I still had an Ashmead ticket in my pocket. I couldn't even begin to contemplate
the rest of my life being unable to fish there again. Yes, I had landed the biggest fish in the
lake twice, but occasionally I would have liked to have been able to fish the greatest place
I had ever cast a rod. At the time I thought it was okay to feel that way, but unbeknown to

**Ashmead in all her glory.**

me, my visit the following Monday would be my penultimate session on the Avalon Flats.

I drove past Stonehenge as the light of dawn was filling the sky, which took the chill level down a notch. The smile got even broader as I passed the massive pig farm on the left a little farther on. They were just a couple of things that made the journey to Ashmead so special. I bounced down the long and bumpy track to discover there was only one car in the car park, and after a brief chat with the owner I went in search of carp. They were evident everywhere I looked, really, and when they were like that there, it always made the fishing a little more tricky. You see, if I could find the majority of the fish in one area, invariably I could play on their competition for food. Being so spread out it was a little harder to get them in the mood, but there was one bit of good news. I found the big girl, Single Scale, suitably settled in a channel at the far side of the fishery, which meant that I could set up as far away from her as possible. In the end I fished three rods a foot from the bank on a little peninsula, and set up as far back from the rods as the topography would allow. I was just sitting contemplating the meaning of life, and all that, when a barn owl appeared, flying ever so slowly towards me, and hovered just above my head for few seconds before continuing his stealthy journey. I would have paid my syndicate money for that single experience alone, and all I could think was how good it was to be back. A carp now would have been a bonus, and at 6.00 a.m. that bonus arrived. The fish ran around like a lunatic, finding every clump of weed in the 50 or so square yards in front of me. It gathered so much in the end that I couldn't actually see what was on the end of my line. Eventually, I had to take to the water in my chesties, and spent a minute or two wrestling the maniac into the net. Once back on dry land the dark 25lb mirror made the most arresting sight. He was a typical Ashmead mirror, and when I discovered he was called Turbo I could understand why. Yet again, as I lifted the sides of the unhooking mat around

*Turbo would be the last mirror I would ever catch from Ashmead.*

him to slip him back, I could see just how much bait he had got through in the night. It always makes me smile as I think about when I had inquired about the fishing there, when I was told not to use much bait, and anything but boilies. It's a good job I never listen to anyone, isn't it? The rest of the session was relatively quiet, and the peace and tranquility of the Somerset Flats were only interrupted by two small commons. I had no idea when I would be back, but I think I knew it was all over. I didn't realise it at the time, but I would only open those gates once more as a member, and old Turbo would be the last mirror I would ever catch from there.

Again, the long journey home was spent thinking about my fishing. I was no nearer to an answer, and to be perfectly frank, that thought would have to go on the back burner, for a while at least. I had to make some plans for the TV series once again, and eventually decided I was going to a private stretch of river in the South of England, and I'm not allowed to give any more details than that, I'm afraid. We were going to make a half-hour programme for the *Chilly on Carp* series with Fishing.TV, and a segment for Sky's *Tight Lines*. I was truly excited, and although I had broken my carping virginity on the rivers a year or so before, I couldn't wait to get going. Before that, though, I could do some fishing for myself and for whatever reason I decided I would make a return to the North Lake at Yateley. I had fished there when CEMEX had re-stocked the place, as you have read, and I guess I just wanted to see how the fish had fared. It was still under CEMEX's control at the time, although I believe the sale was already arranged. So, before I lost my ticket to fish there I went along for a two-week sabbatical. I only fished five nights of those two weeks, before you think that I was there for a fortnight, something which I can assure you I would find terribly boring. The fish had settled in, and by all accounts were doing well. Speaking to a couple of the lads fishing there I was told that boilies were not on the list of the carp's favourites, and

*It was crazy fishing!*

*I left having landed so many fish to 36lb.*

seeds were the way forward. "That is a bit of a problem for you," one of them said, "seeing as you like boilies and all that." I smiled back and wandered off to my van, to load the barrow and place the only bait I had with me on top. Yep, you guessed it, two air-dry bags of 10 and 15mm Hybrid. I only fished one swim in that time, which was in the middle of the works bank, and I cannot for the life of me remember its name. Again, on arrival with my barrow, I was told that it wasn't the one to fish as it had a massive open area in front of it and the carp shied away from it all the time. I must have trodden in something that morning because things kicked off right from the start. I never want to make a meal out of carp that I have caught before, and some of the fish I landed, I recognised. It was incredible fishing, however, and all of them fell to the unfashionable mass-boilie approach. Fishing as near to the weed at the far side of the clearing was the answer for me, and eventually l left having landed commons to 36lb and mirrors to over 34lb. It was crazy fishing, which often saw me having to swim out, with a life jacket on of course, to get fish out of the weed that was flourishing. I was so pleased that the lake was once again becoming something to be reckoned with. Basil was dead, but the North Lake was, and still is, very much alive.

With my time at the North Lake, and almost certainly with Yateley itself, now over, I could concentrate on the next mission in my mad life. I met up with my friend John Dunford, the cameraman, at the southern river the evening before the fishing and, because we couldn't sleep on the land, we would bivvy up nearby. We met up with the river manager the following morning, the 16th June, and stood transfixed as we watched the swirls of mist dance their way down the river and across the long grassy banks. There was a small group of friends who had permission to fish this stretch, but they do so very infrequently, and when they do, it is mainly for the perch. However, there were a fair few carp in the river, and you would have thought

*It was probably the best day's fishing I had had in a very long time.*

that with only three or four of them having been caught, this would be like taking candy from a baby. I can assure you, it was nothing of the sort. With filming in mind, it was the sort of morning that we could only dream of. And once John had had his fill of filming it, we went in search of carp. In truth, it didn't take long to find a couple of fish, and I was also encouraged to see that they found my pellet and corn concoction to their liking. It all looked so easy, but actually angling for them became the most frustrating fishing I had done in a very long time. The whole day was so visual; there was no problem finding and filming them, and even the underwater camera picked up loads of fishy action. Getting them to pick up a hookbait wasn't that hard either, but actually hooking one became almost impossible. I stood and watched carp after carp pick up the hookbait and simply put it back down and carry on feeding. Bear in mind here that they had never been fished for in this way. Intelligence, as it's always been claimed, has nothing to do with it; they simply allow the advanced filtration system in their mouth to sort out the stuff that it wants to eat from that which it doesn't... such as my hook!

I made a few tweaks to the setup, all of which made no difference at all, as they invariably don't anyway. I believe all that happens is the fish start to feed strongly enough to get themselves caught, and eventually they did just that. I landed two commons in the end, and whilst they weren't the biggest fish I will ever catch, they were both landed on my centrepin reels, and in such an intimate environment. It was possibly the best day's fishing I had had for some time. And then someone who will remain nameless brought me right back down to earth with a bit of a thump. I was told I was missing out on so much, and if I had used a Chod Rig then I would have caught loads of them. Really? It was the era when this rig became the only one to use, if you wanted any street cred of course, and to me that was wrong on so many levels. Not least is the fact that it shows how much carp fishing is dominated by fashion, and not the individual's ability to think their way around a particular problem. And let's not forget here, if that was the only rig being used on a water, then that was the only rig which would catch fish. There are so many more interesting avenues to explore, and in many ways that is what makes carp fishing so fascinating. I had never used the rig, and I had no intention of doing so, but I get a little inquisitive at times and decided that I would give it one month. I knew I would never use it again, but so many in carp fishing shout and scream about certain things, having never experienced them, or even used them. You need to know what the hell you are going on about before you can do that, surely?

So, the following week I set out to see what all the fuss was about. All I could hope for was that I wouldn't feel as if I came from an area of the country where it was fashionable to marry one's sister! I had, evidently, a 'well wicked' Chod bin, and some seriously 'well carpy geeza' hooklink material. So far so good... I even found some carp to fish for, and at that point the wheels started to fall off. The lake was very weedy and because of the nature of the Chod thing, it is fished rotary style, which meant the lead stayed attached when the fish was hooked. (There are systems which release the lead on these setups, but I didn't have one available to me on that session.) The first fish I hooked came adrift in the weed, and the second one was only landed because I had access to a boat. It was, however, my first Chod-caught carp, for which I apologised as I slipped the 28lb mirror back. I landed two more carp, but nothing endeared me to that setup at all. I guess the conditions that I was faced with would be considered ideal for it, but I know for a fact I would have caught more on my conventional setups, and with a lot less hassle, too. So, I had now used a Chod Rig which means that I can talk from experience; I don't want to marry my sister (if I had one) and I will never use one again! And whilst I was trying desperately to delete the word Chod from my vocabulary, I received a call, and within minutes all thoughts of stupid rigs had been erased.

I had been speaking to a guy, whom many of you would never have heard of at the time,

*I apologised to this 28lb mirror for his Chod experience.*

who went by the name of Dean Fletcher (think the Parrot at 68lb 1oz and you will know him now), and he ran a lake near Reading called Tipping's Lane. I am not suggesting that we were bestest buds and all that, but I often bumped into Dean as I travelled around, and thoroughly enjoyed his company. Anyway, he had told me about his lake, and that if I ever wanted to escape I was more than welcome to come and have a go. I had left him a message a few days before, and he had called back to confirm that I was more than welcome. I told him I would be up the following Monday and arranged to meet up later that day. The lake itself was a water that was really in its infancy, and although it looked fantastic, and the stock was great, there were no monsters for me to target, not at that time anyway. Be that as it may, I liked it there and was determined to catch a few over the coming weeks, as I once again tried to find somewhere to hang my hat. I never really did see many of the members, and busied myself catching a few of the lake's doubles. I knew it wouldn't last long, and after a couple of trips, fate decided to play me a decent hand. I had set up in a swim that was right beside a public footpath that ran the length of one bank, when a guy said, "Hello, Mr Chillcott." I hadn't seen him for about 12 years, and he went by the name of Jason Boucher. We had last fished together at Yateley, and it was great to see he was still chasing some carp around. He told me about Tipping's, and with his limited time it was the perfect place for him to angle. He also mentioned another lake a little further up the way, and that was when my radar acquired a target, although at first it sounded like the biggest dump on the planet. It was a 20-acre lake situated in the middle of a massive housing estate, which automatically conjured up pictures of locals ruining the fishing and treading on used hypodermic needles. He said it really wasn't like that, and the carp were quite spectacular; old scaly fish that had been around for a very long time. They sounded very interesting, but the

**My Southlake adventure began.**

location did not. However, never one to dismiss anything out of hand, we arranged to meet up the following week and go take a look. Jason had told me it was shut down for a short close season, and in the right conditions we should see some carp. Okay, nothing ventured, nothing gained and all that. As we chatted I remembered a young lad whom I had spoken to a week before, and he was telling me about a 33lb scaly mirror he had landed a month or two ago. That had been from a water 'just up the road' and I wondered if I had found it.

As arranged, I met up with Jason and we drove over to take a look. We pulled up in the car park next to some flats and, I must admit, I nearly turned around. But once we had walked through the buildings, there lay the most fantastic-looking lake. Probably the greatest thing as we started to walk around, was that I didn't see a single used needle, and there was no litter

**At 21lb this dark mirror made a great start to proceedings.**

at all. By the time we came to an island at one end of the lake, I was quite literally dribbling down my chin. It looked unbelievable, and that reaction was further enhanced by the sight of about 70 to 80 carp sunning themselves in about 2ft of water. I even took my trainers off and waded down towards them. I didn't see any absolute monsters, but there were enough 30s and scaly beasts to keep any man happy. I liked the Southlake a lot, and as soon as I was home the secretary took my details and my payment. I had a ticket, or the promise of one anyway, and all that was left to do was sort out my gear for an early start the next Monday.

Things didn't start off too well, to be honest, and it wasn't my fault at all… I don't think. As a bit of a technophobe, I was amazed to arrive at the lake around an hour before first light. You see, it was the first time I had ever used a satnav, and I wondered why I hadn't bothered before. The lake looked fantastic as the light started to fill the sky, and the words of a couple of people I had asked about the place still rang in my ears. Evidently, it was a fairly easy place, and I would have been hugely unlucky if every other fish wasn't a scaly 30-pounder. It all sounded so good in the telling, but the truth, for me at least, was a little different.

The lake itself is incredibly shallow, and in an effort not to get tied into fishing one of the two most popular swims, I fished an area of slightly deeper water for the first night, a night, incidentally, in which I listened to carp leaping continuously in the 'popular' swims some 75 yards to my left. I decided there and then to move at first light, but first of all I had to survive a visit from the bailiff. It was dark, and I was lying on my bedchair sipping a brew when he arrived and asked me for my ticket, to which I explained that I had been accepted and they had taken my money, but it just so happened the ticket hadn't arrived when I left that morning. Oh Lordy, his smile nearly split his face in half, and at one point I thought he was going to disappear into the bushes to fiddle with himself. "You're Ian Chillcott and you haven't got your ticket with you? You are going to have to leave, and probably will be facing a lengthy ban," he gleefully announced. I asked if he would ring the treasurer, but he was adamant that I was now banned. He rang the guy in the end, and things settled down a little after that, but I couldn't help thinking how sad some people can be. He left in the end, and I wondered if I had made a mistake joining the lake. Oh well, as long as I wasn't on the end of a public flogging next time around, I guessed I ought to try to enjoy myself, so I did.

By early morning I had two stiff link pop-ups launched over to the shallows that the popular swim covered. A scattering of boilies completed the traps, and I sat down to wait for events to unfold. During the night I had to remove tackle from three fish that were towing the most horrendous rigs around, and I wasn't happy at all. Thankfully, at first light I got a proper bite, and after a bit of a dour fight I was able to lead a lot of weed, plus a carp, into my net. At 21lb the dark mirror made a great start to my time on the lake, and that night I landed five more fish, all upper-doubles. I couldn't help wondering what the "every other one's a 30" was all about. I did land one more fish before I left, and that was a truly handsome, scaly, 21lb mirror which was more like the fish I had gone there to catch. The MNDA event at Linear Fisheries kept me away the following week, a week in which I shared some time with my mates. With Dave Lane, Adam Penning and Paul Forward, amongst others, it made the raising of over £20,000 a special time. I returned to the Southlake the next week and again caught carp, all doubles apart from one which was a 25lb 8oz common.

Sorting out the bigger fish was a problem I would have to work out at a later date, however, because I was off to Italy the following week for the World Carp Classic with my World Champion buddy, Lee Jackson. Just to get as much out of the trip as possible, I would be travelling with cameraman John Dunford, hoping to do as much filming as we could, although none of us could have known what a complete and utter disaster it would end up being. I could probably write a book about that one trip alone, and whilst it wouldn't include a single carp caught by any of us, it would encompass some of the biggest disasters I have ever had to endure. Our six-man team was Tim Paisley and Steve Briggs, Martin Locke and Tom Duncan-Dunlop, and me and Lee, and all was going well until we got off the ferry. My phone didn't work, and if I can't talk to Lynn 24/7 it just isn't happening. John said I could use his phone, so we cracked on in convoy. I got a pay-as-you-go phone in Italy, and all was well for about five minutes. The draw saw all three pairs in the same section, a section incidentally that didn't produce one carp in the match. We had to set up on a sandy beach, and as we were doing so, the local landowner started hollering and shouting at us. I was all for filling him in, but Jacko decided to talk to the guy, and for a while all was sort of settled. That was until we were hit by a 30-yard-wide tornado. It absolutely obliterated everything, sending pieces of kit hundreds of yards away. Everything was soaked and broken, and I would have run for home right there and then. At which point the wind changed, and although Jacko wouldn't admit it, our chances washed away on the waves that were now moving away from us. It was a spectacular place, some 25,000 acres of volcanic lake, but John and I felt like we were castaways on a desert island. In the end, we travelled around and filmed what we could, and as we went, more and more things went hopelessly wrong. Eventually, it was time to go and we left a day earlier than the others, and the problem was, things just got worse. Our TomTom satnav wouldn't work and John thought we should buy another one. It took about three hours to do that, and he raced out of the shop he bought it from like he had won the World Cup. The excitement was short-lived, as we couldn't get that one working either. How I didn't kill someone I will never know, but on we went. The best I could come up with was keeping the sun on our left side, so at least we knew we were generally travelling north, but we still got hopelessly lost. I did most of the driving whilst John spoke to his mum and dad back in Blighty

*The Italian trip was a bit of a disaster, but it wasn't a bad
social event. With friends prior to the match.*

to try to sort out the satnav thingy. I just didn't think that it could get any worse... but it did!

We had pulled into a service station, having seen our first sign for Switzerland, and although we were still basically lost, it seemed like the first indication that we were going in the right direction. I grabbed a brew and went in search of a map at the station over a bridge, on the other side of the motorway. I didn't realise John had gone over there, too, and when we RVed back at the van he discovered he had lost the bloody keys. I had to walk away. I was as mad as I had ever been, and I simply concentrated on not letting the red veil of doom cloud my judgement. We had no idea where they could be, and it was probably an hour before I ended up over the bridge and at the petrol station once again. As I arrived, I spotted some crazy bloke dancing on a bench waving something over his head. They were John's keys, and this lunatic showed a marked reluctance to hand them over to me. Without thinking twice I launched the best uppercut I have ever delivered. He flew over the back of the chair and the keys skidded across the tarmac. Some guy thought he should intervene, but he got the good news, too. There was utter silence as I turned and marched up the stairs and across the bridge, but I had the keys and we were going home... to hell with 'em! Unbelievably the satnav started working, thanks totally to John's mum, and we completed the ten-hour drive to the ferry in France. I breathed a huge sigh of relief, but just as I thought we could cross the Channel and leave all this crap behind us, the British Port Authority guy discovered my passport was out of date. I held my head in my hands as he discussed the problem with his boss, as his mate was telling me I would probably have to spend a few days at the Embassy in Paris before it was sorted. I was once again ready to hurt someone when the guy returned. It was only a couple of weeks out of date and they had decided that I could travel on the boat. I was so glad they did, because that trip to Paris may just have been a little longer, had I done what was on my mind at the time. In all, it took around 20 hours to get home, and all I wanted to do when I got there was lay down in a darkened room for a day or two. And yet there are those who say, "Oh, it's easy for him isn't it?" Well no, it bloody well isn't, actually!

I desperately needed a change of pace, something to calm me down a little, and I had on the horizon the one thing that would eventually be the trip of a lifetime, something I had said I would never do. I just don't like living in the past. I have little doubt that knowing where you came from will help to shape your future, I believe that about all aspects of my life, but what happened shortly after my return from Italy probably helped me, more than most, to come to terms with things that happened in the past; things which I had ignored for many years. Much of the time I have no wish to visit places that have had an influence on me, preferring instead to allow the things I have heard and read about them to satisfy my thirst for knowledge. One such place is Redmire Pool, lying on the estate of Bernithan Court in the village of Llangarron, a couple of miles from Ross-on-Wye. Growing up as a budding fisherman, I was under the spell of Richard Walker and his exploits, especially the catching of a 44lb common from this fabled pool in 1952. It was this fish that I gawped at most during my formative years, and the pages of his book, *Still-Water Angling*, bear testament to that fact. However, I had never had a wish to visit the famous lake; I just wanted to remember how I thought it would look from what I had read about it. That resolve was tested to the full when I lived in Hereford for many years. At one point I was courting a young lady in Ross-on-Wye, and although I was rarely in this country, her little house there was where I spent my time. I was probably as fit as any man on the planet back then, and much of my downtime was spent either running or in the gym. Being 14 miles from my Hereford base made it an ideal running distance, which meant that every morning and evening I would run, or occasionally cycle, past the road that lead to Redmire. Without fail, I would always glance left or right, depending on which direction I was running in, and think about Walker, his friends, and the pool itself. But I never went to visit the lake that had shaped me into the angler I am today. I had been invited on several occasions, but still I had never wanted to go.

My whole Redmire abstinence changed whilst talking on the phone to Tim Paisley one day. We talk regularly, but this time he asked if I would like to accompany him on a trip to the fabled pool. It was ironic, really, because the day before I had been speaking to Mark Walsingham, Ashmead owner and Golden Scale Member, and he happened to say that he was sharing the visit with Tim. As Mark and I spoke I couldn't help feeling what splendid company that would be, but I could never have imagined that I would be invited, too. It was for the company, as much as fishing the pool, that I agreed to go, but I could have had no idea just how emotional those few days would be. Again, I was distracted by magazine work and charity events before I could fulfil the ambition I had no idea existed. I had read Walker's book in 1966, and now I was going. I left home very early on the Sunday we were required to arrive, not because I could have a look at the pool, but because I wanted to visit two graveyards in Hereford before I went to Llangarron. I had some respects to pay, and, in all, I visited seven graves of warriors that go way beyond anything that carp fishing represents. I sat and talked with each of them for a few minutes, and eventually drove into Hereford itself. The barracks are no longer there, but I drove past and did some more remembering. I even drove to, and parked up outside, the two houses that I used to own there, and let the memories flood over me. It may have put me in a bit of a sombre mood, but I would never have forgiven myself if I had not visited those places, and the people who had meant so much to me, and still do.

When I managed to tear myself away, I set out for the one road I said I would never travel down. It was a surreal moment, but before I could enter Bernithan Court I met up

**The Redmire visit was a truly emotion trip.**

with Mark in a nearby hostelry, and we shared some local beef and a pint of the finest local mead. It really was the perfect way to shake off my maudlin mood. Tim arrived and we set off for the hallowed ground of Redmire. It was the place I dreamed of as a child, and I was far from disappointed as we opened the gate and walked through. It was probably the greatest moment in my fishing life. Sure some things have changed, but it looked so far removed from a commercial fishery that I actually let out a little cheer. I left the other two to get on with their thing, and wandered off to find some carp to fish for, although I wasn't too sure that I needed to fish, to be honest; just being there was enough. But eventually I found a few small commons cruising up towards the shallows, and settled in a swim called Keffords. You can use four rods there, but it just seemed so over the top and crass for my liking, so I used two. The fishing was quiet, and I wondered if I would ever get a chance to play a Redmire carp. The other two guys were catching nothing either, but I nearly had a heart attack when, early on the second morning, my buzzer indicated a stuttery take. We danced the dance and after a few minutes I lifted the net around a Redmire common carp! The ghosts of my forefathers had allowed me the greatest honour, and I held the little fish up for a picture or two. I was away the following day, and even as I drove off I knew I would never be able to find the words that would describe just how humble and ridiculously pleased I was to have actually been there.

I drove home full of joy, but I did give some thought as to what I was going to do that winter. 2012 was marching on, and I just couldn't find any direction to my fishing. I was happy, however, although I needed to find a target for the winter just to give me and my fishing a little uplift. I wracked my brains once again until, like a bolt of lightning, it came to me. I had just been to the most historical carp lake in the world, so decided I would revisit a little slice of my own nostalgic past. I would return to somewhere that is very dear

**It was truly an honour to land a Redmire common.**

to me, but somewhere I hadn't fished in almost 15 years, not properly anyway. With my gear packed and a cartload of 10 and 15mm boilies on board, I set off for Oxfordshire and, more precisely, Manor Farm Lake on the Linear complex. As I drove I only had one fish on my mind. Spike was probably the biggest fish in the lake at the time, and if I was going to be fishing a very busy day ticket water, then what better way to motivate myself than targeting the biggest carp in there? Well, we are all allowed to dream, aren't we?

I had fished a social session there the year before, but the thing that trip taught me was that maggots dominated the place. Now, if I was fishing it for a while then there was no way I would be using maggots. I understand that infrequent visitors want to get a bite, and maggots may be a good way of doing that but, ultimately, their constant use will affect the fish, and the fishing, terribly. Subsequently, the 40-pounders in the lake as winter sets in will invariably weigh much less come the beginning of March. I have witnessed this on many waters, unfortunately. Consequently, I arrived armed with a new bait from Mainline. Now, I am not the best at changing baits, and Mainline have never asked me to, because I prefer to get the best from my bait over a period of time. However, on this trip I was going to a new water, and this was probably the best time to try out some new carp tucker. Oddly enough, I had missed out on probably the greatest bait revolution since the Hair Rig, and the original Grange, by not using the Cell. The biggest-selling boilie in history had never been cast out by me, and I was now armed with the Hybrid, a mixture of Active-8 and Cell, along with a few winners from Steve Morgan of course! I have never failed with any bait Kev Knight has provided me with, and there should have been no doubt this time, especially as I had landed my target fish, Hendrix at 44lb, the first night I changed over to, and used, the New Grange! Whilst I couldn't possibly expect the same result, I had high

*Manor is a little nostalgic slice of my own past.*

hopes for the new bait, and they would be seeing plenty of it over the coming months.

I had no idea in advance, but when I arrived Fox had booked the first two swims on the road bank to do some promotional work. They hadn't been shut down and baited for them, and I even talked to the paying customers who were just vacating the swims. I was keen to fish away from them, and eventually settled in swim four, where I had seen a fish show, and that is where my Manor campaign would start. The day was windless, and the high pressure was winning the battle in the sky. Not great conditions, but I got three stiff link pop-up hookbaits in position at around 110 yards, behind a massive bank of weed. It felt good to me and I spent the rest of the day looking across the water for any signs of carp. As I settled down for the night the radio informed me that the pressure was going to drop, with some wind and rain on the cards. I dozed off that night hoping the weatherman would keep his word.

By morning, although I had heard several fish in the night, I was remarkably fishless. I sat by my rods, looking for inspiration, and it came riding along on the southerly wind that was strengthening from my right. In the ripple, I spotted the tiniest oil trail at about 70–80 yards, in front of swim five. I grabbed my brew and walked down to investigate, and as I got there I noticed a subsurface roll, which was all the encouragement I needed, really. In short order I had reeled my rods in, and checked one of the pop-ups. It sank like a brick, but it was still popped up, and that would have to do. Along with the landing net, and one buzzer on a bankstick, I went back, casting the rig about 30 yards beyond the epicentre of the oil slick. I trapped the lead on the surface, reeled it along the surface back to the spot, and then gently lowered it to the deck. It landed with a decent thump, and I simply slackened off the line a little and placed the rod on the rest. My backside didn't even get a chance to sit on the ground before the rod was away. A lively battle ensued before I was able to scoop up my prize, a 24lb

**Spike was mine, all 44lb 6oz of him.**

mirror. I was off the mark, and in no time at all my gear was in swim five and I was ready to rock and roll. I fished two rods on that spot, again with stiff link pop-ups, and baited with about 2kg of 10 and 15mm Hybrid. I also used a similar amount of the Hybrid Response Pellets, and as I sat down I was very pleased with my efforts, and extremely confident.

At some ungodly hour that night I was running to the rods, as one of them was in meltdown mode. Even with the rod in my hand I could make no impression on the fish, and for some time I felt wonderfully out of control. I kept the pressure on and it turned, and as carefully as I could, I drew the fish towards me. It lunged around in the deep margins, feeling all the time like a very good fish, and when it hit the surface my suspicions were confirmed. A big, long mirror slid into the net, and although I suspected which fish it was, it wasn't until I had got my headtorch on that I was sure. The first thing I noticed, as I shone the red glow into the net, was a spiky rear dorsal fin, and after taking in once more its enormous length, I knew for sure. Spike was mine, all 44lb 6oz of him! Although it was horribly unsociable, I rang Roy Parsons, who gave me permission to sack the fish until the lads arrived from Fox in a couple of hours. At first light we set about getting the pictures done, and soon enough I watched as that magnificent mirror swam casually away, an epic day-ticket carp and, much as I had done at Cleverley Mere, my target fish had been caught using a new bait for the first time. Lightning really can strike twice! All I could think about then was – where the hell was I going next? I visited the lake twice more with friends, but the spell had been broken, and it really was time to move on. And it appeared that I was moving on with my diary that I wrote every month, because the next one I wrote would start an association with *Total Carp* magazine. It looked as if it really was a clean slate, and all I needed to do was find something to illustrate it with.

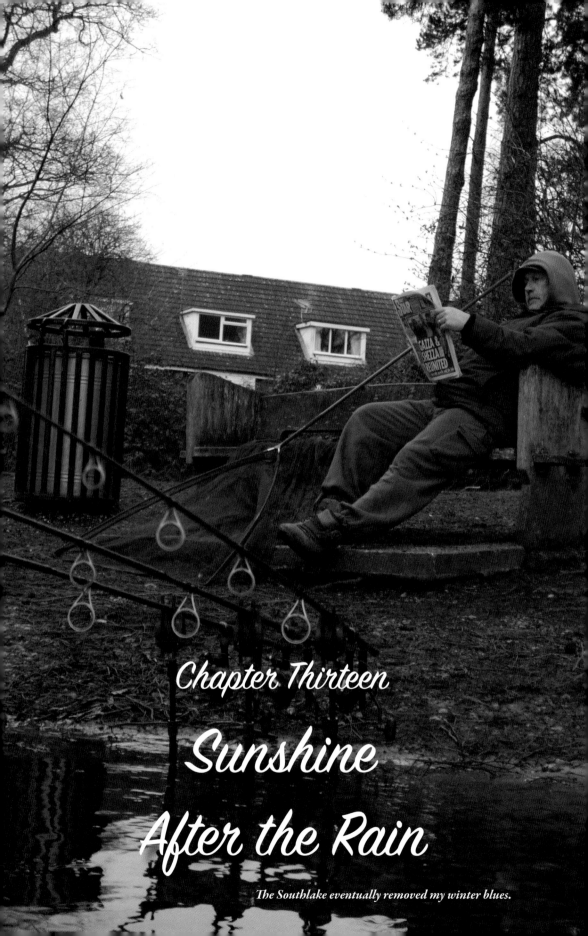

Chapter Thirteen

Sunshine
After the Rain

The Southlake eventually removed my winter blues.

*The Basingstoke Canal wasn't going to be easy.*

It was the winter of 2012/2013, I had caught my target for the colder months within two days, and I had absolutely no idea what to do next. This, to all intents and purposes, brings us back to the situation you have found me in a few times over the past hundred thousand or so words. Just so we are sure on this point, I am not complaining about catching a fish I desperately wanted in the first session on the water, but I didn't expect to be moving on that quickly. I sat at home and pondered the situation. For a kick-off it would be hard to get into a campaign this late into the colder months. And secondly, although I could never have known it, as I sat and thought about what to do, we were just about to experience one of the coldest winters on record. I rarely speak to anyone about carp fishing once I am at home; I like to switch off from it as much as I can and explore some of the other equally important aspects of life. However, there can be no better people to speak to than some of my friends, and Laney and Adam Penning were the first to be subjected to the Chilly cry for help, although even those guys were at a loss as to what to do. I did, however, arrange a social with Laney and his buddy, Paddy, back up at Linear Fisheries, although by the end of that session I was probably even further away from finding out what I wanted to do. There was one other little situation, and that was beginning my diary in *Total Carp*. It's kind of nice to start off with a bit of a bang; however, it looked as if the fishing I could be portraying would be anything but successful.

That said, the downtime did make me think about the filming I had been doing with *Fishing.TV*, and I thought maybe it was time to do another programme. The guys there had been telling me about smart TVs, and apps, and a whole host of other things that I have absolutely no friggin' idea about! This all meant, evidently, that our audience had increased massively. Nice! Just up the road from me is the Basingstoke Canal, a very accessible, and often productive, carp-fishing environment. The problem was that I hadn't carp fished it for over twenty years, which made the challenge a little more interesting. By way of a recce, I did a magazine feature there the following week, so at the very least I would know if I could catch a carp or two from the selected area. It would also give me somewhere to bait up, and that just happened to be the worst thing I could possibly have done. John Dunford and I turned up and barrowed all our gear the 500 yards to the spot I had selected one cold and miserable morning at the beginning of December. The first thing to do was get fishing, which I did immediately, and after doing a few little bits to the camera, I decided to redo one of the rods. I was amazed to see the crayfish had attacked the hookbait, and from then on I wasn't sure what had responded best to my baiting efforts. I was pretty sure, however, that the crayfish and the mallards had won the day. This wasn't going to be easy and, to be honest, it just got worse. I noticed a little later that an increasing amount of weed was drifting down on what looked like a flow in the normally still canal. An hour later the place looked more like a river, and the weed wiped my lines out every couple of minutes.

We found out they had shut off the canal some two miles up to our right and were pumping water in from the other side of the barrier. How bloody wonderful! I was struggling to see the funny side of things, and when a vagrant tried to nick one of the cameras and the bailiff's dog ran off with my chicken dinner, I was starting to think that I had wasted everyone's time. The mood lightened when I chased the hobo out of the area; it looked so funny as the old wino tried to sprint down the towpath! And the bailiff returned, minus his dog of course, having visited the nearest shops, bringing me some more chicken. The bream and the crayfish meant that by first light I was only fishing with one rod. I hadn't been this pissed off in a while, but as I sipped a brew I saw a large boil over the remaining hookbait. For a second I thought another mallard would reappear, but the bobbin lifted and the rod arched round. With much nervous chatter I played and landed the mid-double mirror, and right there and then he became the greatest carp I had ever caught! The programme was complete, and both John and I ran for home as quickly as we could.

My next trip was to the Pads Lake at Yateley, but by the first morning the lake was solid with ice. Winter was definitely there. I had arranged to do some angling with Penning the following week, and yet again I would have John Dunford along to do some filming. The weather, however, was really starting to turn, and the 'Beast from the

*A frozen Yateley Pads Lake.*

East' as the weatherman described it, was starting to make its presence felt. The company of those two guys was just about as good as it gets, and we got some great stuff on the camera, but yet again the lake froze and we were driven away a day early. I knocked it all on the head and headed down to spend Christmas with my folks in Plymouth.

The New Year frivolities had become a distant memory by the time I got the rods dusted off and ready for action again. With the folding of CEMEX Angling I had lost a lot of

*Trying to do some filming with Adam, but everything kept freezing.*

waters where I could confidently expect to catch winter carp. Perhaps I had been living in a bit of a comfort zone but, whatever the case, I needed to go fishing. I actually had no idea where I was off to when I left my house early one morning the following January, 2013, and I didn't make my mind up until I was a few miles from home. I belonged to a couple of private syndicate waters, and I headed towards one of those. Both lakes contained huge carp, but the one I was going to now had recently had an introduction of some small stockies, and I looked forward to seeing how they were doing. There was also the not-insignificant fact that if I could get them rooting around for a bite to eat, they might just arouse the interest of their bigger brothers and sisters. As normal, a spread of 10 and 15mm boilies completed my traps and I settled down to wait, then, as a light dusting of snow covered the ground at first light, I got myself a bite. From the off I knew it was a stockie, but after a little over fifty years I had, for the first time, landed a carp in the snow, which seems remarkable to me, seeing as I had fished relentlessly through the previous twenty winters without doing so. It was followed shortly after by another of similar size. The bigger fish had eluded me, but I would be back once the weather warmed just a little more. Dream on, Chilly boy!

I was gazing around a rather boring-looking lake the following week, and decided to give Adam a call. After telling him my tides of woe, he suggested that we fish a little dayticket water near his home in Essex. I didn't need any further encouragement and was soon RVing with him in Ingatestone, and ten minutes later we were turning into Churchwood Fisheries. I had no idea what to expect, but when the bailiff, Alex Bauer, arrived and offered a lift to the lake on a quad bike, I decided I liked it there a lot, and nothing that happened over the two days we were there changed my view! Steve Sands and his wife, Helen, run a very exclusive dayticket set up, and even before the session finished I hoped I would soon be back. The session was

*A great social with Penning at Churchwood, and I even caught carp!*

a great social, and I even managed to catch two upper-double mirrors. The sad part about it, and it was probably the first time I had really given it any thought, was that I was happy because I had landed fish to write about in my diary. At that time I had been penning an article about my fishing (amongst many others) once a month for thirteen years, and I had had no idea just how much it controlled and dominated my life. In saying that, I was a fortunate man, and as I love carp fishing, I could think of absolutely no reason to stop... so I didn't!

My seasonal maladjustment was kicking in big style, but I figured that spring was nearly upon me. I tried to fish at Fryerning Fisheries, and that froze over, as it did the following week too, and as I packed up on the second session, I made a couple of calls. I was chatting to my mate Gary 'Milky' Lowe, and he suggested a venue called Churchgate Lakes, near Southend. It could be very productive, and a couple of his mates had landed a few from there of late, so I dialled up the coordinates on the satnav and headed off. The first thing to do was make sure the water was wobbly on my arrival, and I let out a cheer when I saw that I could actually get a lead in the wet stuff. I had Max Hendry coming from DHP to do some pictures for an article the following morning, so I set up with this in mind. A spread of the obvious 10 and 15mm boilies were fired out over the two hookbaits, and I waited. I watched a young lad up to my right land a couple of fish, and by 3.00 p.m. I was starting to get a little twitchy. I should not have worried because by 11.00 p.m. I was 20 fish to the good. It was crazy fishing, and to save some action for the camera, I baited the area and left the rigs in the butt rings. The daylight wasn't as productive, but I landed a few fish to around 19lb for the feature, and even stayed another night. The sizes of the fish were irrelevant; it had been an enormous slice of fun, especially when the conditions were considered. By morning I was ready for the off, but a chance conversation with the guy who ran the place changed all that. "Have a go on the

*Two 21-pounders and a 23lb 4oz made it a winter trip to remember.*

members' lake, the fish are a little bigger in there." Well, if you insist! I fished two rods to the far margin reeds at around 30 yards and baited with just a couple of pouches of boilies over each. The third rod was fished as a single a little way up the margin to my left. All that was left to do was sip brews and smile the rest of the day away. I loved carp fishing again, which was the complete opposite to how I felt only a few days before! A couple of mid-double commons started the action, and around midnight I landed my first mirror of 23lb. They were getting bigger. At first light I was playing another fish, and as I got that in the net one of the other rods chirped into life. Then, as I played that one, the last rod joined in the fun. It wasn't pretty, but eventually I had three 20lb mirrors in my two landing nets, a right result at any time of year, but during this awful winter, it was nothing short of biblical! I couldn't help giggling to myself as I sorted it all out. Conditions were absolutely freezing, and I even broke up some cat ice in the margins as I lifted each fish onto the mat. Two 21-pounders and a 23lb 14oz made it a trip to remember and, as I packed away, one last fish of 20lb 12oz bade me farewell. And yet there are still those who think winter carping is a waste of time. Pick the right water and anything is possible; it just depends if you have the balls to do it, doesn't it?

I went to Linear Fisheries after that, once for a social with Penning, and a second time to try to find some bigger fish on Unity Lake, neither of which lit my fire. Easter was fast approaching and I still had no direction to my fishing. The weather was colder at this time of year than anyone could remember, and there seemed no end to it all. As much as I was in the doldrums, there was one thing I had to do around that time, and probably the last thing I could believe I would ever do, especially when you think about my history... I was off to Russia! I have travelled the world many times over, and seen just about everything that is on offer. However, for much of my adult life I trained to either repel a Russian invasion, or to

**The view of Moscow from my hotel room.**

invade the Soviet Union itself. I had always believed if I was heading that way, my first view of the country would be as I exited a Hercules aircraft under a parachute at around 700ft. It felt so unnatural to be visiting this country in my new guise as a carp angler, but Fox had a stand at a show out there, and we were going to be hosted by a group of guys at the very heart of the emerging Russian carp-fishing market. To be honest, I had no idea what to expect, but I was going to be truly surprised, not only by the country, but also the people. The whole trip left me feeling, much as I had always done, that it is governments that want to kill people, not the people themselves, a profound statement, but the Russians were so polite and friendly it was they who made the trip for me. The first thing to endure was the flight. God, I would rather jump out of planes than I would land in them! Alix, our host, picked us up from one of the four Moscow airports and we eventually arrived at the hotel. As we drove I couldn't help thinking how big everything looked; even the side roads had ten lanes on each side, and the hotel, which was built for the 1984 Olympics, didn't disappoint either. It was like a small city, all on its own, with all the normal city things going on, as we were to find out. We met up in one of the many bars, and straight away we were approached by the ladies of the night (and day, bless 'em). Once they had sussed out we were English (although most thought we were Australian, for some reason) the first one approached our table. "DO YOU WANT SEX?" she hollered at the top of her voice. "No," I said, "I did not," and once the rest of the lads had refused her offer, she turned away on her six-inch heels and tottered off. Within a minute another was screaming for custom. This went on for about half an hour before they got the message, and eventually we were able to relax a little.

The show itself was remarkable for so many reasons, but I guess the most remarkable for me happened on the first morning. I had been to classes to learn a little colloquial

*Instructing the captain and vice-captain of the Russian volleyball team on rig mechanics.*

Russian before I left. I hate the fact that most Brits expect everyone to speak English when they go abroad. I was keen to try out my new-found skills (cough, cough) and eventually found a T-shirt on a stand that I wanted to buy, and asked the guy how much it was, in Russian of course. He replied in English, and said that he was amazed and honoured to see me in his country, and would I do him a favour and sign his book. Of course I would, but I had no idea he and his friends would drive 1,200 kilometres to get those books! The following morning I signed their copies of my 2007 book, *Tackling Carp*. Now that was just as about as humbling as it gets. Even the captain and vice-captain of the Russian volleyball team came to visit, simply to get a picture with me. It was the most fantastic trip. However, looking at their cold and miserable weather reminded me of what I had endured that winter, and I only hoped it would have improved by the time I got home.

On the flight back I decided I wanted to be fishing for some bigger fish, but there was one issue I was determined to get my head around. The Southlake at Reading was a little thorn in my side, because I just couldn't understand why I hadn't caught one of the 30-pounders that lived there. It would be factored into proceedings over the coming months, but first up was a visit to one of the syndicate waters. The problem was that the easterly air flow was still making life very difficult indeed, and my first mission after the Russian trip was cut short by the lake freezing yet again. Undeterred, I set off the following Monday, and after finding a fairly deep channel in the relatively shallow lake, I scattered maybe a hundred boilies over the three hookbaits that had come to rest in it. For the first time in a very long while I actually felt like I was fishing effectively, but only the carp could confirm my thoughts, of course. I was probably fishing for at least six fish in excess of 40lb, and a good head of 30-pounders too, so you will understand why my heart was in my mouth when I got a jittery take a few hours later.

*An historic Tight Lines segment was filmed at Hollybush Lakes.*

As soon as the rod was in my hand I could tell it was one of the stockies, and soon enough a mid-double common was in the net. Whilst I sorted him out I had another bite and landed another stockie of similar size. Okay, they weren't big fish in the scheme of things, but as I felt like I was just about to freeze to death, it wasn't a bad start to proceedings. I landed a few more fish before I headed for home, and on the journey I was once again asked by Mick Brais at *Tight Lines* if I could do a little fishing segment for the programme. Bearing in mind that carp-fishing historian Chris Ball would be in the studio, I reckoned I had the perfect place to go. It was a complex of lakes, five in all, where I first cast out a Hair Rig in anger back in the '80s. It also contained a lake that had caught the interest of the entire Redmire syndicate way back in 1974, when a fellow by the name of Dennis Langley landed a 37lb 8oz mirror there, the biggest carp reported in this country that year. So, with national history and a little history of my own on my mind, I was off to Hollybush Lakes about a mile from my house... perfect!

My focus of attention was Pit Four, although as I wasn't sure I could get a bite from there, I did make sure to look at Pit 3 (now called Station Lake) which was probably my best chance of getting a fish for the camera. The weather was appalling, once again, but I landed a few fish from Pit 3 the night before the cameras arrived, so at least I had one to hold up and show the audience. The angling itself was a total waste of time on the day, but it did make a brilliant segment for the programme; great carp-fishing history. I made the decision to go to the Southlake the following week and see if I could get a little closer to landing a 30 from there. Having spoken to a mate of mine up that way, and listening to him telling me nothing of note had been landed from the lake since November, I probably wasn't that excited. However, in my own inimitable way, I convinced myself I was going to get a bite, and off I went. When I went for a look around I came across one of the two anglers on the

*Soon enough I was sorting out a dark mirror of 27lb 4oz.*

lake, and remarkably he had a fish in his landing net. My timing, I surmised, was perfect. That 26lb mirror provided me with all the encouragement I needed, and I bade him farewell and carried on with my travels. I had spotted a couple of tench roll in and around the buoys on the other side of the lake, and it was there that I eventually set up. The problem with this incredibly shallow lake were the tufties and coots. They really were a nightmare, and to that end I did something I very rarely do; I fished three single hookbaits. In short order three

Hi-Viz Pineapple pop-ups came to rest on three firm spots I had found in the silt. Apart from the odd pickup from the birds all was quiet, and I was soon knocking out the Zs. That was until around 5.00 a.m. when one of the rods ripped into life. The fight was unspectacular, and stupidly I had left my wellies in the van. This meant I had to wade out barefooted to land the little blighter. A very painful experience I can tell you! Once in the net though, I started to warm up as I peered down on an awesome, dark linear. At 24lb 1oz he made the most arresting sight as I held him up for a fellow angler to photograph. It was a great start for sure. It got even better the following night, when again I had to wade out in my bare feet. How I forgot to get my boots from the van I have no idea, but I wasn't about to let a bit of frostbite get in the way of proceedings. The fight wasn't really a fight at all, and soon enough I was sorting out a dark chestnut-flanked mirror of 27lb 4oz. My two-night visit had ticked all the right boxes, and just maybe I was a session closer to my ultimate goal.

Whatever I wanted to do at Reading, it was going to have to wait, because as the weather improved, albeit very slowly, I had a whole host of filming tasks to take care of. Interestingly, the photographer who had helped out on the Southlake asked me a very interesting question, after listening to me talking about the camera work coming up. "Do you get fed up with it all, not being able to fish for targets and not catching those targets because of your work?" There can be little doubt that it sometimes gets in the way of what I want to achieve on a personal level, but it is what I signed up for. I get as much pleasure doing stuff and catching for the cameras, as I do achieving my individual goals. That may sound a little crazy, but the pressure of a camera can be very daunting, and is a huge challenge in itself. Life, for me, is all about overcoming hurdles, dealing with different situations, and stretching the boundaries. Yes, I want to catch big, elusive carp, but spending all my time doing that would certainly drive me round the bend. Carp fishing offers a host of adventures, all of which have to be approached in certain ways and dealt with differently. It is the eclectic nature of what's available that drives me on. I want to experience it all then, at the very least, I can comment with reasonable authority on most subjects.

During the course of the winter, Fox had been putting a DVD together about the new Edges range of end tackle, and Scott Day and I were going to fish together, and do the links between the segments. Harry Charrington also told me it wasn't important for me to catch, so I was looking forward to a mellow session in good company, although that's not to say I wasn't going to try to get a bite, of course! The weather was still pants, but I arrived before the guys, got myself set up, and chose where I did because I saw a couple of carp show, bless 'em. However, it wasn't until the following day that I got myself a bite. A cracking little mirror made the trip worthwhile and we completed the filming, but not before Scott bagged himself a cracker of 31lb 12oz. This just goes to show that we think we know what we are talking about when it comes to the weather, but in reality we know bugger all.

The following week was all about getting some short-form filming done for *Fishing.TV*. Whilst it may have been nice to catch one that session, I didn't, not whilst John the cameraman was there anyway. But he hadn't been gone more than an hour when I landed two stockies. Bites didn't seem to be the problem at that time, but the size of the fish was, and on the drive home I decided that I was going to do something about it. It is amazing what can be achieved when you put your mind to it. So the following week I eventually kicked 2013 into high gear.

Just to put a little more sparkle on events, I tarted up my rods and loaded new line onto my reels. A few hooklinks were tied up, and once I had loaded the air-dry bags I was positively salivating at the thought of an early-morning start. I left so early that the roads were all but deserted, and arrived well before first light. Low pressure and clouds had been forecast, and for the first time in ages the day felt reasonably warm. In fact it was positively tropical by the

*Scot bagged himself a cracker of 31lb 12oz.*

time I had completed my first lap. There had been a couple of fish out at the weekend, and it wasn't hard to see why when I arrived at the shallow end of the 12-acre lake. The wind was pumping in there, and in only a few minutes I saw a couple of big fish boom out in the waves, so it didn't take long to barrow my gear round. Before I cast out I baited a few margin areas which I could check the following day, and eventually set three traps along an island margin at about 80 yards. I baited with 4 kilos of my boilies, and with a smug grin on my face, I once again settled down to wait. About two hours later one of the rods bleeped and heaved over. It was another small stock fish, and another followed him 30 minutes later. What the hell did I have to do to get myself a bigger one? The answer was simply to be patient, and an hour later I got exactly what I was craving. The bite again was just a couple of bleeps – I couldn't let them have line fishing that close to the island – and as the rod arched over in the rests I picked it up. From the off it was obviously a better fish, which I probably played far too carefully, but after a while I was leading the carp into the outstretched net. Now that's what I was taking about! At 33lb 12oz I was over the moon, and placed her in a retainer whilst I sorted out and recast the rod. I got my camera set up, and with the pictures done, it was celebratory brew time. As I sipped it one of the other rods bleeped and heaved over, too. Again, the fish plodded around steadily; this was another good one, and once it was in the net I was sure it was a 30. I repeated the same well-practised procedure and recorded a weight of 30lb 12oz. Now we were cooking on gas! It could have stopped right there and then for all I cared, but things were going to get even better. It is amazing how just a couple of bites can change everything. Winter was forgotten in a heartbeat; spring had arrived and I was well and truly making hay.

A 27lb mirror just as it got dark finished the action for the day, and as I settled down for the night I smiled myself to sleep. The morning was quiet, too, with only a small stockie

***I found myself connected to a bit of an animal.***

finding the bottom of my net. However, later that afternoon I found myself connected to an absolute animal. The battle was breathtaking, and a little scary at times, but a large slice of patience helped me lead a big old mirror into the net. With her scattered scales and massive rounded tail, she looked absolutely perfect, and at 36lb 5oz that is exactly what she was. I settled down with a brew after freshening up the spots with some more bait, and was surprised to play and land a 27lb mirror an hour later. The fish had woken up for sure, and indeed everything seemed to be active; it really was the first day of spring. As I watched the water in the morning I landed yet another 27lb mirror, and as I played it I saw a fish roll over the margin spot to my left. As soon as I had a few pictures of the fish, I was off with a couple of rods to see if I could get one from the prebaited spot right in the edge. What happened next was amazing . I had only just lowered the second rod onto the spot, when the first was away, and as I picked up that rod the other one decided to join in the fun. It took some doing but eventually, after much cussing and swearing, I had a low-double and a 26lb 4oz mirror in the net. I chuckled as I made my way back to my swim; this was carp angling at its very best. The night was quiet, but as dawn approached I was playing another fish, a long 22lb mirror, and as it slipped into the mesh one of the other rods bleeped for my attention. This fish took my breath away, and whilst I have no idea how long we fought for, it seemed a painfully long time before she gave me a chance to net her. She was a beautifully-proportioned fish of 34lb 3oz. This was the last action of the trip, but what a session it had been: four 30s and a few 20s, too. The winter was definitely over, and it had been the worst I had ever known. However, one thing was for sure, there could be no doubting that it is the bad times that make the good times good!

*The stalking was amazing.*

*She was a beautifully-proportioned fish of 34lb 3oz.*

# Chapter Fourteen
## No More Looking Back

*The Mangrove was a very special place.*

I often wonder just how much (along with a few other issues) conditions play a part in our fishing. I only say that because I can think of countless occasions when I have landed a carp or two, at a time when the resident 'experts' say I shouldn't. It's a bit like rig and bait talk I suppose. The author will tell the reader that he landed his fish because he had changed from a Size 6 hook to a Size seven, or the bite came because he used a dumbbell-shaped hookbait as opposed to a normal round one, something I have always found to be the biggest load of horseshit known to man! I have spent much of my carp-fishing life using two rigs I am most confident in, along with my boilie approach, to catch my carp. Without all that alternative silliness running amok in my brain, I can concentrate on the most important aspect of carp fishing, finding the right place to put the bait. I had all those thoughts racing around in my head as I set out early one dismal morning in May. I had believed that spring was finally in the air, but in truth I think it had taken a break, and was simply waiting for summer to begin. I arrived at the syndicate lake again, and as I opened the car door, I wished I had packed some more cold-weather clothing; it was bloody freezing! However, I was buoyed by the previous week's results and although I could see two bivvies set up on the lake, neither of them were anywhere near the area I had fished a few days before. Now that was handy. The first person I got to was just packing up. Having had nothing he blamed the weather, along with a whole host of things that, as far as I could tell, had nothing to do with blanking. Why can't people blame themselves sometimes? After all, I suspect that in 95% of 'not catching events' it is the angler who got it all around his neck, not the tackle he is using. The other bivvy occupant had also blanked, which I found a little odd. The weekend had produced three fish, which was pretty good for that lake; surely the carp had switched on, regardless of the weather?

I sat and watched, then nearly burst into flames when two big mirrors boomed out in the swim I had occupied the week before. Strangely, one of the anglers told me that no one had been in that plot because of the fish I had landed from there. It was obviously where they wanted to be, and half an hour later I had my loaded barrow parked at the back of the swim once again. Much the same as the week before, I positioned three rods, all armed with stiff link pop-ups (no change there then), a rod length away from the island margin, and spread 4 kilos of 10 and 15mm Hybrid over them (no change there, either). The day was quiet, but as the sun disappeared behind the trees I landed my first fish, which was a truly handsome 14lb fully-scaled. It wasn't until first light that I was once again staring up at a very bent rod. This fish was trying to rip my arms from my body, and nothing I did made any difference. But just as I thought it would never end, it simply gave up and allowed me to reel it quickly into the net. The extremely dark mirror spun the scales round to 31lb. The second night produced a couple more doubles, and I packed up happy with my results, and also knowing I wouldn't be back for a very long time. I really needed to find me a carp to fish for, but the conversation I had on the way home kind of told me that it would be a while before that was ever going to happen. It was John Dunford again from *Fishing.TV* and we discussed the third series of *Chilly on Carp*. I was determined, once again, to fish waters that I had never fished, or even seen before. To that end I had arranged for us to visit a holiday lake in Devon, and to fish The Mangrove in Shropshire. The icing on the cake, however, was that while I was at The Mangrove I would carry out an in-depth interview with my friend, Tim Paisley. I just hadn't realised how quickly this was going to happen, and the next couple of weeks were a bit ball-busting to say the least!

As I rang off from John I started to think, most of all about the weather, because it looked as if spring had definitely been cancelled. That said, I could not have imagined just how well the filming would go. First port of call was a place called Stenhill Fishery in Devon, 15 miles north of Exeter. I had never heard of the place, but thankfully Fox's specialist angling consultant, Julian Chigley, had. He arranged for me and John to be on the water for a couple

*A dark 31lb mirror.*

of days to do the *Chilly on Carp* programmes. I had no idea what to expect, but as I pulled into the lake the following week, I was greeted by the guy who had hired the place that weekend playing and landing a 19lb linear. Now this was looking good. I met up with Brian Cox, who, along with wife Caroline, owns the fishery. It was run as a holiday destination, having all the comforts of home, and as it wasn't a syndicate or day-ticket water, I would have the place to myself. Nice! The first thing I wanted to do was have a wander around, which of course John filmed. However, I took along my stalking gear, which happened to include a rod armed with my favourite centrepin reel. With around a hundred fish in the 1½-acre lake, I reckoned they wouldn't be too hard to find, which they weren't. The problem was getting them to feed, and that took quite a bit of work. They showed a little interest in the first couple of areas I baited, but I am impatient and was sure I could find somewhere to get a quicker bite. Eventually, I lowered one of my normal PVA bags of 10 and 15mm boilies onto my third spot. A 30lb common was the first to show a bit of interest, but it wasn't until a few of his buddies arrived that things got interesting. The water got so cloudy that in the end all I could see were the tail patterns of the carp as they fed. I was confident of a bite, but I still nearly jumped out of my skin when the rod heaved round and the 'pin' sang her tune. The fight was spectacular, but soon enough the first carp of the programme lay on my mat. At just over 20lb she made the perfect start, and a little later I was setting up at the other end of the lake in the slightly deeper water. All three rods were fished in the margins, which involved me having to walk around the bank to my right with two of them to place them accurately. By nightfall I had landed four more carp, topped by the most handsome 26lb 10oz scattered linear. He was the biggest fish of the trip, and meant the programme was coming together nicely. A big apple-slice-scaled mirror arrived early in the morning, and it was then that Brian told me about the

*The fight was spectacular on my centrepin.*

*A very handsome 26lb 10oz linear.*

*Chilling at the Mangrove, a lake that inspired me.*

fish being the Leney strain of carp. This trip was just getting better and better! I spent the following day stalking and casting at showing fish, which resulted in another load of scaly carp, and we finally finished off the filming that evening after landing 14 fish in just 36 hours.

John and I were on fire, and when you are on a roll you just have to ride with it. The Mangrove was our next destination, but I was still very unsure if we could do a *Chilly on Carp*, and get an interview with Tim done, whilst ensuring we did justice to both. There was also the fact that I would be fishing a lake I had read so much about over the years, stories that at times had driven me to greater things. By way of a recce, I decided to go up on the Sunday and get a feel for what was going on. Tim recommended I fish either the Fallen Tree or the Lightning Tree swims, from what he had seen there the week before. It was all the encouragement I needed, and as quickly as I could, I loaded up a boat and went on my way to Lightning Tree. I had read and heard people talk about the place, and a few thing of interest were: they only feed in the silt; hemp and small baits are the way forward and bottom baits are the only way to get bites. Really? There was no way I was going to do anything different because the way I fish has worked everywhere I have been, and I could see no reason why it wouldn't work there. I did spend an hour or so having a cast around with a marker, finding several areas of very firm bottom, along with a large mussel bed, the latter of which demanded a couple of my stiff link pop-ups, and around 3 kilos of boilies, of course. The other two rods were fished left and right on the edge of the vast lily beds that abounded around the swim. It all looked the nuts, and as I excitedly settled down for the night, I couldn't help remembering Leney's influence on this historic water. I woke early the next morning wondering if I had got my side of the equation right, but whilst I fretted one of the rods on the heavily baited mussel bed roared into life. The fish chugged around for a minute or two before I lifted the mesh around

*This Mangrove mirror of 28lb 6oz made all the effort worthwhile.*

*Sorting out the interview with Tim.*

my first Mangrove carp, a 28lb 2oz common. I was over the moon, and after securing her in a retainer, I rang John. We had a carp with which to open the programme! That said, things went very quiet, and it wasn't until the following evening that it started to liven up again. I was in a mood with the weather as it had stopped us doing our interview with Tim, but my smile returned when I landed a 16lb 5oz mirror just as darkness was falling. A 23lb mirror in the morning broadened that smile still further, and as my mood brightened so did the weather, which meant we could get round to see Tim, and interview him. The word 'legend' is so overused these days, but there was no doubt in my mind that I was talking to one that day.

And then it was back to the fishing. I had baited the spots before we went over to Tim, so all I had to do was cast out. There they stayed until the early morning when the heavily baited area produced another bite. The fight wasn't overly-exciting, but as I gazed down on the contents of my landing net a few minutes later, I knew the programme was a good 'un. The stunning mirror weighed 28lb 6oz, but it was the way the fish looked that made all the effort so worthwhile. Tim had landed a couple of fish while we were there to 27lb and it rounded the mission off nicely; I really couldn't have asked for more.

I drove home full of myself. Yet again my tactics had worked, but I couldn't help wondering why people follow fashion rather than their own instincts. Strange. My fishing was going so well that I was kind of forgetting about the most important thing in my life, which was Lynn. I knew all was not well when I got home, as it so often isn't for her, and right there and then I decided I needed to be at home before she yet again ended up in hospital. Unbelievably, she is the first to insist that I go fishing because she doesn't want her illness to get in the way of the things I want to do. Be that as it may, I very often have to show some discipline, and this was one such occasion. So, amid a lot of complaining from Lynn that I needed to go fishing, I settled down to try to be domesticated for a few days, something I was never put on this earth to be, if I'm being truthful! By the Monday I think she could see that my being home for a few more days wasn't quite what the doctor ordered, and I reluctantly (honestly) agreed to go if I could find somewhere close to home to fish. I eventually spoke to a guy called Nick, who had bought Sandhurst Lake from CEMEX, and he sorted me out with the combination. Knowing how busy the lake can be, I was surprised to see so few cars in either of the car parks. From memory I think there were two anglers on the lake, and one of them was fishing for bream, of all things. This meant that I could take my time, which I didn't actually need because the six fish I saw show were all about 70 yards in front of the Car Park Swim. I normally hate to fish the convenient areas, but if that was where they were, then that was where I was fishing. I got all three rods baited, and in the clips, ready to be cast to a big clear area at around 75 yards. All that was left to do was bait up, and I wondered if I may just have overdone it with 7 kilos of my boilie concoction. With everything sorted, I positioned the hookbaits and sat down for a brew. I have written it before, I know, but I have never understood this 'little bit of bait and nick a bite' thingy that people go on about, much preferring to put a lot of bait in and nick a lot of bites. Consequently, 10 minutes after finishing my brew I was playing my first carp... fancy that, eh? The 16lb mirror was a great start, and a little later I landed a cracking mirror of 28lb. Things didn't really slow down, and I ended the session with 12 fish after 20 hours of fishing, and 10kg of bait. It is a truly remarkable lake, but unfortunately I have never been back. That being said, I had eventually found somewhere I wanted to be. In a lake called the Quarry, run by my old buddy Ben Lofting, lived the most spectacular mid-40lb common called Ray, and I decided I wanted to catch him.

Monday came and, with Ray in mind, I loaded my gear and set off for Essex. A couple of hours later I was opening the gate to the fishery. There were a few anglers on, as expected, and I spent a while just soaking up the atmosphere and having a good look around. The

*Sandhurst is a remarkable lake that holds some great memories for me.*

first person I spoke to had landed a 31lb linear in the night, but apart from that, all was quiet. I already had a good idea where I wanted to set up, but made sure I investigated all areas of the lake. The main thing was I felt comfortable there, and that would do for me. I had been told that the majority of the fishing, apart from the shallows, was done around the two islands. I wanted to do completely the opposite, as usual, and the carp I had seen showing, and sending up enormous sheets of bubbles, were 50 yards in front of a corner swim. A clear strip in the weed at that range was soon accommodating my three stiff link pop-ups, along with 5 kilos of 10 and 15mm Hybrid boilies. A couple of tench made things a little uncomfortable in the early evening, but at 4.00 a.m. I was playing my first Quarry carp, and what a battle it was too. Along with a large ball of weed I scooped up my prize, an incredibly long and handsome mirror of 29lb 1oz. What a way to start the campaign! I quickly recast that rod and set about removing some of the floating weed from my line. As I did so, the recast rod burst into life once again. Again the weed was a problem, but I was soon sorting out another mirror of 22lb 7oz. I liked it there, no doubt about that. I moved into the shallows later that day, mainly because the carp seemed to have moved away from me. No point in fishing for carp if there are no carp there to be caught. To be honest the carp looked as if they may spawn, but I did land mirrors of 16 and 23lb before the urge got the better of them. As they thrashed the water to a foam in the annual sexfest I left them to it. It would be a couple of weeks before I could get back; Ben would let his carp get over their spawning before angling would be allowed again. This is something all fishery owners should do, if they want their carp to have a long, healthy life, of course.

Just up the road from Lynn and me are a family who have in many ways restored my faith in humanity. Twenty-year-old (well he was at the time) Stuart Dawes and his brothers, along

*I couldn't think of a better way to start my Quarry campaign.*

*My neighbour Cameron and his first 20lb common.*

*At 23lb 4oz Stuart was suitably blown away.*

with mum Tracy, seem to be the only people in this area who are not driven by hatred or jealousy, and Stuart and his brother, Cameron, had recently got into carp fishing. Indeed, at a charity event Stuart landed his personal best of 19lb 8oz. Work and family keep him from the bank most of the time, but I asked him if he would like to come with me to have a look at a couple of local lakes that had recently been connected to create one water. I had spoken to fishery manager, Stu McDermott, and he agreed to allow him in. We made our way to Hollybush Lakes at Farnborough, and, interestingly, one of the lakes was where I landed my first 20 some 30 years before. We drove around in Stu's 4x4 and eventually settled on an area to fish. The bubbling was incredible, and I allowed Stuart first dibs on which swim to fish. He went where there was most activity, and soon enough had a couple of rods in the area armed with a big PVA bag of Hybrid boilies. I did the same some way down to his right. Nothing happened for a couple of hours, so Stuart came for a brew, and just as he arrived one of my rods chirped into life. From the off it was obviously not one of the stock fish, and it plodded around for ages. Stu, the fishery manager, had noticed the action and came round to man the net, which soon contained a common that we all thought was over 30lb. However, there was no time to celebrate because one of Stuart's rods called for his attention. Leaving my fish in the net I went up to offer my advice, but he didn't need it, even though the fish was fighting like a lunatic. It was with immense pride that, on looking in the net, we saw that he had landed his first 20-pounder! Ironically, he had landed it only feet from where I had landed my first 20 all those years ago. At 23lb 4oz he was suitably blown away, as I was when my common spun the scales round to 31lb 7oz. I am sure it will be a day that he will never forget; I know I never will.

It was back to the Quarry the following week, and I was truly excited about returning. It was the first day we were allowed to fish after the spawning, and I was surprised to find

**Nineteen at 33lb 2oz.**

no cars or anglers anywhere. I took my time and, once again, discovered carp in the same swim as the last time I was there. All that was left to do was set up in exactly the same way as before and, the same as before, the tench were a bit of a pain. They stopped during the dark hours, but I must admit to being a little surprised at not getting a carp. I had seen a few fish showing right over the other side of the lake, and was just in the throes of packing my gear when one of the bobbins pulled up tight and the buzzer howled. I had to coax it from the weed, and then it kited at speed to my right. It was impossible to stop it getting beyond a fallen tree, and I had to take to the boat once my life jacket was on. After that it was all over bar the shouting. I scooped up my fish and returned to shore, where one of the locals, Chris, gave me a hand. It was a fish called Nineteen; why I have no idea, and weighing 33lb 2oz she confirmed I had made the right choice about going to this water. Unfortunately, it would be a long time before I could get back.

The need to be near home was paramount once again. I would never have achieved many of the things in my life if it hadn't been for Lynn, and the very least I can do is be on hand when she needs me most. She also needed a whole host of hospital visits for tests, and monitoring, and to that end I turned back to Hollybush for a week or two. I also have moments in my life where I get so sidetracked by the things I do, that I forget some things need to be sorted before it gets too messed up! Consequently, I fried my brain with some paperwork which Lynn normally has to sort out, bless her! With that at an end, I packed my gear and headed off to Hollybush just as soon as I was able. The carp were so obvious it wasn't hard to find them at all, and as two other guys were just turning up I quickly got set up in the area of most activity. It was supposed to be a simple case of positioning two bottom bait rigs with a PVA bag of boilies in each area, but as the bankside vegetation had been completely stripped in

*I think I was more knackered than this 33lb mirror.*

the revamp, it took a long time to do it with any success. I must have done something right, because thirty seconds later the rod fished down the left margin arched over, and the fight began. Once on the surface I could see it was a big common, but it was the same one I had landed the first time I fished there. I already had some good shots, so sent her quickly on her way. I'm never happy with recaptures, but had to admit it was a great start to proceedings. With Lynn's illness ever on my mind, it was a fantastic way to spend a day or two, and I even landed a couple of fish for a magazine feature. But once I was on my own, and packing up, I received one last bite. It has often been written that a particular battle was the hardest fight the angler had ever experienced, and this was one of those. Nothing I did made a hoot of difference for ages, and the only way I could get near it was to keep walking down the bank with the net. Of course the pressure finally paid off, but I think I was far more knackered than the 33lb, long and handsome mirror, which eventually found its way into my net.

A few days with Lynn recharged her batteries, as well as mine, and then I was off to the Carping4Heroes event. It had been thirteen years since I had left the Army, and I had done quite a bit to support Help for Heroes, but this was the first time I would be spending time with a load of military men in ages. Simon Bangert heroically organised the event, and I had a wonderful, if not occasionally very wobbly, time. It also gave me a chance to speak in detail to many who had served in Afghanistan. It certainly opened my eyes, and our country will never be able to do enough for these brave men and women. My respect and gratitude will always be with you all.

I was desperate to get back to the Quarry, but I had to bite the bullet for a little longer. Lynn wanted me to go to Essex, but I wasn't sure and made arrangements to go back to Hollybush for a 24-hour session – and that turned into a sleepless bout of mayhem. The weed was incredible on one side of the lake, but that was where the fish wanted to be, of course. In the end I found an area that wasn't too bad, and one from which I thought I could land a fish safely, so, with a huge digger machine for company, I got a couple of rods in position and a scattering of my boilies over the top. I was just wondering what effect all the noise the digger was causing would have on the fishing when one of the bobbins pulled up tight. 'Not a lot' was the obvious answer to that question as I tried to bully the carp from the weed. With several spectators, including the digger driver, I managed to net my prize, all 30lb 4oz of her. The bait, tackle and tactics were working well. Once the area was topped up again, I shared a brew with Stu, the fishery manager. After he had gone I was in action again with a 21lb common and a high-double mirror. I expected the night to be busy, but it wasn't, apart from a million liners, which left me feeling absolutely shattered by morning. I had tried everything, including Zigs and floaters. As the liners stopped at first light, I tried to get my head down, but the carp weren't having any of that, either. Stunning mirrors of 21, 25 and 26lb made sure I went home in desperate need of sleep, and I couldn't have been happier about that if I tried.

The weather had been stiflingly hot, and as the heatwave continued, I was once again back on the trail of Ray, the Quarry's big common. The lake was very quiet when I arrived, with only one angler in residence. He was about a mile from the nearest carp, as they were all up in the shallow arm, and it didn't take too long to find an opportunity. A small clearing in the marginal weed was baited with about a kilo of the 10 and 15mm boilie mixture, and I crept back a long way to prepare a rod. The rig was the same bottom bait setup I use at whatever range, and once I had baited it with a small PVA bag of free offerings I moved back into position. I watched several fish, some well in excess of 30lb, visit the spot and eventually they gave me a window of opportunity. I lowered the rig down no more than a rod length from the bank, and was just about to lay the rod down when the second-biggest fish cruised round the weed and tilted his head towards the trap. As he moved, I watched fascinated as the bag started to melt, and no sooner had it done so than the fish hoovered up the whole lot. The line tightened, I picked up the rod and quite literally pulled the fish into my net. It took no longer to do that than it has taken me to write those two sentences. The problem was she was an ancient fish, and I had no wish to remove her from the water, if possible. I recruited the guy farther down the lake and as I lifted her from the net we got a couple of pictures. For the record she went by the name of Shoulders, weighing 34lb 10oz, and I worried about that fish probably more than any other I have ever caught. She still lives to this day, and my mate Laney landed her in January 2016 at well over 40lb, and it was probably the same age as him, too! It was just nice to know she was okay. As well as she was, I had been told that Ray the common had died, the first target I had had for a long time. I was gutted, and this really ended my time at the Quarry. It was, and still is, a fantastic lake, run as a day-ticket water now, but I couldn't see myself going back any time soon.

With the summer raging on I had a fair number of commitments to attend to, and the first of those was a Fox weekender at Cottington Lakes near Deal in Kent. It was somewhere I had been thinking about fishing, and I used the weekend as a bit of a recce. We caught some carp, too, and had a great time. Then it was back to Hollybush, before I attended the next weekender that was to be held on the Isle of Wight. The Hollybush session was as productive as ever, but one incident reminded me just how lucky I can be at times. I had landed a few fish and was sharing a brew with Stu McDermott once again, when he told me about a big leather that had been spotted cruising around, but as yet hadn't been caught. As he stood to leave I told him I would inform him just how big it was by morning.

The night was punctuated with several fish up to 24lb, and as the sun appeared over the trees I hooked a bit of an animal. On and on we battled until my perseverance paid off

*She went by the name of Shoulders and weighed 34lb 10oz.*

and I led a nice fish into the net. As I gazed down I couldn't help wondering where all the scales had gone! That would be the leather, then! At 28lb 2oz he may not have been as big as everyone expected, but he made a great sight as I held him up for the camera; a fantastic end to the session. It was back to making a complete wreck of the paperwork at home, and generally trying to catch up with life once again. Lynn, doctors and hospitals kept me busy, and by way of a change for my wife one day, I decided to take Lynn to the Station Lake at Hollybush. It was a beautiful day, but I have to admit that I knew I had a bit of a problem as soon as I got out of the van. I tried not to look at the fish sunning themselves all over the lake, and concentrated on helping Lynn walk around the water's edge. After about 50 yards she calmly asked why I wasn't going to fish for them, at which point all reason went out of the window. I left my poor wife soaking up the rays and went back for my surface gear. Selfish, I know, but needs must and all that, eh? I scattered some mixers around a weedbed, and within minutes they were taking them. I fished away from the weed for safety reasons, and unbelievably a nice fish peeled away from the pack, zeroed in on my hookbait and took it. Fortunately the carp didn't do too much and soon enough I was looking down on a quite spectacular mirror. At 20lb 8oz she made a fine result for 20 minutes of my time, and, with Lynn very impressed with my carp-catching prowess, we were soon home for tea and tiffin!

I was away again that weekend to Rookley Country Park on the Isle of Wight for the next Fox weekender, and again it was somewhere I had been thinking about for some winter fishing. It really was a great place to spend a little time, and we even caught some carp. I landed two, and the first came in front of a huge gallery of people, most of whom had absolutely no interest in fishing at all. Whatever the case, many remarked on how well the fish was treated on the bank, and at 29lb 2oz it was the biggest fish

**Garfield was introduced to the crowd at Rookley.**

any of them had ever seen. The funniest thing, though, was when they were told it had a name. Garfield was introduced to the crowd, who clapped appreciatively as he swam off back to his home. An early-morning mirror of 28lb completed my Isle of Wight adventure. I gazed over the Solent on the return journey and I couldn't help thinking just how much fun I was having of late, and there still wasn't a target fish in sight.

Next up was a stalking segment for the Fox *Edges* DVD. Harry Charrington suggested Cottington, and I could find no reason to disagree with his decision. I went down the day before he was due to arrive, and in time-honoured tradition I think I caught all the carp I possibly could before Harry got there. I just can't help myself; if they are there to catch then I just have to have a go. We were doing the filming on Christine Lake, and I baited a couple of spots in the edge, fishing at night on an open-water spot with plenty of boilies. By early evening I had landed four fish, three of which were over 20lb. A couple of doubles in the night kept things interesting, but a bite at first light was the icing on the cake. In the shallow water the fight was very spectacular, and once the fish was in the net the sight of it was no different. The 29lb 3oz linear was just about as good as it could get, but Harry was nowhere to be seen. On his arrival the fishing decided to get rock hard, but perseverance finally won the day; I stalked a low-twenty from the edge and my job was done. That being said, it wouldn't be the last time I would visit this amazing little complex of lakes.

Whilst I didn't have a target in mind, I had set myself a couple of 'things to do'. One was at Hollybush, and revolved around a fish of around 37-38lb that I simply wanted to catch. And then, of course, there was the Southlake at Reading and the longed for 30-pounder from there. It may surprise some of you that I would put a fish of that size at the top of my hit-list, but my fishing isn't all about the size of the fish I am fishing for. Hollybush had fish swimming in it

*My biggest Southlake mirror so far at 28lb 5oz.*

that were older than me, and I don't think size comes into that particular equation at all. They are history and I want to catch them. The Southlake also contained some spectacular scaly carp, and as much as a 30 would be nice, it wasn't the be-all and end-all... thank goodness. Again, let's be frank here, even if you are driven by 'big is best', I reckon you are in the wrong game if you didn't want to catch such fish. In the end, I decided that if Lynn needed me near to home then I would be fishing at Hollybush, and if she was well enough then I would head off to Reading. It seemed like a plan, and as an ex-soldier it helped me to organise my life. With Lynn not doing too badly I made a decision it would be the Southlake for the time being.

The next phase of my carp-fishing journey should have been doomed from the very start, when I narrowly missed a black cat at the end of the road (although, in all honesty, I wish I had mowed the little blighter down for shitting in my garden all the time!). And as I arrived in the swim I would fish, a single magpie cackled at me for an age. It got even more sinister when the spot I selected to fish my two rods was at thirteen wraps; spooky stuff. The weed was flourishing and the priority, after finding the fish first, of course, was to try to discover some holes in it. I didn't want to thrash the water to a foam, so thirteen wraps it would be. The lake was almost deserted, with only two anglers on, and once I had baited my traps I sat down to let events unfold. Liners all night kept me awake for most of it, but in the wee small hours a 23lb 6oz mirror, along with 23lb of weed, made me smile. No sooner I had repositioned the rod than it was away again, and this time the weed was even worse. It was just a case of pumping it all into the net with no fight at all, but when I cleared the weed the 25lb 10oz mirror reminded me why I was there. Stunning! The days were unbelievably quiet, probably due to the hot weather, but I was confident of more action as the night progressed. Mirrors of 21lb 5oz, 22lb 2oz and 25lb 10oz made it a great night, but once again I found myself wondering where all these 30-pounders were that everyone was talking about. I baited up mid-morning, and after having a detailed look around the lake, set the traps once more. It was 6.00 a.m. before I was called to arms, and a lively 19lb mirror lay in the net, then, just as I released him, the other rod melted off. Weed again hampered the carp's attempts to fight, but I did land my biggest Southlake fish so far, a 28lb 5oz mirror. I just needed to keep on keeping on.

It is sometimes so hard to make it all sound incredibly interesting, especially when your tactics are working and you can't change them, or do anything differently. And to that end I was once again in the same swim fishing in exactly the same way the following Monday. It really was déjà vu when the bobbins started dancing in the early hours. Once again the first fish had his fighting ability subdued by the weed, but the long 26lb 4oz mirror was most welcome. Then, what happened next will live with me for a long time. With both rods fishing the same spot, I was loath to recast and decided to leave the one rod to do the business. As I looked out, the most enormous bow wave erupted over my area, and a fraction of a second later the buzzer was struggling to keep up with the speed at which the line was leaving the spool. I have no idea how long we argued, but it felt like an age, and not once did the weed slow the fish down. I held on as best I could, and never for a second felt like I had any control until it lay in the folds of my net. One look at its tail indicated why the 28lb 12oz common took so long to subdue. I really thought she was the one, but coming up a little short of 30lb didn't concern me at all. The 20s kept coming over the next 24 hours, but the following week the lake started to pay me back for having such a ball. The tufties and coots became a freakin' nightmare, as did the tench, and when I throw in the fact that I was wiped out by a fish towing tackle five bloody times, you start to get the message. I still managed a smile on the way home though. You see, if carp fishing became too predictable, with carp being caught every time we went, then surely the lure and the challenge of it all would fade and die?

I spent the next two months bobbing around like a lonely turd, not really knowing what to do other than my technical articles and, of course, getting something to write about in my monthly diary. I did fish a match at Fishabil in France with my friend Tim Paisley, which included as much wine-tasting as it did fishing. However, whilst I was there, and in an effort to give my fishing a little more of an edge, I decided that I would return to Cottington, in Kent. Tiny little day-ticket waters aren't my idea of fun, I must admit, but I reasoned that it wouldn't be so busy in the winter. And as the big linear had been out at around 47lb, I decided that it was well worth investigating. It was early November, and I spent a very excited hour or so getting my gear ready to go one Sunday evening, ready for a death o'clock start the next morning. I find it hard to sleep when I am going to a new water, and embark on a new adventure, so to that end I was looking at the alarm clock when it sounded. The drive was a little over two hours, and whilst I was motoring down there I started to think. I had probably left it a little late to be starting a winter campaign, especially as my only experience of the place was the Fox event in the summer. That said, it was only a small water, so surely it couldn't be that hard to find? It wasn't, of course, but the small intimate nature of the place, although I didn't realise it at the time, was to be as close to claustrophobic as I had ever felt in the great outdoors.

I didn't know until I arrived, but my first visit coincided with the capture of the big linear. The lake was packed, and obviously my options were very limited. As I walked round I couldn't help wondering how the hell anything got caught from there. Eventually I settled into a swim into which a nice southerly breeze was blowing, and it was there that I was to meet the first of my 'new friends'. Now, I am quite sure that everything I came across in the immediate future wasn't done with any malice, but Sir Cast-a-lot in a swim over to my left rather spoiled my visit. The place was tiny and you are never far from the next person, and to that end the

*The huge-tailed common of 28lb 12oz.*

carp are under the most intense pressure. I would have thought, in those circumstances, that it would be best to set your traps and leave them be for at least a few hours. I couldn't believe that matey boy recast every 15 minutes or so, and his rigs were landing only a couple of yards from mine. I wasn't happy, but I couldn't say a word as any kind of reaction from me tends to get woefully taken out of context, so I sat there and tried to soak up the punishment.

Eventually darkness fell and mercifully he stopped casting. It got so quiet, in fact, that I got my first bite about an hour before dawn. Now there's a surprise! The little 12lb common was no monster, but at the very least the campaign had started with a capture. As quietly as possible I repositioned the rod, which was away again minutes later. Another small common found the bottom of my net, and then, of course, the casting started all over again. I reeled in and went for a walk, even bumping into the guy who had last landed the big one. I shook his hand and he showed me the pictures, which only strengthened my resolve just a little more. But that didn't last too long. Back at the 'casting arena', I discovered I had even more neighbours, and I could only assume they went by the names of Buzz Lightbulb and Timmy Mallet. The noise and night-time light display had to be seen to be believed. Again, I landed a small common in the early hours of the morning, but on the drive home I really had to ask myself if risking my sanity was worth the effort.

The following week I arrived and shared a brew with Billy in the shop at Cottington. He gave me a look at some pictures from when the lakes were extended, and I studied them. It was a bit of a revelation really, and I eventually ended up in a swim which was in the new piece of real-estate. Although it was on the back of the wind, I couldn't help feeling that if I was a carp that is where I would be, given what I had seen in those pictures in the shop. I swiftly got my gear sorted and soon had two rigs just beyond a shallow plateau at 25 yards. They were baited

**I looked down on a gloriously scaled mirror.**

with 2 kilos of Hybrid boilies, and at long last I felt like I was actually fishing effectively. I spent the rest of the day dreading someone would turn up and ruin my chances, but as darkness fell I was pretty much on my own in this area of the lake. A jittery take at midnight saw me dealing with another small common, which turned out to be one from last week, but at least I was in an area where carp were prepared to feed. The rain hammered down all night and had just abated when I got an absolute nose-bleeding bite at around 6.00 a.m. This was no small common for sure, and we settled down to a dour and prolonged scrap. She let me scoop her up at long last and I looked down on a gloriously scaly mirror. In an effort to get back in the ball game pronto, I unhooked her in the net and quickly recast the rod back on the spot. I sorted out the fish that spun the scales round to 32lb 10oz, which was just what I had wanted from this mission. It was raining so hard that I secured her in a retainer for a while until it stopped. The celebratory cuppa was only half finished when I was called back into action. The same rod was away again, and if anything was an even more explosive bite. The same dour fight ensued, but this one took even longer, and of course, she took every opportunity to show me her impressive scale-covered flanks. However, with shaking hands and a huge sigh of relief, I led her into the net. This one looked even bigger and, at 34lb 2oz, indeed she was. Soon enough she came to rest in a retainer alongside her friend, probably one of the most impressive braces of carp I have ever had the honour to land. I had one more 18lb mirror after that, and then the masses moved in. It really took the pleasure away, having several hookbaits no more than inches from my own. The spell had been broken once again, and apart from one more visit to Christine Lake over the river, that was the end of my time at Cottington.

Lynn had some bad news when I arrived home, in that we had been summoned to see one of her consultants at the hospital. I say 'bad news' because nothing good ever comes from

*At 34lb 2oz she was my biggest Cottington carp.*

these meetings. That was the next day, so by way of cheering things up, hopefully, Lynn and I got in a taxi and went out to Camberley just up the road from me. To be quite frank, I just needed her along to ensure I didn't faint when I was told the price of one of my moments of madness. You see, I own a Dodge truck, and had decided to have some cosmetic work done on her. The problem was, I never asked how much it would all cost... silly really. The truck looked magnificent, I was over the moon, but Lynn had to grab my arm to stop me toppling over when I was told what my moment of indulgence had cost me. My wife, however, had a fit of the giggles so at least I had cheered her up! Maybe I will grow up one day, but don't hold your breath. It got worse. I took Lynn to the hospital the next day, and whilst we drove in my van, there was the most horrible noise coming from it. I am no mechanic – what a bull elephant is to a china shop – and carried on regardless. That was until it gave up completely as the gearbox self-destructed which, to cut a long story short, cost me another £2,000. They say that bad things come in threes, and occasionally they do. Lynn was in a spot of bother again, bother that would require at least two operations a month, or two down the line. She really is the most remarkable person I have ever met, and as we left the hospital she said that I should go fishing as soon as I could. It is all to do with her state of mind, rather than mine, I believe. As long as life carries on as normally as it can, she seems to be able to handle anything. Hollybush it would be then, as it is only two minutes from my door, and for the next few days I started to bait an area. I worry that someone else will take advantage of my work of course, but it was winter now and I was sure my little ploy would go undetected. Soon enough, it was time to find out if they had responded to the copious amounts of bait I had given them. The spot was on the far side of a bank of very fresh weed that stretched between two islands 60 yards apart. By 10.00 a.m. the next Monday I had

*A cracking Hollybush common of 31lb 9oz.*

three stiff link pop-ups baited with several kilos of my Hybrid boilie mix in position, and all that was left to do was wait. And as I waited I couldn't help but reflect about my time on this historic complex. These were the first waters where I used a Hair Rig, back in the '80s. I landed my first 20 from there, and also my first 20 off the top; a very special place indeed.

All was quiet until around first light, when I received a short, sharp take. The fish had buried itself in the weed, but with a bit of effort I soon got it moving into the open water. It was fully fifteen minutes before I was able to lift the mesh around the angry fish, and at 27lb 2oz the torpedo-shaped mirror looked stunning in the early-morning winter sunshine. He came to rest in a retainer, and no sooner had I secured the rope than one of the other rods burst into life. It plodded around in the open water and my jaw almost hit the ground as a stunning common rolled over the net cord. At 31lb 9oz she completed a memorable brace as she came to rest next to her buddy. I landed several of the smaller stock fish after that, and baited up once again as I left, promising to return as often as I could to bait up before the next session. On the way out I spoke to Stu about the weight gains of the smaller fish, and of course, we both wondered what the weights of the older fish would be doing. In no small way, we were about to find out.

I had a chat and a brew with Stu and his dad at the front gate the following Monday morning, before heading off to the lake. Again we talked of the old originals, the biggest of which seemed to be the dinks that were stocked just after I terminated my time at the lakes in 1995. Stu remarked that their weights had stopped increasing quite a few years before because the water in the lakes had almost become stagnant. The new environment they were in now was sure to have a positive effect, and things could get very interesting indeed. As I left them Stu's dad, Mac, said it was about time I caught the big one, and then

*The historic Hollybush Lakes' first 40 at 40lb 10oz.*

we would know for sure. I told them I would certainly give it my best shot, and went off to set up. The night was quiet. I didn't hear a single fish and was up and about at 4.00 a.m. It was cold, very cold, and in the bright moonlight sky I gazed at the stars. Several cups of tea later, I was still gazing when one of the rods registered a stuttery take. Once the rod was in hand I was sure a stockie was responsible. All I could feel was a faint knocking and masses of weed slipping down the line. I concentrated on getting the whole thing moving towards me, that was until the weed fell off the line and my little stockie turned into an angry raging bull! Again and again it stripped yards of line from the reel in powerful, almost unstoppable, surges that left me breathless. It began to tire, of course, but it wasn't going to make life easy for me. Its deep rolls broke the surface time and time again, but inch by inch the obviously big fish made its way inexorably towards my outstretched net. And once it was in there I nearly swallowed my tongue when I saw the size of the beast.

Sorry to repeat myself here, but in 1974 Dennis Langley played and landed his first carp from Hollybush and the monster weighed 37lb 4oz, a capture that aroused the interest of many of the carp-fishing legends of the day. It was, in fact, the biggest carp reported that year and remained, until this fateful day, the biggest carp the complex had ever produced. Knowing what these lakes mean to me on a personal level, and what influence they have had on my life, made this capture so much more meaningful. I suppose someone had to catch it, I am just amazed that it was me. Stu and his dad came over to do the pictures and I held up for the camera the historic Hollybush Lakes' first 40 at 40lb 10oz, and in December, too. I cannot even begin to tell you how proud I am of that!

# Chapter Fifteen

## Mayhem

*I was still searching for a Southlake 30.*

The problem now, if I could call it that, was that I had landed the biggest fish in the lake. Not being one to callously rob others of their dreams, I couldn't help feeling it was time to move on, but where? Christmas was just around the corner, and Lynn was far from well, and expecting to be in hospital soon. I would sort out the fishing once Santa had been and allow the joy of a New Year to guide me. I was shocked, as I suspect the rest of the country was, at the flooding over the festive period. My heart went out to all those who were affected, and still does; it was truly shocking. It's times like this that remind me that fishing is supposed to be enjoyable, and an escape from the trials and tribulations of everyday life. As January came out of the starting blocks the weather wasn't actually getting any better, and more to the point, neither was my wife. Only days before we travelled to Plymouth to spend time with my parents, she had been operated on. But as normal, thinking of others before herself, she insisted that we should make the journey. I wasn't so sure, and once we were home a few days later she went to bed and didn't get out again until New Year's Eve. I must admit I was a little stir-crazy by then, and once she had spotted what a disaster the bungalow was, she gently reminded me that there was some fishing to be done.

I remembered to pack a few more bivvy pegs. Although I am a brolly user, I have never quite seen the point in living in a darkened tent with the door down, doing whatever one does with the door down, when you are outdoors trying to enjoy and appreciate the surroundings. There is also the fact that you can't see the water, and therefore respond to what the fish are telling you at times. Only my opinion of course! The conditions looked perfect as I nailed my Supa Brolly to the ground, and positioned all three rods in and around a new area of weed. I had been there just once to bait up, and it was there that I saw the only fish show. Things started off well and I landed three commons up to 16lb in the night. However, the following day things started to get a little pant-soiling, when the wind had increased to a frightening strength. The other problem, although I have no idea how they stayed attached to the water, were the bloody tufties. A flock of the villainous little cretins landed on the lake and in no time at all had found my baited area.

*I have to say it was one of the most emotional days I have ever witnessed, when she got on a horse for the first time in over thirty years.*

**Me and my buddy Crystal... who would have thought?**

It was a nightmare as they picked up my hookbaits throughout the night and there was bugger all I could do about it. By morning the wind had increased even more; indeed, I had heard one or two of the lake's conifers smash down in the darkness. The rain had also returned, and I watched through a haze of horizontal water as the tufties took their breakfast at my expense. The will to live was leaving me, and as quickly as I could, I ran for home.

An hour after vigorously waving the white flag of surrender I stood at my front door looking more like a drowned rat than an angler. Lynn giggled, bless her, and an hour later I was sitting in my chair tucking into one of her breeze-block sandwiches and a hot cup of tea... Weather, what weather? I couldn't rest for too long, however, because Lynn wanted to be somewhere else. Since I had met her she wanted to get back into horse riding, but her illnesses just wouldn't allow it. The thing with Lynn is that she will never surrender to anything, and we had eventually got involved at Cow City Livery, run by Drew and Laura, at Arborfield near Reading. I have to say it was one of the most emotional days I have ever witnessed, when she got on a horse for the first time in over 30 years. It got even more emotional when I was offered a ride, too! I nearly shit my pants when I was on-board a massive horse called Rhino. I discovered, eventually, that all horses really wanted to do was bite me, and called a halt to my riding career there and then. I do have one buddy at the stable though, and she goes by the name of Crystal, a tiny Falabella who bites everyone but me. We even win rosettes at agility events... who would have thought?

It took a few days to sort out and dry everything, but soon enough Lynn was hounding me out of the front door. I was very concerned about catching that big mirror again, but as there was hardly anyone fishing there at the time, I hoped it wouldn't matter. In saying that, and so that I don't have to keep repeating myself and the fish, I landed that 40lb mirror several more

*She looked enormous, and at 34lb 10oz, I guess she was.*

times. It was heartbreaking, but at least it was getting fed quite royally! I decided to find some new spots to fish, and the first things I saw when I returned were the black and white devils hanging around the old areas waiting to be fed. Not this time, my evil little friends, because I had arrived armed to the teeth with the strongest laser pen I could find. The other reason to find more spots to fish was that the original ones I baited were huge and clear of weed now, and I couldn't help thinking the carp might find them a little daunting. Although the weathermen were still predicting strong winds, sunshine and showers seemed to be the order of the day. As soon as I had shackled the brolly down I set out to create a feast for the fish. I had no reason to do it, but I upped the bait to around 10 kilos, and as I sat back on my bedchair I thought it may take them ages to get through that lot. It didn't, of course, and an hour and a half later I battled with a 24lb 4oz common. On the mat the fish deposited a cartload of partially digested bait, and I couldn't help thinking just how much they were on the feed.

That night was just about as brutal as it has ever been for me on the bank. Indeed, the guy up to my right was literally blown off the lake at around 1.30 a.m. He had a huge bivvy up, and it ties in nicely with the old sailing quote, 'The more sail you have up, the faster you go'! I sat smugly under my brolly, a little wet, maybe, as I had landed three more doubles by morning. Be that as it may, I was determined to be fishing as effectively as I could, and even though the weather was awful, I had all three rods right on the money. As it happens, it seemed as if all the effort was worthwhile.

I had changed my clothes, which is something I normally don't do. In typical squaddie style I usually climb right back in the sleeping bag and let my body-heat dry things off, however, this time I was far too wet to do so. As the light filled the sky, I thought I would sit and watch the water for as long as I could. I was just revelling in the heat from the sun as it rose behind me when one of the rods let out a few bleeps. In the second it took me to stand up the spool became a blur, and when I picked up the rod, that big-fish plodding began. She got locked in the weed twice, but I was able to move her, and I marvelled as great swathes of green stuff littered the surface in her wake. Once within range I was able to lift the net around her; she looked enormous, and at 34lb 10oz I guess she was. Apart from one scale high on her back she was a leather, and a truly handsome one at that. This winter, despite the problems with Lynn's health, was turning out to be a very good one. I was back as soon as I could and, for the first time in a while, I saw a couple of fish stick their heads out as I walked around. They were in the other, weedless side of the lake, and as I knew there was a shallow bar in this area I decided that would do for me. Two of the rods were fished at the back of the bar, and the other was cast near to a small crop of weed I found. In all, 3kg of boilies found their way to the spots, and as the wind got up again, I spent a little time securing everything. In the early morning I started to get liners, but it was some time before one of the rods behind the bar tore off. It was a lively scrap but soon enough I had a gloriously-scaled mirror of 22lb 3oz in my net. Stu came along later and told me how special that carp was; it was over 50 years old! He was also always seen with another very-rarely-caught carp that was even older. In an ironic twist of fate, I would bump into someone a little later that day who had fished for, and landed, those fish back in the 1960s.

I landed a small mirror around 8.00 a.m., and after rebaiting the spots sat back to wait once more. There was a young lad called Dan, from Sparsholt College, on-site doing work experience and as I saw his car pull up around midday, the bar spot produced another take. This one was stopping for no one, and even when Dan reached me some ten minutes later the fight was still raging on. When a huge set of shoulders hit the surface, I was sure it was the bloody 40 once again. Even as it rolled into the net I was still convinced, and then it rolled onto its side. It wasn't the 40, but a fish I was convinced was related to the 22-pounder I had landed earlier. We both thought she was an upper-30, but I could never have been disappointed when the scales registered 34lb 7oz. I smiled the smile of a contented man as I posed for the pictures. A while later I met up with the fellow who had angled for these fish back in the 60s, Dennis Smailes. He had arrived to do some business with the fishery. It was staggering to hear that the 34 was in excess of 60 years old, having been stocked in 1954!

The next trip saw me cross another one of the Hollybush Lakes' most wanted off my list, as I slipped the net under a truly stunning 24lb 12oz fully-scaled. The lake was fishing well, but I had turned my mind to somewhere else, much to the amusement of Stu, who felt there were still some incredible fish to catch from there. He wasn't wrong, of course, and after I had scratched a longstanding itch I would be back to catch probably the greatest carp I have ever caught. It may surprise some of you, especially in a world that is dominated by the 'biggest is best' culture, but I wanted to return to the Southlake at Reading, and see if there wasn't a 30-pounder with my name on it there. I also had a few tickets in my pocket that gave me access to at least six carp over 50lb, but it was the Reading thing I needed to finish off first.

I was actually amazed by some people's reaction to where I was fishing, and it just went to show that many anglers' vision of carp fishing isn't quite the nice, pleasant vista I always though it should be. Listen, if carp fishing was all about big carp then it would be a remarkably sad place, and by the same token, it wouldn't be the successful commercial venture that it is today, either. I have always believed that life is about setting personal goals, and then striving to achieve them, and thankfully, I still do. "What the hell are you doing fishing for pasties?" was one uneducated comment. One of the others was, "It's a pus-hole, and not really worth the effort." There were a couple of other more colourful viewpoints, but all they did was make me shake my head and wonder what the hell was wrong with carp fishing. They were going to get some more boilies this time around, and I made sure

*This marvellous 22lb 3oz mirror was as old as me!*

*I was staggered to hear the 34-pounder was over 60 years old.*

**Harry and me filming for the Fox Edges DVD.**

the air-dry bags were full before setting the clock and getting my head down. As you have already read, I fished there the year before and did remarkably well with the number of carp I had landed, being termed several times as biblical. That was all well and good, but everyone I spoke to had landed a 30; one chap in particular had only landed two fish from the lake all year and both of them weighed 34lb. As I drove to the lake one Monday morning in early spring, I just reminded myself to fish well and I would soon be moving on. By the time I packed away two days later, with both nets remarkably dry, I was starting to wonder just how soon I would be making that move! It didn't get any better on the next trip either, and by the time 48 hours of purgatory was over, I was wallowing around in a pool of self-pity.

I was back at Hollybush on the Station Lake the next week, filming links for the upcoming Fox *Edges* DVD with Harry Charrington. He reckoned I needed to catch a couple of fish to make things good, but with recent results I felt more likely to fly to the moon! It was tough fishing, but I did land a couple of fish, and once Harry had gone I decided to stay on for the night. It was a night in which I landed nine carp; no big ones, but that wasn't the point. They all made me smile, I was happy, and I was going back to Reading to catch that 30-pounder. So keen was I that I left home an hour earlier than normal. I needed to be looking, and I was sure the carp would tell me what to do. They did, of course, but there was little I could do about it, not in the short term anyway. I was on the second lap when I noticed movement in the swim of most interest. It was a warm morning, and the carp were so evident in front of the guy fishing there, that I was surprised to hear he hadn't had a bite in the two nights he had been there. In fact, he hadn't had a bite all season. I looked longingly at their backs as they creased the surface of the shallow bay, but I wasn't getting in this plot any time soon. He was staying until he caught one, and that was that. I fished up the other end of the lake, blanked

***It is hard to explain how overjoyed I was!***

the night very well indeed, and woke at dawn totally pissed off. That only lasted about an hour, because the bloke from the shallows came round and told me he had landed a 25lb mirror and the swim was now empty. I don't think I have moved that quickly in a very long time, and in short order I was pushing my barrow into the recently-vacated swim. Hallelujah!

There didn't seem to be as many fish around, but I was sure I could get a bite from there. I waded the rods out and cast to the shallow water. There was little point in putting bait out in the daylight, so I waited until dark to deposit about 2kg of 15mm boilies over the area. The night was quiet, and I was up way before the light started to fill the sky. At 5.00 a.m. one of the bobbins pulled up tight, and stayed there as I lifted into what was obviously a small fish. I really didn't care how big it was, to be honest, it was just nice to see a lovely scaly double in my net at long last. I didn't put that rod back out in an effort not to disturb any other fish that may be feeding. Half an hour later I was reaching for the kettle once more, when again one of the remaining bobbins pulled up tight. This one wasn't stopping for anything, though. The battle was fraught in the shallow water, and it wasn't long into the fight when I thought the fish may just be what I went there for. Thankfully, the carp gave up after a while and allowed me to steer her into the net. It looked as if I had done it, and when the scales spun round to 32lb 10oz it is hard to describe just how overjoyed I was. A friend of mine, Boxy, came round to do the pictures, and once I had let her slip from my hands I realised that it was indeed time to move on.

Amongst other tickets in my wallet was one for Vinnetrow, near Chichester. It is situated in a holiday park, and has several more lakes surrounding it. The lake itself contains one of the biggest fish in the country, at the right time of year. It goes by the name of the Half Lin, and was very likely to be over 60lb at the time I was arriving. It had been a while since

I had set my sights on one particular fish, and I wanted to catch this one because of her history. She had got as big as she was under intense, unrelenting, angling pressure, and it wasn't necessarily the weight that got me interested. I must admit that because of my more commercial responsibilities, my start at Vinny never really got off the ground. I have to be zoned in on a water before I feel comfortable, and I just never got into it down in Chichester. My first session was carpless, but it was great to meet a few of the regulars, some of whom I knew from other waters I had fished along the way. Whilst I was there my diary started to fill up with a cartload of filming I needed to do. It may seem once again like I'm complaining, but this is what I signed up for, and the challenge of a camera is just about as intense as it gets. Just down the road from me is a little lake called Shawfields, a beautiful, intimate place that has some very special carp in it. Once I had made a call and got a ticket in my pocket, I decided that this is where I would do a day's filming for *Tight Lines*, followed the next week by a couple of days' filming for Mainline. It all went very well, but whilst I was sorting all that out, I discovered I had one more very important thing to do. *Fishing.TV* was going to make a pilot programme for BT Sports and I was going to co-present it with a guy called Rae Borras. You may have seen him on Discovery in a series called *The Compleat Angler*, and at the time of writing he is on air with *The Game Fisher's Diary*. Basically, we would be introducing segments for a fishing programme, and it went very well indeed. What I could never have realised was that the next few years of my life would be filled with *The Fishing TV Show*, and I became incredibly proud to be involved. All of that was yet to come of course, and once I had done my thing in the business of show, it was time to head back to Vinny.

I really did try to get into the fishing down in Chichester, but never did. I just couldn't get on with the place, and it had nothing to do with the difficulty of the fishing either. I had fished plenty of places that were considerably tougher, but if I don't like being there, then I ain't staying. It was summertime, too, and that normally has me scratching my head, because invariably the carp would have spawned, leaving them looking far from their best, and very much down in weight. I am not keen on catching them because their immune defences may be weakened, yet I still see anglers, if you can call them that, setting up and casting at spawning fish. Yes, I understand that time is limited, but carp just don't deserve to be treated like that, do they? Then there was my family to consider. While this isn't necessarily about fishing, personal issues can have a massive bearing on my angling, as they do for most people, I would imagine. There are those who believe such talk is irrelevant, but I am not some mindless little idiot who believes the only thing which should concern us in our lives is carp fishing. There are infinitely more important things than that. Lynn had been 'reasonably' well for a while, but we are always on stand-by for the next thing to upset the apple-cart, which it was just about to do. I was at home far more than usual, trying to take care of business as she lay in a hospital bed, and there she would stay for some considerable time. As I was coming to terms with that my phone chirped into life, and my father told me my mum had gone into hospital all the way down in Plymouth. There wasn't a lot I could do about things down in the West Country at that moment because of the situation with Lynn. And just to compound things further, I had a horrible toothache, and eventually it ended up in the dentist rubbish bin. My life was in turmoil, and I have to say, I was falling out of love with carp fishing. I drove myself on, but I didn't want to even get up and go. I did, of course, and immersed myself in surface fishing for a while so I didn't have to do any nights. Remember, I was writing a monthly diary and had to catch carp to write about. All I was doing was 'enough', and I have never been happy with that in any walk of life I have ventured into. Filming became a great way of getting something to include in my writing, but I have to say that with everything that was going on, my heart just wasn't in it. At one point I believed I would never go carp fishing again, and started to look at what alternatives were available to me. I hadn't been this unhappy for a very long time, but I thought I had a couple of things that may just brighten me up. Once, of course, the most important two women in my life were the right way up.

I had my name down on several waters' waiting lists, and two of them had come to fruition that year. The first was The Mangrove Swamp up in Shropshire, a ticket that I had waited for, for several years. The second was Farriers Lake, up in the Cotswolds, and I reckoned that as soon as I was able I needed to pay a visit, and see how I felt about them. The first port of call was going to be The Mangrove, but once again I was shocked by the odd person's opinions of this decision. "What you doing going there, there's nothing big in it," and other such juvenile comments. Listen, I do my own fishing; I am not driven by what others think I should be doing. Which all means that I invariably enjoy myself, and a lot more people ought to try doing that at some stage in their sad lives. You may well think I was a little fed up with others trying to influence my decisions, and you would be right of course! And so I set off for Shropshire early the next Monday morning. The drive was about three and a half hours and went without a hitch, which for me is something of a miracle. There was only one other person on the water, so I sat for a little, soaking up the atmosphere. I thought of all the articles I had read that talked of the fishing there, and of the people who had fished it. It certainly had a special place in my heart, but I was there to fish and after loading up a boat, I set sail. I didn't go too far, and ended up in a swim called The Field. I quickly found a few firmer spots to fish on the unremarkable lakebed, and once all four rods were out, I sat back to take it all in. 24 hours later I hadn't seen a single thing, and moved to the other end of the lake to a plot called The New West. That effort provided no rewards, but it most certainly is a magical place; the only problem I had was that on the drive home I decided I would not return. It was a ton of money to waste on just one visit, but on the fishing front, the water never really spoke to me, which is kind of sad really. I was also thinking just how much out of love with carp fishing I was, if that didn't stoke the fires a little.

So once again I returned to Hollybush to try to sort my brain out. It is a complex of lakes that have helped me recover from myself from time to time, and I hoped it wasn't too fed up with putting me back on the road. And on my next outing it probably let me know a little of its displeasure. I had been asked to do another segment for *Tight Lines*, and as I was having a fair bit of action at Hollybush with my surface fishing, I decided it should be done there. We started off stalking on the first lake in the complex, Station Lake, and it went very well indeed. I was keen to see if I could get a fish off the top, and eventually turned up on the new lake at the back of the fishery. I had landed plenty of fish with my surface tactics, and as soon as I spread some mixers on the surface at the far end of the lake, the fish responded. I got them tearing up the surface before presenting a single hookbait to them. It drifted in perfectly and in the blink of an eye the little trimmed-down pop-up disappeared into a cavernous mouth. The weed was horrendous, and it didn't take too long for the carp to bury itself into it. I said some rather shaky words to the camera before ringing up the management to see if they could get a boat out. They did that in no time at all, and soon enough I was over the top of the fish, and had it moving. What happened next will live with me forever. The second time I got it out of the weed, I did so by hand-lining it, not always the best move, but what was even worse, as the fished turned and dived, was that I held on to the line. I have watched the segment countless times, and cannot believe what a complete cock I was. It snapped the light hooklink in seconds, of course, and I turned away in embarrassment for losing the biggest carp in the lake... on camera! Who says that everyone in my position knows what they are doing? I certainly don't! It really was symptomatic of the way life was for me at that time. I was like the little duck trying to paddle his way

*Out filming for Mainline with cameraman John Dunford.*

*Rae and me doing our bit for the BT Sport pilot programme.*

*The Fishing TV Show got under way with some carp fishing, of course.*

*I hadn't fly-fished for trout in a very long time.*

*Julian Shambrook and a hard-earned thornback ray.*

*My day filming with Des was magical.*

upstream. It all looked cool on the surface, but below it was total and utter mayhem.

It was probably a whole host of things that eventually had me chewing at the bit to go carp fishing once again, and I don't think it began until early September of that year. In the meantime, I had a couple of issues to take my mind off things, and most of that revolved around *Fishing.TV*. I mentioned a while ago that we had made a pilot for BT Sports of *The Fishing TV Show,* and they had asked us to produce a dozen half-hour programmes along those lines. We were all very excited, and I cannot tell you how proud I was to be involved. There were plenty of little bits to sort out first, but all too soon we were ready to rock and roll. I wanted to start off fishing for carp, and chose the Station Lake, Hollybush. It was there that the show took its first breath. Lynn was still going in and out of hospital, but was improving slowly. My mother was still not well, but again, she was starting to get on the mend. It had upset me more than I was prepared to admit, but both of them are such strong, courageous women, and all they wanted was for me to get on with my life... so I wasn't about to argue with that! After exploiting the surface action at Hollybush, I turned my attention to the filming. I wanted it to be about carp, but Rae, who is the boss and the dollar behind it all, wanted a bit of his obsession first. I was off to Avington Trout Fishery, where we would do two of the shows. It was the first time I had fly-fished for trout in a very long time and, the day before, I was remarkably like a child at Christmas. It was an incredible day as Rae and I cast a whole host of different flies around. I never stopped saying that we should put a worm on, but my suggestion fell on deaf ears. Doing all the stuff to camera isn't the way forward where fishing is concerned, as the crew were going to find out, and this was no different. By the time we got fishing, the trout were more than a little fed up with being fished for; in fact most of them had been caught and were in the smoker already! Eventually, using a fly that looked more like a painted hook, I played and landed our first trout, all 7lb of it! We caught a couple more, and both programmes were in the can, as they say in the business that is show.

Next up was the filming of the first programme, and we went to Hollybush for that. The lake was so good to us, and we even got some great footage of me stalking a 20lb mirror from the edge. I was loving it, and as soon as we had finished that, we loaded the cars and headed off to Taunton. We managed about four hours' kip before we were up and about, this time with a guy called Julian Shambrook. We would be fishing from the shore into the Bristol Channel, and do two programmes again, but it turned into a very hard day. The terrain was more akin to a lunar landscape, but we got the job done, with Julian landing a small conger eel and a lovely thornback ray. Bloody hell, we worked hard for those fish, but no matter how shattered we were, it was off to Shropshire at 7.00 p.m. and an early-morning date with Des Taylor. We had even less sleep that night, but from the moment we met up with Des I didn't stop laughing. In fact, it was one of the best day's fishing I had had in a very long time. I would go so far as to say that Des rekindled my passion for fishing, and the lovely barbel he landed probably had a hand in that, too.

The last few months had been hard for me; not as hard as it had been for those around me, like Lynn and my mum, but it had all taken its toll. Looking back, it would appear that I handled it all very well, but not for a second did I think so. Throw into the mix the TV programmes we were doing for BT Sport, and my carp diary, and I don't suppose it is hard to see why I had no rhythm to my life, let alone my fishing. I was still very much convinced that I had lost the plot, but in the end I discovered I had done nothing of the sort; I had simply mislaid it for a little while. I still wasn't enjoying my fishing, but I could never have guessed that a chance meeting with a guy called Gaz, and a 28lb common, was just about to change all of that. I was starting to see the wood for the trees by the time August came along, and it was now that I visited the second water that I had been granted permission to fish. With little idea how life was going to pan out for those closest to me, I could have had no idea just how much this water, and the people I would meet there, were going to change everything.

Chapter Sixteen

# More Than a Memory

*I prepared for the fishing just as I had for any other water.*

For a very long time I have got into the habit of never looking at the details of waters that I am going to fish. That may sound a little counterproductive when we are very often told to find out as much as we can about any venue we are interested in. For many years I had been on a bit of a mission to prove that I can take my mainstay tactic to any water, and catch carp, and so far I haven't been let down. To that end, as I set out for Farriers Lake, I prepared for the fishing just as I had for every other water; boilies, boilies and more boilies were going to be the way forward. The only error I made was to take along 5kg of 10mm'ers... that would prove to be a painful mistake. With everything prepared I set off from home around 4.00 a.m., and headed towards the Cotswolds. One of the greatest things about carp fishing is actually going carp fishing, and by the time I was on the M4, I was racing along with my hair on fire. An hour and a half later I was entering the gate code, and I got my first look at the water. I stood in one of the car park swims and marvelled at how many carp I saw show about 45 yards out. I should have simply chucked a couple of single hookbaits out, but I wanted to see the rest of the lake. So, after depositing my water butt in there I went for a look-see. Lee Collings from Birmingham Angling Centre was the first friendly face I came across, and after we had caught up for a while, I continued on my travels. To be honest, as nice as it was to have a look around, I just wanted to get back to the swim with the fish in it and start angling. The two rods were armed with stiff link pop-ups and cast 45 yards, and then I fed them with several kilos of the 10 and 15mm Hybrid boilies. All I could think of once I had finished, was, 'How big and how many?' Silly, really...

At around 3.30 a.m. I was starting to lose the will to live as I returned my fifteenth

*I had no idea how it happened, but I had caught a carp.*

tench of the night, which suggested the carp had done the off. I was totally knackered, and as I popped the tea bag in the cup for another brew, the bobbin cracked into the rod and the buzzer sang her tune. That was probably a carp then! The next ten minutes were spent desperately trying to extract it from one weedbed after another, until eventually it rolled into the net. I had no idea how it had happened, but I had caught a carp, and at 27lb 2oz I really couldn't have been happier. It was a great start to my Farriers' campaign, but I could never have realised just how much the tench would ruin things. Someone once famously wrote about the baiting pyramid, and how it worked, but I can assure you he never fished at Farriers. The next twenty-four hours were a nightmare, and I had thought up a million ways to kill a tench, which is a little unfortunate really, because they are such magnificent fish. In an effort to get away from them, and having spotted a couple of fish at the far end of the lake, I moved just as fast as my legs would take me. A few fish had come out around the lake, and I wanted a bit of that action, but I can only think the tench had moved just as fast as I had. It was another horrible night, and by the morning I had written in my diary in big red letters, 'Leave the 10mm'ers at home next time, you twat!!' The MNDA event at Linear Fisheries was to keep me from the bank at Farriers, but when you are part of raising over £34,000, you really can't complain. It is always an honour to be there, and amongst friends.

I was more than keen to get back to the Cotswolds. Word on the street, although I was trying to avoid talk of the lake, was that it was fishing very well with a couple of good fish coming out. Maybe with the 10mm'ers taking a session or two off in the freezer at home I could get in on a bit of that action? All I was looking for on my arrival at the start of the following week was a swim with no tench in it, and eventually I ended up in an area at the top end. I had found a little bit of raised lakebed the last time I was there, and although I was loath to call it a bar, it was certainly a feature in an otherwise featureless world. Behind it was a strip of silt, and I could think of nowhere else I would want to place my two pop-up hookbaits other than there. It was a comfortable 60 yards out and in no time at all I had 4kg of 15mm'ers doing their best to get me a bite. For the first time in ages, as I put the kettle on, I felt like I was fishing in a reasonable manner. That's when I met Gaz. He walked into my swim and, after a little chat, he asked if I would like some fish and chips. Why not? And about an hour later he duly arrived with a box of Gloucestershire's finest fare. It really was good, too, but it was the conversation that made me realise what I had been missing all this time. Good company. We spoke about everything but carp fishing, and by the time my belly was full I felt more at one with myself and the world than I had done in years. I even caught a couple of tench soon after Gaz had left, but they couldn't upset me this time, no matter how hard they tried, and believe me they tried! I even went into my vast array of rigs, all two of them, and tried a bottom bait, as opposed to a pop-up, but nothing made a hoot of difference.

I had just slipped back another red-eyed hooligan when I received what I thought was another tench bite. It was nothing of the sort, and at long last I was playing a carp. Weedbed after weedbed made life a little difficult, but soon enough I was admiring a cracking 28lb 2oz common. I was delighted, and he completed my recovery from the depths of despair. It wasn't until that very moment that I understood just how depressed with it all I had been since the previous May. I rebaited the area, and sat down to enjoy the day; I hadn't felt so good for so long. Things got very interesting late in the afternoon, as I watched a few plumes of bubbles come up over the hookbaits, along with a few liners. It looked promising for another bite, and it wasn't long in coming. The weed and my other line ensured that it wasn't the most frantic of battles, and eventually the fish got clogged down in the green stuff some ten yards in front of me. An old acquaintance from my Yateley days, John Claridge, came to my rescue, and after donning his chesties, he waded out and wrestled the fish into the net. She

***The MNDA event at Linear is always a joy to attend.***

was a good fish, and when the scales registered 35lb 12oz, at long last all was well in Chilly world! On the drive home I couldn't stop smiling, and also couldn't help thinking just how much I loved carp fishing again. It had dragged me out of a few dark holes in my past, and with Lynn, my mum, and my life in general on the mend, I couldn't have been happier.

For those who don't know about Farriers, it is a water full of very big commons, and what spectacular fish they are! There are about 25 mirrors in there, and to a great extent it is those that many of the members cherish most. The lake itself is very shallow, with an average depth

***Soon enough I was admiring a 28lb 2oz common.***

of around 4ft. The weed was horrendous, but not too limiting, and best of all, I have rarely come across a population of carp that love boilies so much. I was back the following Monday, armed once again with around 10kg of Hybrid 15mm boilies. I looked as thoroughly as I could, but it was the same swim as the previous week that caught my eye. There was no other way to do it really, and in very little time I was set up as before. Two stiff link pop-ups rested in the silt, along with around 6kg of boilies. It felt so damn good, and the carp must have agreed, as an hour later I landed a common of around 20lb. Nice start. Twenty minutes later

**At 35lb 2oz all was well in Chilly World.**

that same rod was away again, and once more Mr Claridge helped out with the netting. There in the net was one of the lake's mirrors, and whilst he may not have been the biggest fish I would catch from there, all 19lb 7oz of him, he was very special. The carp moved out of the bay that night and the tench moved in, but there wasn't a swim for me to move to because the place was as busy as hell. To that end, it wasn't until 7.00 p.m. the next evening that I was once again connected to a carp. The fight was non-existent, as most of them are on this lake, and in about 45 seconds a rather good mirror lay in the folds of my net. At 31lb 5oz I really didn't care what happened after that, but the tench decided to take the night off, the carp came back for more, and I landed five more commons to 24lb. The tackle and tactics were working well, and as I sat watching the light chase away the night, one of the rods simply tore off. No sooner had I picked up the rod than the fish was covered in weed, and it was just a case of pumping the whole lot towards me. The incredibly long fish spun the scales round to 33lb 6oz. My time at Farriers had started with a bang, and I was determined to keep it going.

It is very easy, no matter what your level of experience, to get a little complacent about one's fishing. Whilst I wasn't exactly expecting bites all the time, I did feel that the lake was going to be good to me most of the time. Oh, you poor deluded soul, Chilly! Carp fishing, for me at least, needs to be a challenge, but very occasionally I get lured into thinking that I am on a bit of a roll. This, nine times out of ten, means that I am just about to get a metaphorical kick in the bollocks. I could never have known, of course, but, as I packed my van for a third visit, the lake was just about to tell me that I had to work a little harder to keep the ball rolling. It was early September, and the time to make hay had arrived. I was away by 4.30 a.m. and by the time I turned off the A419 just north of Swindon, I had conjured up a million scenarios, all of which involved several monster carp in the bottom of my net. The lake was very busy, and as it

*At 31lb 5oz I really didn't care what happened after that.*

had been fishing well, who could blame everyone for being there? The far, shallow end of the lake was the place where the carp had been spending much of their time, but I didn't want to fish there, really. I have no wish to start hand-lining fish to the net, it just isn't my idea of fun, and to that end I looked for somewhere I could intercept them if they moved away from the weed at night. One swim that I was determined to find out more about was free, so I placed my water butt in there and made my way back to the van. There had been a couple of 40s out over the weekend, and this news probably quickened my pace as I pushed the barrow into The Slope, as it is known. I leaded around and could only find one spot to fish, the same area that everyone else had, I assumed. Not my cup of tea really, but needs must and all that. Again, two hookbaits and around 2kg of boilies came to rest on the silt just in front of a wall of weed at the back of the spot. I had fished the swim for one night before, landing a 24lb common and losing two others. This time was little different, and two fish had again slipped the hook.

I only had one more night and decided to move, which was actually a bittersweet pill to swallow. Cussing and swearing I got my gear in a swim about 20 yards to the left of The Slope, and as I was setting up, another member moved into the swim I had just vacated. I slept for a while, before some activity in the swim I had departed from woke me up. I trotted over to help, and discovered the guy had landed four fish. I went back to my plot, discussing with myself what an idiot I had been for moving, and, of course drank several cups of tea. The kettle was just going back on at 5.00 a.m., when one of the bobbins pulled up to the rod. I was convinced it was a tench and rather casually lifted in the fish. I still thought it was another red-eyed devil when it was halfway towards me, but shortly after that a lot of weed fell off the line and some bigger ripples spread out across the lake. Okay, maybe it was a really big tench then? It did nothing else and it was only when it neared the net that I could see I had actually hooked

**Maybe it was a really big tench then!**

a carp, and quite a good one, too. At 36lb 6oz I thought I was about to burst into flames, and that probably made up for being so impatient earlier in the session. If it didn't light my fire, I reasoned, then I should bloody well sell my tackle and take up knitting!

Of course, there is always something in my life to take me away from the places that I am concentrating on. Again, I am not complaining because I enjoy the diversity, and as I was about to head off to film another BT Sports programme, I was relishing the challenge. However, this little adventure at the Quarry in Essex had a nice twist to it. I was going to be doing a whole host of filming with Adam Penning, and as good as that is, there was one major life-changing event just about to happen. His girlfriend, Hils, was pregnant, and the due date was that Wednesday. The filming dragged out over four days, but we accomplished most of what we wanted to do, and anyway, I was sort of involved in baby Penning making its first appearance, and I could never be unhappy about that. How Adam kept himself together I have no idea, but towards the end of our session a little life entered the world, who will go by the name of River. Hils didn't have the best time in hospital, but we were glad to hear that eventually mother and baby were doing fine. I wasn't sure about dad though, I don't reckon he will ever get over that... bless him!

I was away too long that week, and the hoped-for return to Farriers was cut short because Lynn had become very ill. I was just walking around the lake when she rang, and within an hour and a half I was home. There can be no if or buts in that situation, if she needs me I'm off. A few days at home and plenty of trips to doctors and hospitals, and Lynn was soon showing me the door. I aim to please, of course, and very soon I was again stalking the banks up in the Cotswolds. Once again it was busy, but as I got to The Slope, I could see the occupant was packing up. I wasn't too sure that I wanted to give the swim

*Filming with the expectant father at the Quarry.*

another chance to give me a good kicking, but I was determined to rectify the situation. By midday I had once again put both rods on the popular area, which may seem like I had invested all my eggs in one basket, but for some reason it just felt right. I'm not totally sure of the reason, but I had changed over to my old-faithful bottom bait rigs and PVA bags this time around. I guess I felt more confident in using them there again. By way of confirmation, an hour later I was slipping back a common of 25lb 6oz, but that was it for the next 24 hours. I wasn't moving, that was for sure, because I think we all know by now what would have happened. And I am so glad I didn't. I lost a fish in the night, and the tench decided to try to make life miserable, but I was determined to stick with it.

The liners started around 3.00 a.m. very exaggerated ones. The carp had obviously come back! By 6.00 a.m. I had landed five, all 20s to 28lb. The action was finally rounded off with a cracking common of 33lb 2oz around 8.00 a.m. I really let 'em have some bait after that, and whilst I was still feeling very smug about proceedings that evening, I landed a 24lb common. But then the lake simply died, or went to sleep. I stayed awake as long as I could, but saw or heard nothing. Even as I gazed across the lake as the dawn was filling the sky, I was still confused about the lack of activity. That was until one of the bobbins smashed into the rod and the buzzer howled. As fast as the run was, the fight wasn't a fight at all, but the handsome common of 35lb 7oz made a spectacular sight in the early, misty morning light. On the drive home I couldn't help feeling lucky to be fishing such a water; the other members were so friendly, and it was producing 40lb commons for fun. I suggested to myself that it was about time I started catching some of the real monsters in the lake. The thing was, I was catching on every trip, so there was no problem with either of my rig choices. Bait, as it never has been, wasn't a concern either as they simply loved

*She made a spectacular sight in the early-morning mist.*

it. And I could see nothing wrong with the amounts I was putting in, either, because every fish had shown its appreciation by depositing a good load of bait on my mat, or in a retainer. It was just that old adage once again, 'just keep on keeping on', so that is what I did.

To that end, I once again loaded the air-dry bags with as much 15mm Hybrid as they could carry, and set the alarm for an early call at 4.00 a.m. I was away after a quick brew, and just as the weatherman had said, the conditions were perfect. The problem was, I had been working so hard at home that I was shattered, and for the first time in my life, as I pulled up in the car park, I fell asleep behind the wheel. I woke at just gone 7.00 a.m. and rather embarrassingly had been beaten to two of the most productive swims on the lake... Oops! Not surprisingly the lake was still busy, but I reckoned a lot of the plots would become vacant as the morning wore on. I wasn't too concerned, but I definitely needed a bit more sleep. One swim that had aroused my interest was just about to become available, and, best of all, the guy who was moving out had caught three fish that weekend. It was an area I hadn't fished before, so the first thing was to have a lead around. As I have already mentioned elsewhere, I don't like to fish the obvious spots, but something made me change my mind this time around. The lake contained a couple of koi carp, and it was one of those I could just about make out, as it visited the area. He wasn't on his own, for sure, and as soon as I was able I had two bottom bait rigs, armed once again with a PVA bag, in position. The silty gully was only about 20 yards out, and very quickly I got a couple of kilos of boilies spread around my rigs. At which point I handed proceedings over to the carp...

As I was fishing on the back of the wind, the calm water allowed me to monitor the fish's movements, and later that day a couple of them moved in. I was fascinated as the stream of bubbles they sent up criss-crossed the area, but still nearly jumped out of my skin when one

*At 37lb 2oz she was one of the most perfect commons I had ever seen.*

of the rods literally tore off. The fish hit the weed straight away but I kept constant pressure on it, and after a few minutes it was rolling on the surface. The close proximity meant that I could see it was a good fish, and once in the net this was confirmed. It was one of the most perfect commons I had ever seen, and at 37lb 7oz I beamed over her back as the pictures were done. After that the area looked like someone had thrown a hand grenade in, and I couldn't see a single fish anywhere. It was 5.00 in the morning when the line bites started; big, lazy carp-like liners. They were out there feeding for sure, but it took an hour before the bite came. The difference this time was that the fish wasn't stopping for anyone, and literally crashed through the weedy barrier at the back of the baited area. I slowed him, of course, but as I drew him towards me the line picked up more and more weed until eventually he stopped fighting altogether. With the waders on, I marched out with the net and scooped up everything. It took a couple of minutes to remove most of the weed, and when I did I nearly swallowed my tongue. It was bigger than the last one, and I was sure I had landed my first 40 from the lake. He fell a little shy at 39lb 12oz, but I could never have been unhappy. It was one of the lake's better-known carp called John Doe, and was the last of the action I had that session. I did spend some time leading about in other areas, just to get a little more knowledge, then headed for home. On the drive to the lake the next Monday, I was determined not to fall asleep in the car park, and just as determined to get back in a swim called The Slope. It is not something I would normally do, preselecting swims is usually a recipe for disaster, but for whatever reason, I was sure that was where I needed to be. And I was just about to find out why.

The swim was occupied, as I knew it would be, but I was pleased to hear that he would be gone by 9.00 a.m. The water butt was left there, and I carried on my travels. Strangely, I wasn't looking for anything, I was in the swim I wanted to be in, and that would do for me. By

*John Doe at 39lb 12oz.*

*The scene of the crime.*

*At 46lb 10oz she made sure my fires were blazing!*

around midday I was ready to rock and roll, but I had changed my setup again. You see, the last time out I had convinced myself that bottom baits would get me more fish and, let's be honest, catching my two biggest fish from the lake so far would sort of confirm the notion. However, could it have been coincidence? I wasn't sure, and the only way to prove to myself that that was the case, was to go back to my stiff link pop-ups. It made sense to me anyway! A silty little gully at around 45 yards was the area I was going to fish my two rigs, and positioned them about 7 yards apart. I had also gone back to using 10mm'ers, and once I had put out 4 kilos of them and the normal 15mm'ers, I sat back and wondered just how many tench I was going to be bothered by. I had every confidence in what I had done, but I have to say it was waning, come the morning. I hadn't even had a single bleep, but I wanted to stay put, and as the lake was still very busy there really wasn't a move on anyway. I reeled in, freshened up the spot with a little more bait and visited the shops. Three hours later I was back, repositioning the hookbaits, and when the right-hand one donked down I couldn't help muttering under my breath that that was probably worth a bite. Time would tell of course... and I didn't have long to wait.

As the cloud thickened and the drizzle threatened to soak everything, I was sipping a brew when the bobbin on the 'that's a bite' rod clattered into the rod and fell immediately back to the deck. It looked like one of those instances when something had got away without having its picture taken. I stood wondering if I should reposition the rod when the bobbin lifted again. Before the bite could develop more, I had the rod in hand and a massive swirl erupted over the spot. It shifted so much water that I couldn't help thinking that this was probably a bit of a chunk, and nothing it did for the next couple of minutes made me feel any differently. She stayed on the surface, kiting around to my left and getting stuck in a thick weedbed for a moment. This gave me a chance to put the chest waders on, and once I had launched the landing net out into the lake, I marched straight after it in an effort to claim my prize. Once the fish was out of the weed I was once again able to gain some line, and 10 yards from the net I caught sight of the most massive golden flank. I was actually shaking as I moved it slowly towards me, but I did spare a thought for my tonsils when I thought about my battle cry if I got her in the net. That wasn't too long in coming, actually, because within a minute an absolute giant slid over my net cord and the lake was treated to a deafeningly loud; "Light My Fire!"

She looked ridiculously big in the net, and felt even more outrageous when I lifted her out of the water and onto the mat. I had no doubt that it was a personal best common, and when my neighbour, Justin, confirmed the weight of 46lb 10oz I was torn between two very strong emotions. You see, catching Charlie's Mate from Frimley all those years before was the culmination of a lifetime's dreaming, a lifetime that had a thread weaving though it which led me to catch a common comparable to Walker's record. I wasn't sure, just for a second, that I wanted to actually beat that milestone. I hoped that Walker would smile down on me, and be happy for me that it was time to move on. I had no thoughts of creating a new personal best common when I started at Farriers, I was simply trying to find myself again, and rekindle the passion for my fishing that had meandered through my life. From Runcton and Vinnetrow in the south, to Tim Paisley's Mangrove in the north, I had searched for my soul, and right there and then I knew I had found it safe and well.

## Chapter Seventeen

# It's a New Dawn, It's a New Day

*The best time of day, a new dawn.*

*This 27lb common made a fine end to my time at Farriers... for now.*

I spent the entire night reliving the capture of that magnificent Farriers' common, but I couldn't help thinking about what I was going to do next. The obvious choice was to stay in the Cotswolds, but two things made my eventual decision to move on a little easier. First of all, the lake didn't have a very good winter track record, even with the number of carp it contained. And secondly, I wasn't sure how many big common carp in excess of 40lb I wanted to catch. To me, it seemed like having your favourite meal every day of your life. Very quickly it wouldn't be your favourite meal, and it wouldn't be special any more. We are all driven, thankfully, by different things and, to me, catching big carp constantly means that with each capture they will become just that little less special. I want to chase big carp around, indeed I have caught an awful lot of them in this country, but I want the fish to mean something more to me, not just adding another number to a list. Carp fishing is all about enjoying myself, not an exercise to get my ego massaged, and to that end I tried to find somewhere to spend my time that winter. The choices got fewer when I arrived home, because Lynn had received the results from her most recent tests. I would need to be near to home again, and as worrying as that was, at her insistence, life simply had to go on. There was something else that was just about to change the winter ahead, and that came via a call I received as Lynn and I were having lunch one day. It was Paul Cooper from *Fishing.TV*, who informed me that the viewing figures from *The Fishing TV Show* on BT Sports had far exceeded those the channel had hoped for. Consequently, we needed to make a new series, as well as do the last programme in the first series, just as quickly as we could. That was all fine and dandy with me, so plans were made. We put dates in the diary, and ran a few ideas around when I returned to Farriers the following week. I don't think I had ever been so chilled in my life, and the capture of two perfect commons of 24 and 27lb made a fine end to my time on the water, for now. I wasn't sure I would even be back, but as I drove home I just couldn't wait for the ensuing madness to begin!

*It had been 18 months since I was last on the Isle of Wight.*

The first order of business was to sort out the last programme in series one, and this time I would be spending my time with the ultimate fishing icon, Chris Yates. For me, a day's fishing cannot get any better than that. I had done a big interview with Chris about three years previously for the online channel, *Fishing.TV*, and after we had finished Chris told me that about 40 per cent of what he said he had never spoken about before. We had got on so well, and the interview was such a huge success, I could only hope this meeting would be no different. We met up the evening before for a meal with Chris and the crew at a small hunting hotel, and the conversation that night went way beyond fishing, thank goodness. It was a rather civilised 8.30 a.m. when Chris led us through the countryside to a little secret lake, which simply took my breath away. The conversation, and the filming, went remarkably well, but the fishing did not. To that end, Chris took us to another lake that was nearly a thousand years old (yes, one thousand) and there the fishing side of things was completed, too. I told anyone who would listen that the last time we had met was my greatest day's fishing I had ever had, and now I had a new 'best day' to file way in the memory banks.

I still had no idea what for, or where, to fish that winter, and decided to investigate a few places I fancied for my cold-weather fishing. Jones Pit in Leighton Buzzard was one such place, but it never lit my fire. The Basingstoke Canal was another option, but I wasn't happy there either. A couple of other waters came to mind, but it was to be Hollybush Clearwater once again. However, that didn't have a very settled feel to it either, because the filming schedule was just about to kick into high gear. From carp fishing at Farlows, to pike fishing at Wraysbury, it all kept me busy, but probably the best, and certainly the most amusing sequence, was watching Jerry Hammond playing and landing a 25lb catfish on a Zig from a half-frozen lake for one programme! I cleared the decks as fast as I could, and was just about to settle into a bit of my own fishing when things turned decidedly colder in the latter part of January 2015. In fact, everywhere froze, and I was confined to the bungalow for nearly two weeks. I was just about to go completely stir-crazy when something dawned on me. About 18 months before I had been over on the Isle of Wight with Fox for a weekend event. We had fished at Rookley Country Park, and I remembered how much I had enjoyed fishery manager, Tim Oakley's company. I had promised I would return one day, and as he had a fountain on the lake to keep it partially clear of ice, I reckoned that now would be as good a time as any. Tim couldn't have been more helpful, and even allowed me to book a swim for the following morning as there was no one on the lake at the time. How cool was that? It was a no-brainer really, and my name was put on the famous Corner Swim. The ferry was booked, and all that was left to do was fill the air-dry bags with boilies once again. I am probably the most boring bloke on the planet, and I know I have mentioned it before, but it is how I catch fish no matter what the 'experts' tell me.

The problem I had when I arrived at Rookley was that my air-dry bags were still in the freezer back in Aldershot. Doh! Yes, I could have fished single hookbaits, but I catch carp at whatever time of year using bait, so I sat and sulked for a while, before Tim turned up to open his shop. Maggots aren't my favourite bait, but I had no choice really, and in the end I purchased about six pints of the red and white wrigglers. They were my best option, as Tim pointed out, so that was what I would be using. I had a lead around and found a large firm area for two rods at about 40 yards' range, and a small hump to the right of that for the third. The maggot hookbaits, along with a PVA bag of the same, came to rest on the spots, and I baited with about four pints of the grubs. It all looked and felt so good, and it got even better when an hour and a half later I was playing a Rookley carp. I probably played him far too carefully, but soon I was posing behind a lovely 25lb 10oz mirror. My overriding feeling was that there was so much more to carp fishing than catching big carp, and when a 21-pounder came to visit an hour after that, I thought I was going to burst into flames! The weather was freezing, and horrible, but things got even better. I kept the maggots trickling in, and landed two more chunky 20s before dawn on the last day. The lake had become busy (I wonder why), and my baited area now resembled the beaten zone from a General Purpose Machine Gun, but amazingly I got another bite just as I was about to pack up. The fish fought deep and hard, but patience won the day, and all of a sudden I was holding up a 31lb 2oz mirror. The mission was complete in every sense, but while he got his breath back in the net, I hooked another. I thought at one point the fish was purposely trying to make me late for my ferry, so long did the fight go on, but the final fish eventually found its way into my net. What a way to end it all, with a cracking 28lb 7oz scaly mirror. It was great to spend time with Tim, and it also reminded me, once again, about how much more I had to discover about carp fishing.

Then my life got busy all over again. I had the honour to represent Fox in Russia once again, and nothing happened on that trip to change my mind about how special the average Russian is. However, something did happen that I was sure was going to make a huge impact on carp-fishing history. Paul Reeve, Shaun McSpadden and Scott Day had to spend the last evening in a business meeting, which meant that the hired help could go off and enjoy themselves. I was keen to have a good look at the Kremlin, so our host Alix decided that we should have a meal nearer the centre of Moscow, and then we could travel in once the traffic had died down. Rob Hughes, Alix and I enjoyed a fantastic meal, and eventually bundled into Alix's van to continue our journey. We visited Gorky Park, the Soviet version of the White House, and several other historical sites before eventually coming to the Kremlin. We parked a little way from the massive buildings,

*My final Rookley mirror of 28lb 7oz.*

and ran up to take some pictures, which is a difficult task when you have Rob trying, for whatever reason, to photobomb all my efforts. Anyway, with that done we headed back to our hotel and had a couple of beers with the other lads, then headed off to our rooms.

The hotel was like a furnace, so I woke very early, decided to make a brew, then switched on the TV. On the screen was a grainy picture, obviously from a security camera, of the very area we had parked in the night before. And there, in the middle, was a big van that looked remarkably like the one we had been in. I glanced at the time clock on the screen, and realised it was indeed us! The van, which we were in of course, moved off and disappeared from in front of the camera. A few moments later a figure appeared, walked round to a parked car and shot another grainy figure four times. I was amazed, and as soon as I was able, briefed the lads on the night's exciting events. Rob was totally convinced that he and I were about to be arrested, then interrogated by the Politsiya, eventually ending up

***The day just blew me away.***

*At 43lb 5oz he most certainly was a monster!*

in some Siberian labour camp until the British Government could get us released. I was already writing the book in my head, but Rob was having none of it. All he could think about was getting out of the country as soon as possible. I asked him several times where his sense of adventure had gone, but in all honesty he probably had a point, especially when you consider my background! I still maintain that it would have been an interesting experience, but when we got to the airport it was time to get back to the real world.

I had a great day out with Des Taylor on his favourite River Test, him catching chub and me catching grayling, something I hadn't done for over 30 years. It was a day that took me back to my youth, and reminded me of my fishing roots. A trip to Farlows with Harry Charrington, this time doing the links and catching carp, for the latest Fox *Edges* DVD, and finally I was off again with Chris Yates, which just blew me away once again. They were all, in their own different ways, great days spent in the greatest company and I can only hope I get the chance to do it all again one day. The last of my filming duties happened to be a bit of fly-fishing, and I did so practically from the back garden of Pink Floyd's Roger Waters. I am not the best at fluff-chucking, but Rae Borras and I landed several fish to over 4lb, and all of a sudden I was as ready as I would ever be to get back into some serious carp fishing.

I don't want to dwell on what happened next, but some unpleasantness surfaced during the next phase of my journey. I had eventually got a ticket for the Roach Pit, down in Dorset, a truly exceptional water. On my first visit, I spotted several carp in the snags covered in great big sores. Contrary to what some believe, I did tell the fishery owner about the things I saw, and voiced my concerns. He didn't seem bothered and said it would all sort itself out. Oh, it was going to do that all right! The second visit was no better, and once again I informed the owner of what I had seen. It appeared even worse the next time I arrived, when I found three fish that I could have literally scooped out of the margin. It was obvious nothing was being done, and no one wanted to rock the boat by complaining to the management. I posted my concerns on Facebook, and one or two cowards really had a cyber dig at me, saying there wasn't a problem at all. However, within a month the fishery was dead. I am not saying that if anything had been done when I first voiced my concerns it would have helped, but at least, as a group of anglers, we would have shown that we care about the fish we fish for. Interestingly, the cowards who had a pop on the old 'intro web' never apologised for suggesting I was wrong to be concerned. Strange how hard you become when you don't have to physically put your head above the parapet, isn't it?

Onward and upwards... I had decided that I wanted to return to Farriers. I had no other tickets, after all, and it was the best place to try to put the Dorset disaster behind me. Yes, I held the lake record, but I reckoned there were one or two bigger fish in there to catch, and in any case, the biggest mirror, The Jewel, a most stunning linear, was yet to grace my net. I had a long discussion with Penning, whilst doing another programme for BT Sport, and he agreed with me. "Fill your boots and enjoy yourself," were his parting words... and I was about to do just that! The weather had become positively balmy, so when I got home from that filming trip I busied myself with getting my gear ready for the first mission to Farriers that year. It was going to be all about boilies, once again, and when I had wedged as many 15mm'ers as possible into my air-dry bags, I set the alarm for silly o'clock the next day. By 4.30 I was on my way, as excited as I had ever been, and as the sky started to lighten I turned off the A419 towards the Cotswolds. It was certainly good to be back. The lake was as busy as I had ever seen it, and with the arrival of spring, who could

*That was no double! The dark and handsome stalked 27lb 2oz mirror.*

blame everyone for wanting to be on the bank? I wasn't sure if I would even get a swim, but one of the bailiffs, Ian, said he was leaving a little later, so I booked the swim. Now that was handy, a packed lake, and I was going to be in my favourite plot! I was amazed at the lack of weed, but what that did was ensure I could investigate the lakebed a bit more thoroughly. The usual spot was, as I suspected, clear, but just behind it I could get into about 5ft of water; now that was deep in this area. Eventually, two stiff link pop-ups were fishing about 5 yards apart, and baited with around 3 kilos of 15mm boilies. The wind was so bad that it became a little uncomfortable, but later that day I landed a splendid 31lb common, which made a great start to my second Farriers' mission. Trying to reposition the rod was a task in itself; I could hardly feel the lead down, so powerful were the gusts. I must have got it right, however, because an hour later the same rod was away again. I don't think I even had to put any pressure on the fish as the wind blew it straight towards me, but the 27-pounder made sure I slept that night with a huge smile on my face. One more 14lb common completed the trip, and I was glad I was renewing my ticket. The people were wonderful, as they had always been, and the fishing wasn't too bad either!

I had quickly got into my rhythm again, and the next week followed the exact same path. The lake was packed, but a lot of the guys were fishing the Sunday nights, and heading off to work at around 6.30 a.m. Sunshine, showers and wind were the order of the day, and as I walked, and looked, it seemed that the carp wanted to be on the back of the weather, as they always seemed to be there. It was pretty much stitched-up down that end, but I could see the odd person packing up already. The one swim that should put me right on the money would be available a little later, so I placed my water butt behind the guy, and waited. The guy reckoned I should fish his spots, but I could think of nothing I wanted to do less. Now on my own, the koi once again gave the game away for his friends. It was a clear strip of silt at around 30 yards, and same as before I put stiff link pop-ups at either end of it, about 7 yards apart. 3kg of Hybrid completed the traps, and I was soon sipping my first brew of the trip. It was 4.00 p.m. when I got one of the fastest runs I had ever seen, and picking up the rod made no difference to the fish at all. On and on it ran until it decided to change direction, and a huge boil appeared out in the middle of the lake. Convinced it was a manic

*It was the most fantastic couple of days.*

*I landed five more carp, all 20s to 28lb 10oz, during a hectic few hours.*

20-pounder, I patiently concentrated on drawing the fish towards my net, but when it got there things changed rather dramatically. No longer did it run around, but settled into a more 'I'm a big bastard' battle. Around ten minutes later a very long fish rolled some 10 yards out, and there was little doubt at that point that this was something a little bit special. My knees started to knock and my heart ended up in my mouth, but gradually the fish neared the outstretched net. I was amazed when his head hit the spreader block and his tail was still hanging over the net cord. This appeared to be a big fish, and at 43lb 5oz he most certainly was! I put him in a retainer for a moment while I found a photographer, and amazingly, a guy called Dave came into my swim to ask if I could do him some pictures, too. He had just landed a monster of 45lb 12oz, so it had obviously been the big-fish hour in the Cotswolds! I sat on my bedchair and

*A beautiful 37lb common, but I had to work hard for it.*

wondered at just how many incredible highs carp fishing had given me over the years. I was smiling like the proverbial Cheshire cat when I closed my eyes that night... but not for long.

I landed five more carp, all 20s to 28lb 10oz, in a hectic night. They all made me grin even more, just as the big one had done. But I had one more surprise as the light started to fill the sky, when one of the bobbins rose to the rod and stayed there. I was thinking tench, and nothing during the rather lame fight made me feel any different, that was until the fish rolled on the surface and a big common was ready for netting. She weighed 34lb 4oz and was the last fish of a very memorable session. I spent the journey home wondering just how much more I could love carp fishing, and also how the hell I could have ever thought of giving it all up. Yes, I had been miserable about it all at times, but I couldn't even contemplate life without it.

The lake continued to be good to me, but I am always nervous around spawning time, and as the action slowed, the more convinced I was that they would spawn soon. That said, and although I could hardly buy a bite in the open water, I did land myself another mirror. I had been trying desperately to find something to fish for one day, when eventually I spied a couple of fish grubbing around under a willow in the little top bay. I thought they were all doubles, but a bite is a bite, right? To that end I spent about an hour getting a hookbait in position, and once it was there I noticed a mirror creep up and suck it in. The water exploded, it shot out of the bay, and we danced the dance for ages until I wrestled it, with a barrowload of weed, into the net. That was no double, and at 27lb 2oz the dark, torpedo-shaped mirror meant that I had now landed three of the 25 mirrors in the lake. I landed a 24lb common the next day, and I was surprised to hear they were the only fish caught whilst I was there. And then they

*Weighing 34lb 10oz, she was a brilliant start to the session.*

spawned, and the lake was shut down for about two weeks; just the way it should be.

I messed around trying to keep myself occupied, but eventually I went on a session that had been about 15 years in the making. I have retained many friends from my Army days, but hardly any of them go fishing. However, two guys who I met at the Army lake in Aldershot, Chalk Farm, way back in the early -'90s, have always been a beacon of light as far as I am concerned. Mark Denton and Mark Browne, both ex-Parachute Regiment soldiers, and I had been trying to arrange a session together, and at long last we succeeded. Brownie and I met up at Hollybush's Clearwater Lake one hot and humid morning. We weren't sure about Denton; he doesn't exactly work to anyone else's agenda, and could arrive at any time, as he did eventually. It was the most fantastic couple of days, and the company just made me miss the Army, something I hadn't really done before. We even all caught carp, with Denton landing the biggest, something which Brownie and I were reminded of constantly, of course!

I was gagging to get back to Farriers and one fine morning I found myself outside the gate at first light. I thought it would be open, but a couple of bailiffs (who had oddly been fishing the lake for a few days) said the gate would be open at around 9.00 a.m. Fair enough, and once I was allowed in I started my walk around. Strangely, it was only me and a guy from Wales who had arrived early, but as good as that was, I didn't see a lot to get my juices flowing. This can often be the case after the carpy sexfest; you may just have to start all over again, and so it proved. I did manage a marvellous 37lb common on that trip, but I had to work for it . The MNDA event was the next thing on the list, and I enjoyed my time there. It was the last one, and I am so proud of the fact that I supported them all, bar one. The problem is I don't see many of my mates from one year to the next, and that was the one event I could spend a little time with a few of them. Maybe something else will come up on the radar, who knows?

*I was gagging to get back to Farriers*

For some reason, whilst I had been away from Farriers, my fishing went into a bit of decline. I have no idea what happened, but I guess many of you will have experienced the same thing from time to time. The most simple of tasks becomes a total impossibility, and a cast that you would normally nail with one or two attempts takes about fifty. By the time you have finished whipping the water to a frothy foam, you sit back and know there won't be a carp within a mile of your frantic efforts! The frustration this causes only makes the whole debacle more of a nightmare. So by the time you have any rational thoughts, you have convinced yourself that it would probably be in your best interests to reel in and head for home before you go completely off your rocker. As bad as I was making things, the carp came to my rescue, and what unfolded over the next few weeks blew me away. In a lot of respects, it's what carp fishing is all about for me. I knew I wouldn't be rejoining Farriers the following year, but I could never have realised that my wonderful

*At 31lb 4oz he was an amazing-looking fish.*

adventure, amongst some wonderful people in the Cotswolds, was almost over.

I was determined to keep my foot on the gas pedal for as long as I could at Farriers, right up to the winter. The last autumn period had been biblical in the extreme, and if I could, I wanted a bit more of that. The freezers at home were overflowing with 10 and 15mm Hybrid boilies, and I had just the place for them. The fishing had been tough and I wasn't surprised to find the lake relatively quiet when I arrived one morning. It was just before dawn, and by the time I had done one lap I was thinking the carp may be on holiday, because I had seen nothing. My favourite swim, The Slope, was free and it sort of played into my plan. I could keep my eye on the shallow end from there, and intercept any carp that were transiting from one end to the other. We were due a few warmish days, and I must say by the time I was set up and angling, I started to look around for the best place to take the pictures. Oh, you poor deluded boy, Chillcott! I woke in the morning and stared at the red vista that was building in the northern sky; it was feeling remarkably carp-less. It was a classic 'shepherd's warning' and I knew it was time to move, which wasn't as easy as it sounds. By mid-morning the sun was warming up rapidly, and in true Farriers' style the carp moved quickly into the weedy shallows. The two swims I would have liked were taken, but the more I looked, the more it seemed that the carp wanted to be elsewhere. I watched them for ages, and the route they took brought them in front of a bank of weed at around 30 yards. This was very handy, because if I was lucky enough to hook one, it was a pretty clear route to get them to the net.

The clear area was about 5 yards wide in only 3ft of water, so I changed my rigs over to my normal long-Haired bottom bait setups. A 15mm dumbbell hookbait was topped with a yellow piece of plastic corn, and once both of them were tooled up with a PVA bag of 10 and 15mm boilies, I got those in position. I catapulted a kilo of 15mm'ers around them and sat back with a smug smile on my face. Even the birds seemed unaware I had done this, and

*The scale read 41lb 6oz, but I'm still not sure.*

I could only hope the carp were as happy with my efforts as I was. It actually didn't take too long to find out. I had been watching the carp travel around the area with their backs glistening in the sunshine and felt my heart speed up a fraction as they rounded the final piece of weed and onto the spot. A few tail patterns creased the surface as they dipped down on the bait. I think I may well have stopped breathing at that point, and only took a breath once one of the bobbins cracked into the rod, and the line pinged from the clip. The take was spectacular, in that twenty bow waves charged off in one direction, whilst only one went the other. The battle was less dramatic, and in about two minutes I had a good common in the folds of my net. At 34lb 10oz she was the best possible start to the session, and a little while later I had a bit of a song and dance with a 21lb lunatic. The night was quiet, as I knew it would be, so as soon as I could see the spot properly in the morning, once again I set my traps. It was early afternoon before the fish ventured into my area, and soon after their arrival I got the most subtle of bites. Something was on there, but because it didn't fight I was wondering what the hell it could be. A huge common soon dispelled any doubts, and I scooped her into the net. She spun the scales round to 36lb 5oz, and I remember looking at her, as I did with so many of those fish, wondering why they simply never fought. I didn't have to wait long for another, either, and about 45 minutes later I was once again steering a carp through the weed and into the net. She was an odd-shaped carp of 34lb 10oz, and was a real character, for sure. Eventually I had a proper row with a fish a little later, and for an age I hung on for grim death, but finally I bundled her into the net and felt sure it was another 30-pounder. She came up an ounce shy, but who the hell cares? It had been a brilliant session, and I was busting a gut to get back, which, as normal, was an hour before first light, at the start of the following week.

I didn't think it could get better, but this remarkable lake was saving things up for me. That said, the next session, although I moved several times, only produced one fish, and I had a sneaky feeling that it was something to do with the amount of bait going in. Everybody was now piling in as much as they could carry and next time around I was going to cut things down a little. I spoke to everyone on the lake the next week, and it seemed that things had slowed down massively. I did spot a couple of fish from a popular swim called Windy Point, and as soon as I was able, wheeled my barrow round to it. I had only fished the swim once before and wanted to take my time. Also I didn't want to create two baited spots, despite the amount of water in front of me, which tied in nicely with keeping the baiting levels down. If they wanted something to eat in that large open area, then there would only be one place to find it. I was doing just two nights that week, and it looked as if things were working well when I landed a 27lb common, along with 27lb of weed! I only rebaited with two spods of boilies, and reset the rod, spending the rest of the day chatting to various visitors. The lake was fishing terribly, so I was chuffed to pieces with my fish, and I got a whole lot more chuffed the following morning, when a couple of big fish boomed out over my area, and the liners started. The bubbles began to streak across the surface too, as the day got brighter and brighter. It was classic stuff, but I still nearly jumped out of my skin when one of the buzzers sang its unmistakable tune. This one practically allowed me to lead it straight into the net, all bar the odd headshake, and rather quickly I had a plump 34lb 4oz common on the mat. The change of tactics had got me bites, although whether I would have got them over lots of bait I have no idea, but as I slipped her home, and headed for mine, I decided to keep the bait to a minimum for a while.

I got back to the lake a few days later, and was a little disappointed to see Windy Point was occupied, although the guy was leaving soon. I did look around the rest of the lake, but nothing floated my boat, and eventually I was unpacking my gear in the popular plot. A sprinkling of boilies over the same spot as the week before kept my hookbaits company, and I was sure a bite was imminent. It wasn't, and I woke in the morning wondering if I had got it round my ear. I decided to stay, and after a visit to the shops, repositioned the hookbaits once again. Then it rained, and boy, did it rain! It cleared eventually, and as it did so I noticed some activity around the area I was fishing. I had just had a full lower leg tattoo done, and I remembered Lynn's warning about getting in the lake without my chest waders on. I was just about to make them a little more accessible when one of the bobbins pulled up tight, and I lifted into a fish. The weed played havoc with the fight and it was fully twenty minutes before I had it anywhere near to netting. And in time-honoured tradition I marched into the lake in my underpants! With Lynn's concerns ringing in my ear, I threw the net ahead of me – needs must and all that – and concentrated on netting one of the lake's stunning linears. With the fish in the net I breathed a huge sigh of relief, and also spared a thought for my tattooed leg, hoping it didn't become infected. The latter thought slipped from my mind as the scales read 31lb 4oz. It was an amazing-looking fish and I slipped her into a retainer for a few minutes while I sorted things out. James the bailiff arrived and we got on with the pictures, although we hadn't even started when the other rod screamed for my attention.

James sorted out the mirror whilst I concentrated on playing another fish. The weed was a nightmare, again, and things came to a standstill when the fish got tangled in my other line. It was comical really, and I couldn't help but giggle about it all. I had my chest waders on this time, and strode into the water to sort things out. Risking a soaking I took one more step, and rather frantically scooped up my prize. It was a huge common, but the weighing didn't go too well. I had, through my own stupidity, half opened the panel on the back of the scales, and water had got in. It took a minute or two

***It was the best I could come up with, and soon enough I had my gear in there.***

to get them going, but I wasn't happy, and to this day I cannot confirm for definite that it weighed the 41lb 6oz the scales said it weighed. It did get caught again eight days later at 41lb 4oz, so it probably was the true weight, but if I am not sure then I cannot call it.

The rest of that session produced two more commons of 29lb 2oz and 31lb. The fishing was out of this world, but on the drive home I couldn't help admitting to myself that my time at Farriers was almost over. I had a session there with Harry Charrington doing a segment for the next instalment of the Fox *Edges* DVD, which produced a mirror of 21lb and a stunning 33lb 15oz common. It just never seemed to let me down, that lake, and a couple of weeks later I turned up for what would be my last-ever session there. I have no idea how the hand of fate works, but Farriers had saved the very best until last, although as I opened the gate that was about the furthest thing from my mind. It was just a little sad really. Farriers had been so good to me; indeed, it was probably one of the best syndicates I have ever fished. And it wasn't just about the fishing either. The people I had met, some of whom I am sure will remain good mates, had made it an 18-month adventure that I will never forget.

The car park was more packed than I had ever seen it, and the first lap revealed that all the best areas were taken, with no likelihood of one of them becoming free any time soon. That said, I was determined to find some fish to fish for, and although it wasn't the hottest of days, I found a few in a very shallow, weedy corner. It was the best I could come up with, and soon enough I had my gear in there. As moribund as I felt, what happened next illustrated exactly why we all go carp fishing, and it went a little something like this. I noticed the fish were doing much the same as the last time I had fished this swim, only this time the water was even shallower. The little silt strip was about 7 yards long, and sat right in front of a big bank of weed, at around 30 yards. Once again, I took off my pop-up rigs and used my ever-faithful bottom bait setups, armed with a mesh PVA bag of 10 and 15mm boilies. There were a hundred gulls just looking to spoil someone's day, so I tied up 20 or so more mesh bags, and baited the area with those. It confused the hell out of the birds, and because I had caught so many fish doing that, I was nearly drowning in a sea of confidence by the time I had finished. The problem was, I hadn't factored in the other birds on the lake. First it was the swans, and then the coots, and over and over again they ruined the traps. It was so frustrating because I could see the carp trying to get to the bait; all I could do was keep recasting, but every time I did, I felt even further away from catching a carp. I was holding my head in my hands when a guy called Andy came down from the swim he was fishing some 75 yards to my right. He had landed a personal best common of 41lb+, and I was more than pleased to go and do some pictures for him. All that was left to do was catch one for myself, but I had absolutely no idea how that could possibly happen.

At around 4.00 p.m., for some inexplicable reason, the birds swam off. Not in dribs and drabs, but as a whole, and within thirty seconds the area was clear of them. It was such strange behaviour, but I wasn't about to ask too many questions and quickly recast the rods once more. For the first time that day I was actually fishing properly; I just needed a carp to tell me so. A jittery take 45 minutes later had me leaning into a fish, but it did absolutely nothing. In fact, if I hadn't put my chest waders on, it would have been in the net in seconds. Be that as it may, as I positioned the net it broke the surface, and I was shocked at the width across its shoulders. I charged out still further and lifted the net around a truly massive fish and stood in the water for a minute or two. I needed to thank her for coming to visit, and also thank the lake for her help in relighting my carp-fishing fires. Eventually, Andy came round to help and together we recorded a weight of 46lb 15oz, a different fish from the previous big one. Stu Morris reeled in his rods, and came round with his camera from the other side

*Together we recorded a weight of 46lb 15oz.*

of the lake. Right there and then I could see all that was good about carp fishing; a truly great fish, great carp fishing, and great company. She was a personal best common, of course, but she was so much more than that. It was as if the lake had let me have one last moment with one of her charges, and that is something I will never forget.

That particular chapter of my life was over, as is this book, and there really couldn't have been a better way for it to end. I still miss Farriers, but I have never been one to rest on my laurels, and the will to move on was upon me. I had no idea where I would end up, and at that point I really didn't care. All I ever wanted was for carp fishing to be fun, and it always has been, although at times during the typing of this tome, I have felt quite out of breath just writing about my crazy carp-fishing life. I can only hope that you have enjoyed coming along for the ride. My life has changed quite dramatically of late, and I am heading off on another carp-fishing voyage of discovery. And whilst I go about sorting that out, having ensured that all my gear is ready for the next phase of my carp-fishing adventure, I shall reach once again for a nice glass of Chateauneuf-du-Pape. I cannot believe just how exciting my life has been since I left the Army, and I cannot even start to think about how exciting it will become in the future. Most of all though, it's going to be fun... and I just can't wait!!

**I just can't wait to do it all over again!!**